LIGHTSTEP™

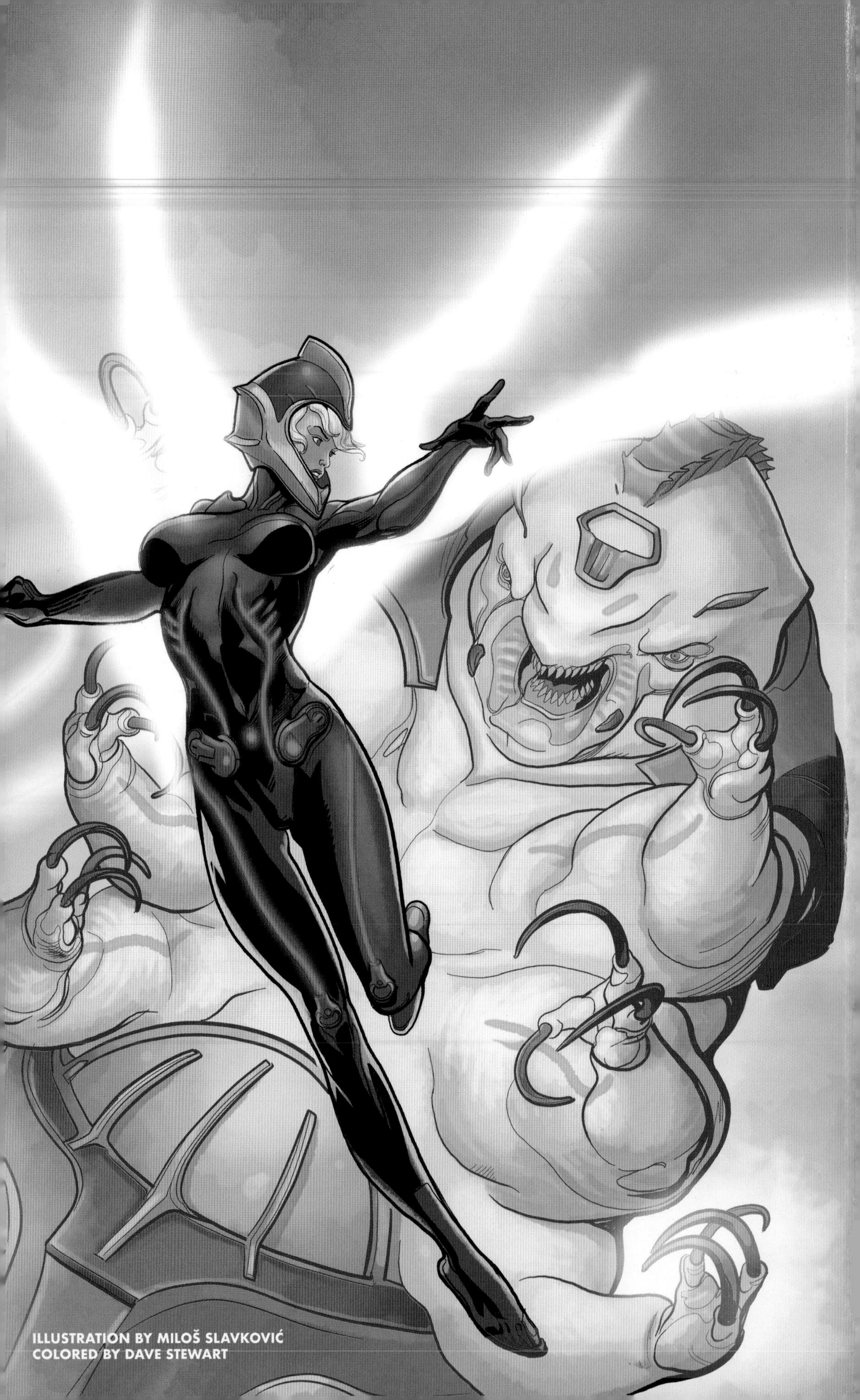

ILLUSTRATION BY MILOŠ SLAVKOVIĆ
COLORED BY DAVE STEWART

LIGHTSTEP ™

SCRIPT
MILOŠ SLAVKOVIĆ
MIRKO TOPALSKI
IVAN BRANKOVIĆ

ART
MILOŠ SLAVKOVIĆ

COLORING
MILOŠ SLAVKOVIĆ
HMT STUDIO

LETTERING
ANDREJ BUNJAĆ

COVER ART
MILOŠ SLAVKOVIĆ WITH DAVE STEWART

EIPIX
COMICS

DARK HORSE BOOKS

EIPIX COMICS

EDITOR IN CHIEF MIRKO TOPALSKI

SERIES EDITOR MIŠO ŽIVANOV ART DIRECTOR HARVEY BUNDA

DARK HORSE COMICS

PRESIDENT AND PUBLISHER MIKE RICHARDSON

EDITOR RANDY STRADLEY ASSISTANT EDITOR JUDY KHUU

DESIGNER SKYLER WEISSENFLUH DIGITAL ART TECHNICIAN SAMANTHA HUMMER

NEIL HANKERSON Executive Vice President • TOM WEDDLE Chief Financial Officer • RANDY STRADLEY Vice President of Publishing • NICK McWHORTER Chief Business Development Officer • DALE LaFOUNTAIN Chief Information Officer MATT PARKINSON Vice President of Marketing • CARA NIECE Vice President of Production and Scheduling • MARK BERNARDI Vice President of Book Trade and Digital Sales • KEN LIZZI General Counsel • DAVE MARSHALL Editor in Chief • DAVEY ESTRADA Editorial Director • CHRIS WARNER Senior Books Editor • CARY GRAZZINI Director of Specialty Projects • LIA RIBACCHI Art Director • VANESSA TODD-HOLMES Director of Print Purchasing • MATT DRYER Director of Digital Art and Prepress • MICHAEL GOMBOS Senior Director of Licensed Publications • KARI YADRO Director of Custom Programs • KARI TORSON Director of International Licensing • SEAN BRICE Director of Trade Sales

LIGHTSTEP

This volume collects the Dark Horse comic book series *Lightstep* #1–#5, originally published November 2018–April 2019.

Published by Dark Horse Books
A division of Dark Horse Comics LLC
10956 SE Main Street
Milwaukie, OR 97222

DarkHorse.com

To find a comics shop in your area, go to www.comicshoplocator.com

Library of Congress Cataloging-in-Publication Data

Names: Slavkovic, Milos, author, artist. | Topalski, Mirko, author. |
  Brankovic, Ivan, author.
Title: Lightstep / script, Milos Slavkovic, Mirko Topalski, Ivan Brankovic ;
  art, Milos Slavkovic ; coloring, Milos Slavkovic, HMT Studio ; lettering,
  Andrej Bunjac ; cover art, Milos Slavkovic with Tiberiu Beka.
Description: First edition. | Milwaukie, OR : Dark Horse Books, 2019. | "This
  volume collects the Dark Horse comic book series Lightstep #1-#5,
  originally published November 2018-April 2019."
Identifiers: LCCN 2019012080 | ISBN 9781506710846 (paperback)
Subjects: LCSH: Graphic novels. | BISAC: COMICS & GRAPHIC NOVELS / Science
  Fiction.
Classification: LCC PN6728.L498 S57 2019 | DDC 741.5/973–dc23
LC record available at https://lccn.loc.gov/2019012080

First edition: July 2019
ISBN: 978-1-50671-084-6

1 3 5 7 9 10 8 6 4 2
Printed in China

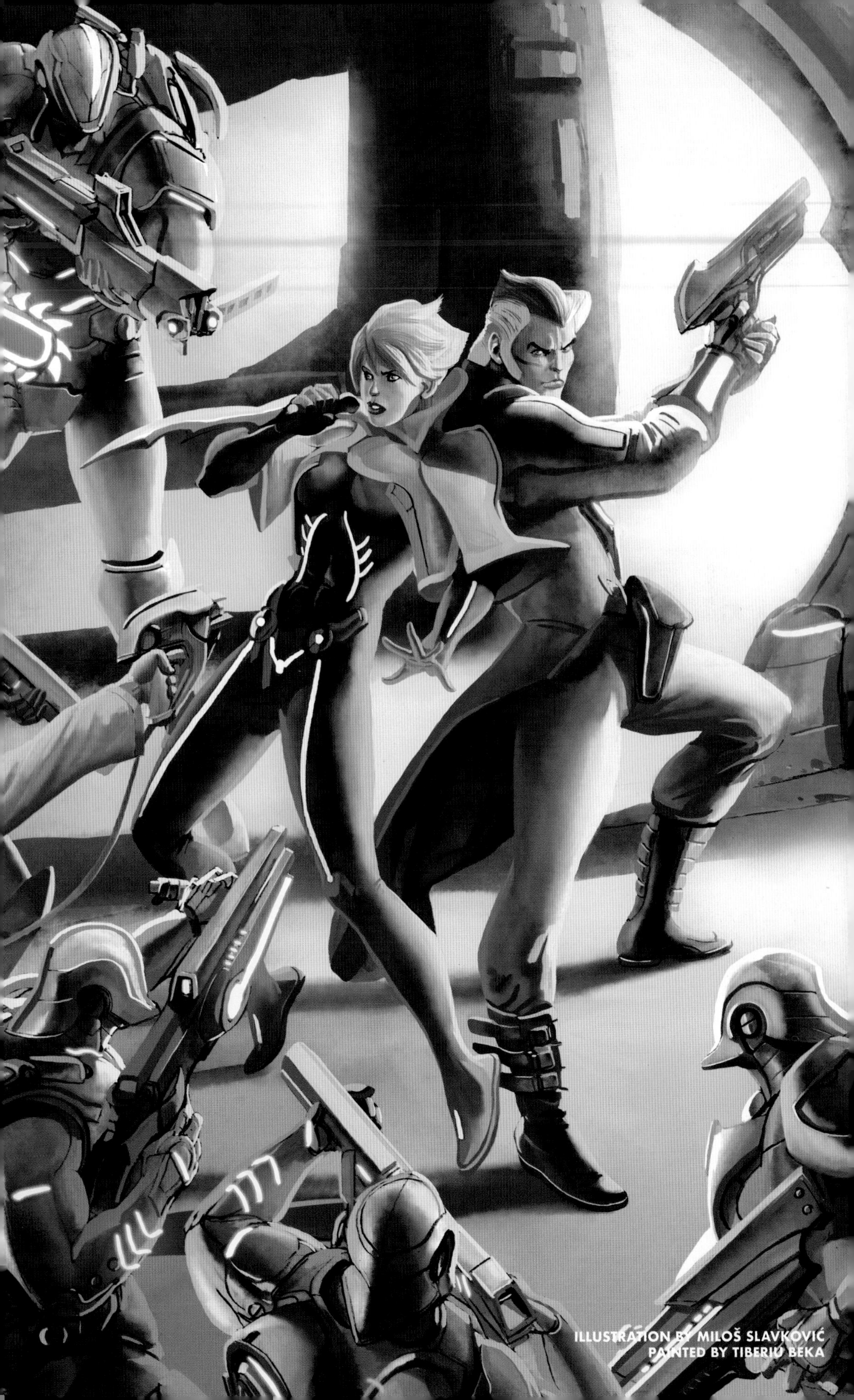

ILLUSTRATION BY MILOŠ SLAVKOVIĆ
PAINTED BY TIBERIU BEKA

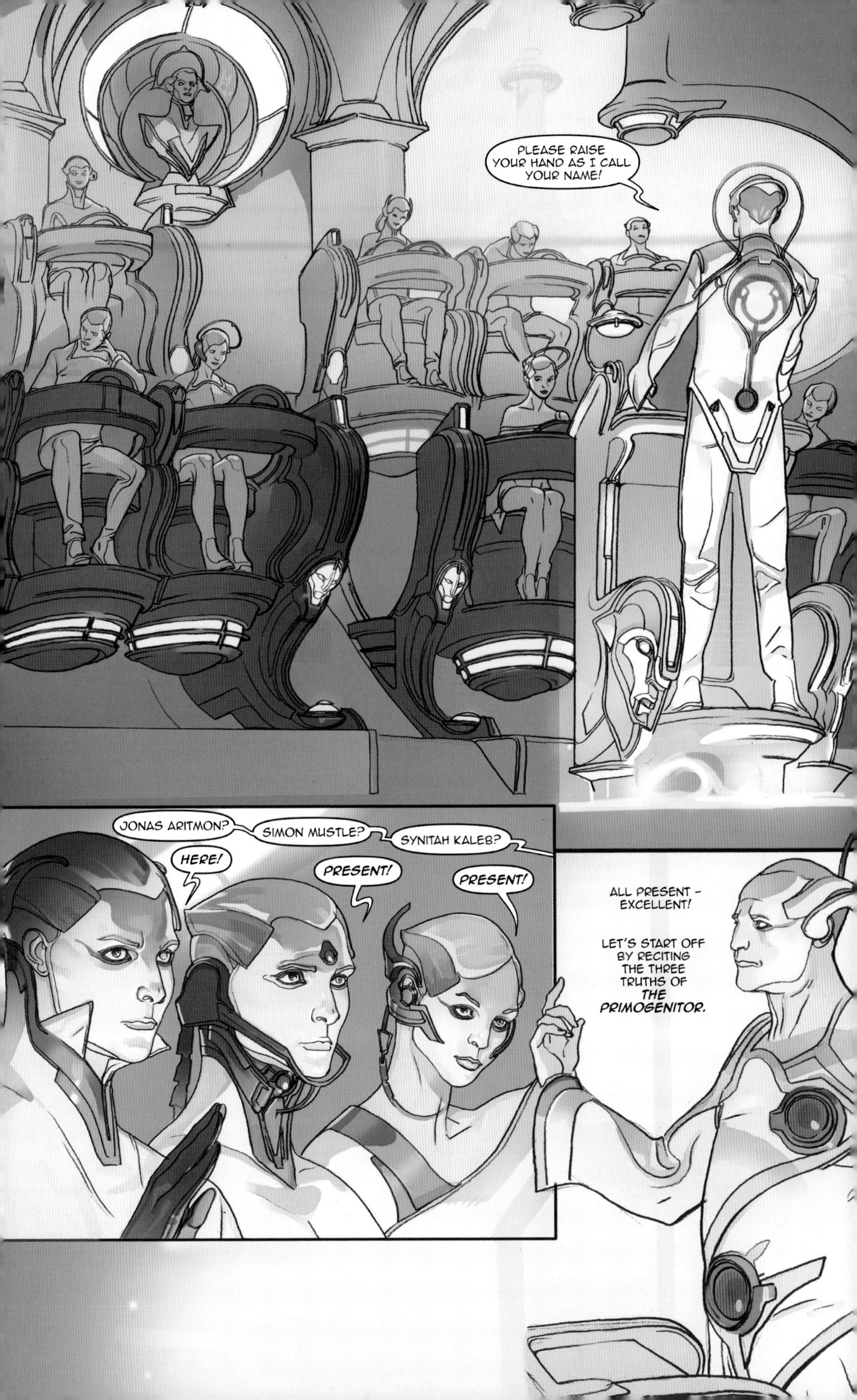
PLEASE RAISE YOUR HAND AS I CALL YOUR NAME!
JONAS ARITMON?
HERE!
SIMON MUSTLE?
PRESENT!
SYNITAH KALEB?
PRESENT!
ALL PRESENT - EXCELLENT!
LET'S START OFF BY RECITING THE THREE TRUTHS OF THE PRIMOGENITOR.

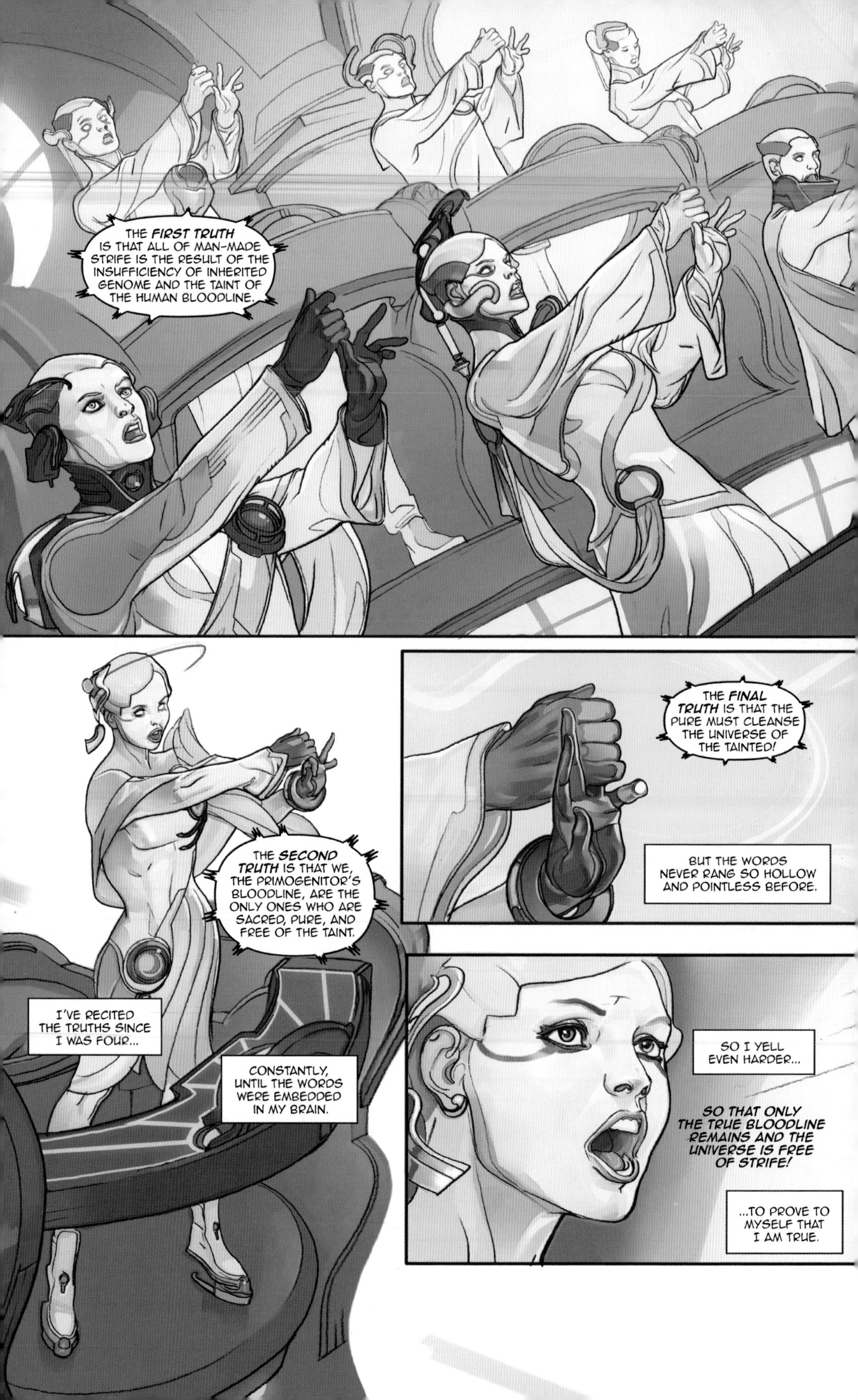
THE FIRST TRUTH IS THAT ALL OF MAN-MADE STRIFE IS THE RESULT OF THE INSUFFICIENCY OF INHERITED GENOME AND THE TAINT OF THE HUMAN BLOODLINE.
THE SECOND TRUTH IS THAT WE, THE PRIMOGENITOR'S BLOODLINE, ARE THE ONLY ONES WHO ARE SACRED, PURE, AND FREE OF THE TAINT.
I'VE RECITED THE TRUTHS SINCE I WAS FOUR...
CONSTANTLY, UNTIL THE WORDS WERE EMBEDDED IN MY BRAIN.
THE FINAL TRUTH IS THAT THE PURE MUST CLEANSE THE UNIVERSE OF THE TAINTED!
BUT THE WORDS NEVER RANG SO HOLLOW AND POINTLESS BEFORE.
SO I YELL EVEN HARDER...
SO THAT ONLY THE TRUE BLOODLINE REMAINS AND THE UNIVERSE IS FREE OF STRIFE!
...TO PROVE TO MYSELF THAT I AM TRUE.

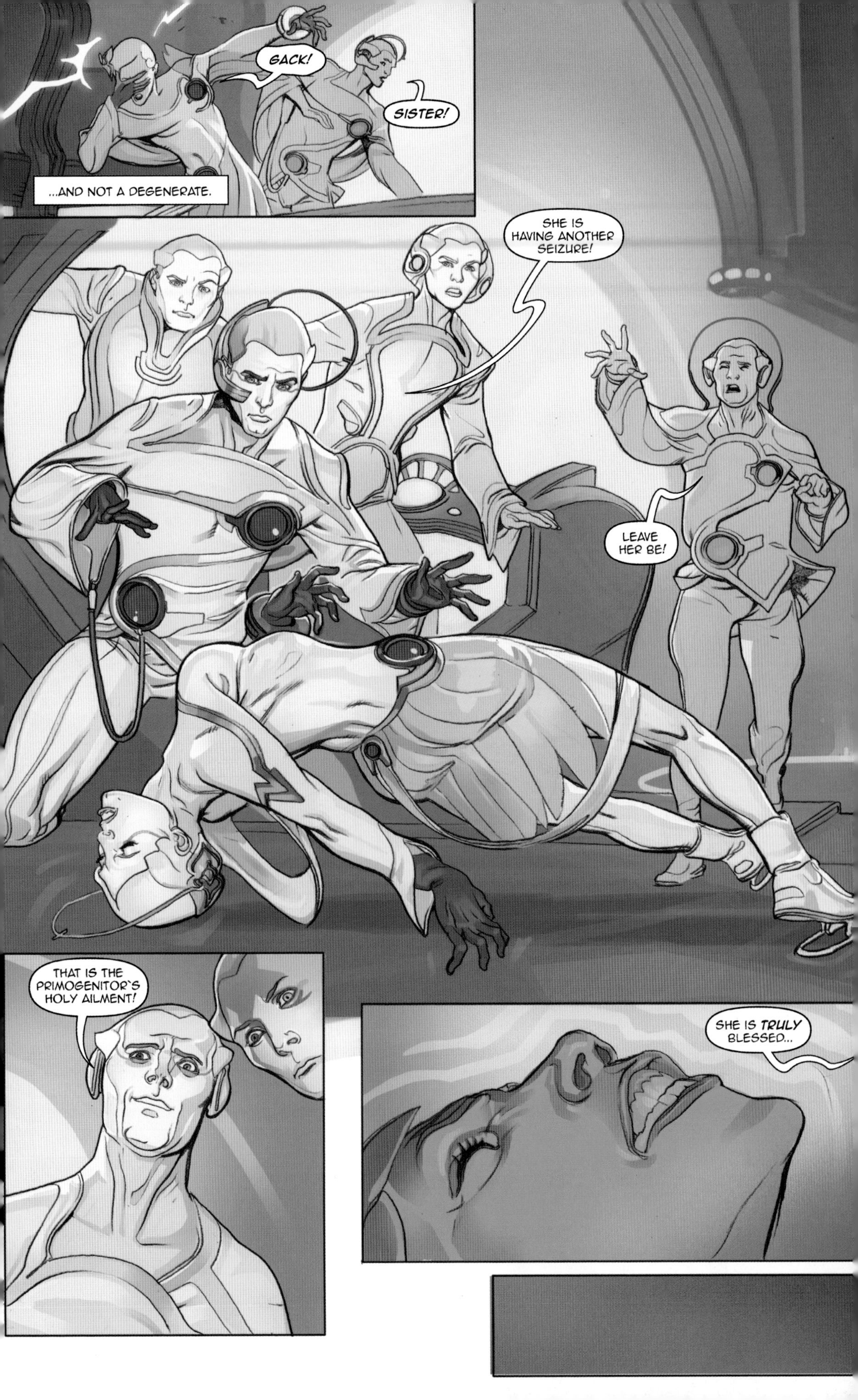
GACK!
SISTER!
...AND NOT A DEGENERATE.
SHE IS HAVING ANOTHER SEIZURE!
LEAVE HER BE!
THAT IS THE PRIMOGENITOR'S HOLY AILMENT!
SHE IS TRULY BLESSED...

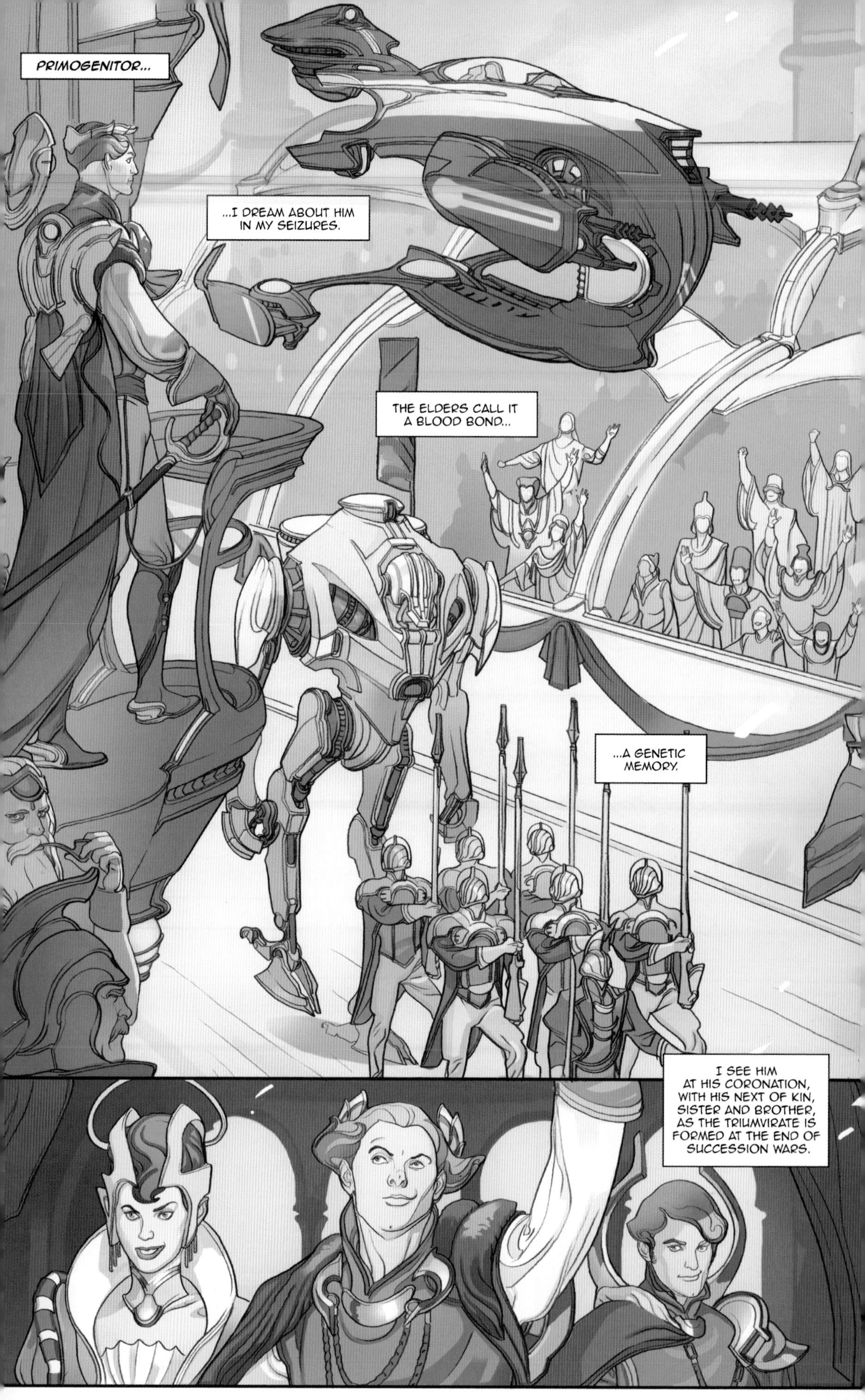
PRIMOGENITOR...
...I DREAM ABOUT HIM IN MY SEIZURES.
THE ELDERS CALL IT A BLOOD BOND...
...A GENETIC MEMORY.
I SEE HIM AT HIS CORONATION, WITH HIS NEXT OF KIN, SISTER AND BROTHER, AS THE TRIUMVIRATE IS FORMED AT THE END OF SUCCESSION WARS.

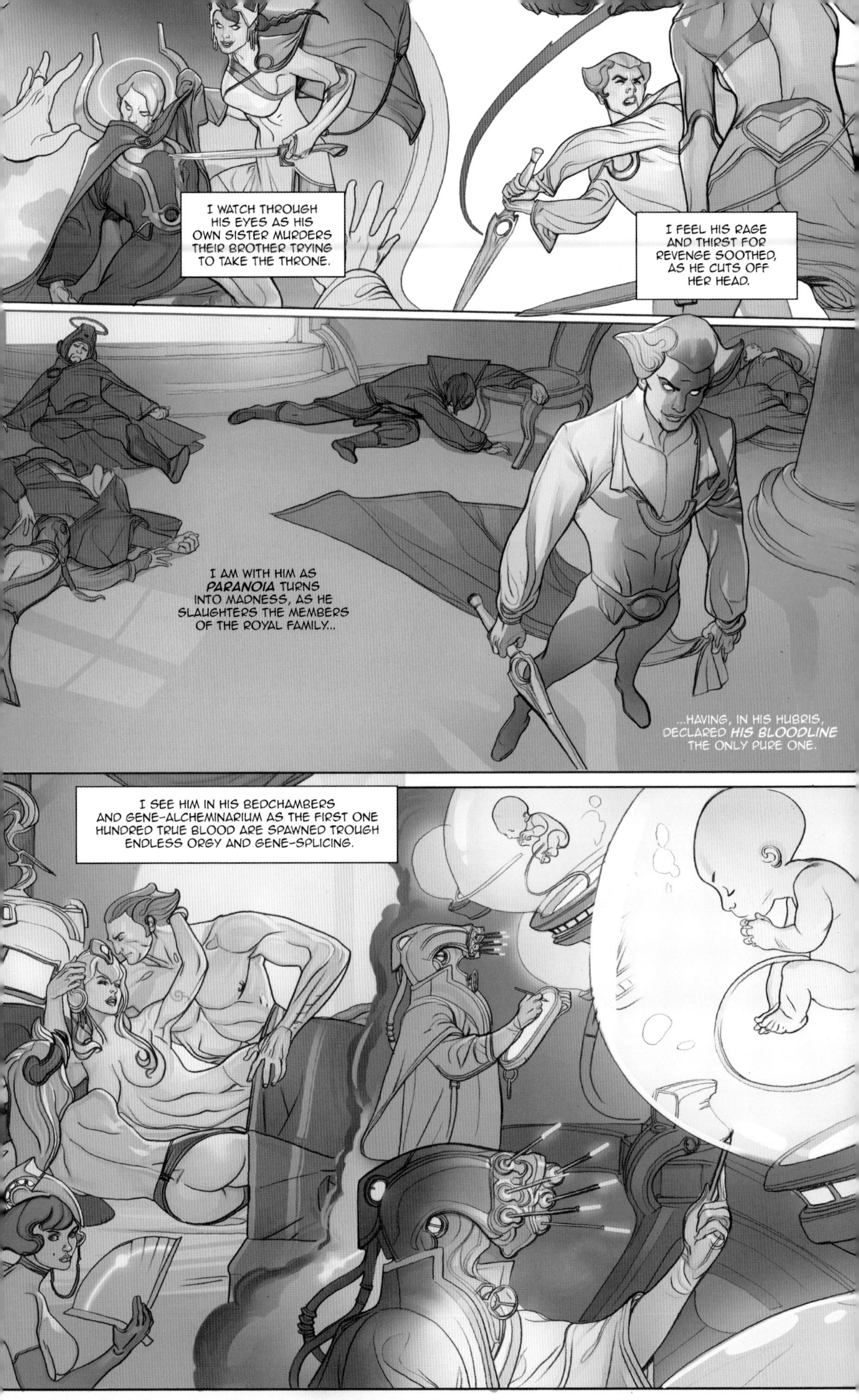
I WATCH THROUGH HIS EYES AS HIS OWN SISTER MURDERS THEIR BROTHER TRYING TO TAKE THE THRONE.
I FEEL HIS RAGE AND THIRST FOR REVENGE SOOTHED, AS HE CUTS OFF HER HEAD.
I AM WITH HIM AS PARANOIA TURNS INTO MADNESS, AS HE SLAUGHTERS THE MEMBERS OF THE ROYAL FAMILY...
...HAVING, IN HIS HUBRIS, DECLARED HIS BLOODLINE THE ONLY PURE ONE.
I SEE HIM IN HIS BEDCHAMBERS AND GENE-ALCHEMINARIUM AS THE FIRST ONE HUNDRED TRUE BLOOD ARE SPAWNED TROUGH ENDLESS ORGY AND GENE-SPLICING.

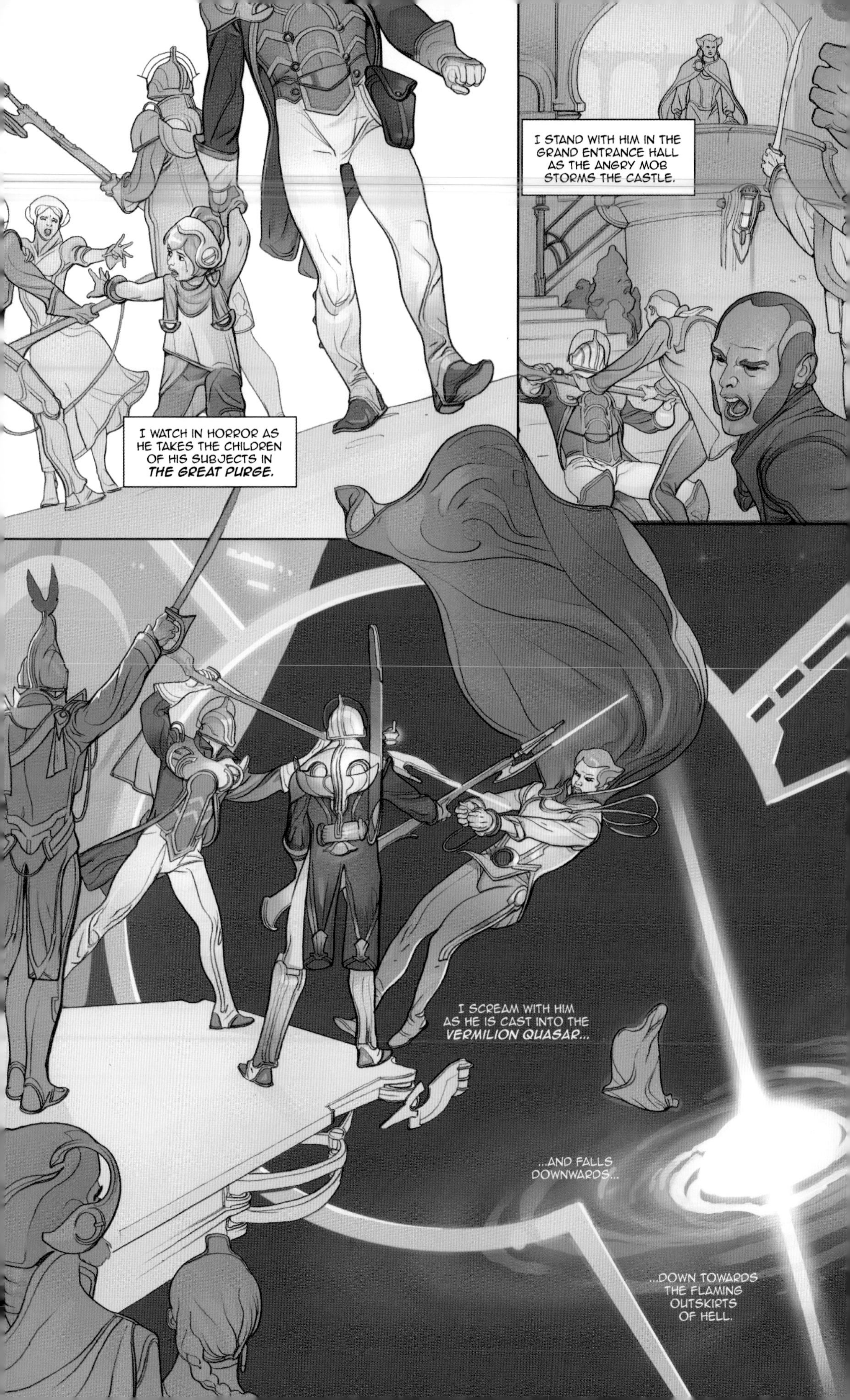

I WATCH IN HORROR AS HE TAKES THE CHILDREN OF HIS SUBJECTS IN *THE GREAT PURGE.*
I STAND WITH HIM IN THE GRAND ENTRANCE HALL AS THE ANGRY MOB STORMS THE CASTLE.
I SCREAM WITH HIM AS HE IS CAST INTO THE *VERMILION QUASAR...*
...AND FALLS DOWNWARDS...
...DOWN TOWARDS THE FLAMING OUTSKIRTS OF HELL.

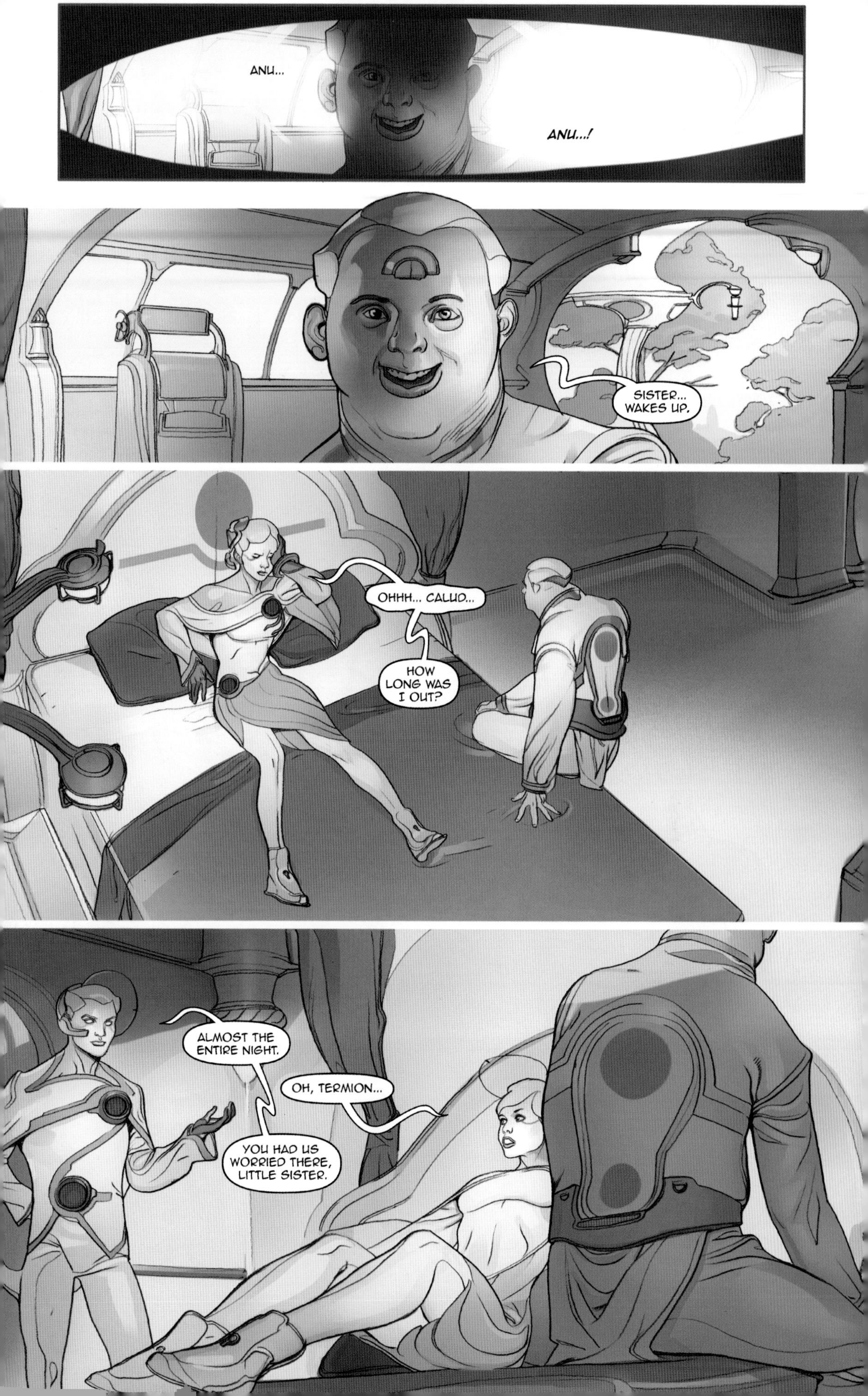
ANU...
ANU...!
SISTER... WAKES UP.
OHHH... CALUD...
HOW LONG WAS I OUT?
ALMOST THE ENTIRE NIGHT.
OH, TERMION...
YOU HAD US WORRIED THERE, LITTLE SISTER.

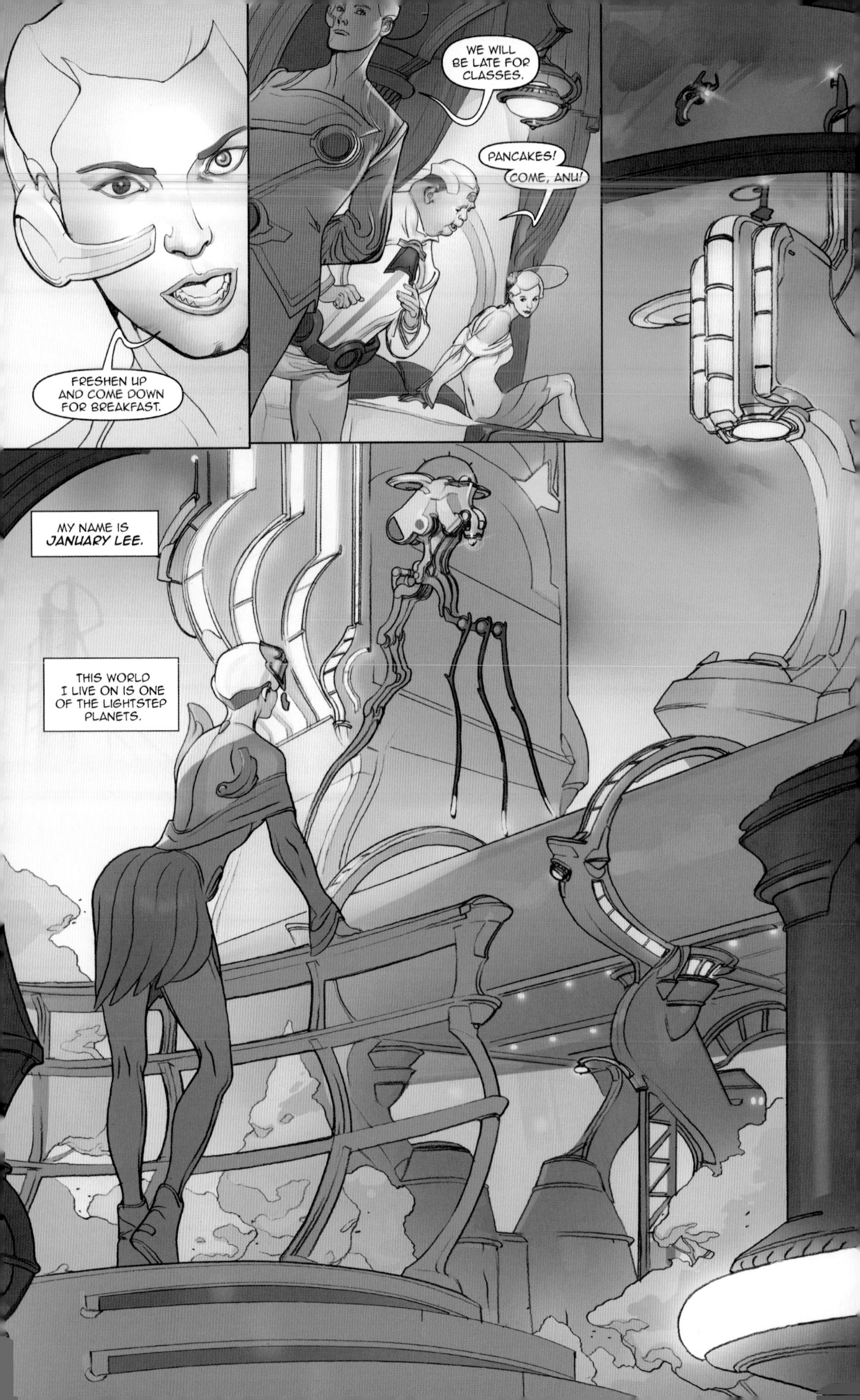
FRESHEN UP AND COME DOWN FOR BREAKFAST.
WE WILL BE LATE FOR CLASSES.
PANCAKES!
COME, ANU!
MY NAME IS *JANUARY LEE.*
THIS WORLD I LIVE ON IS ONE OF THE LIGHTSTEP PLANETS.

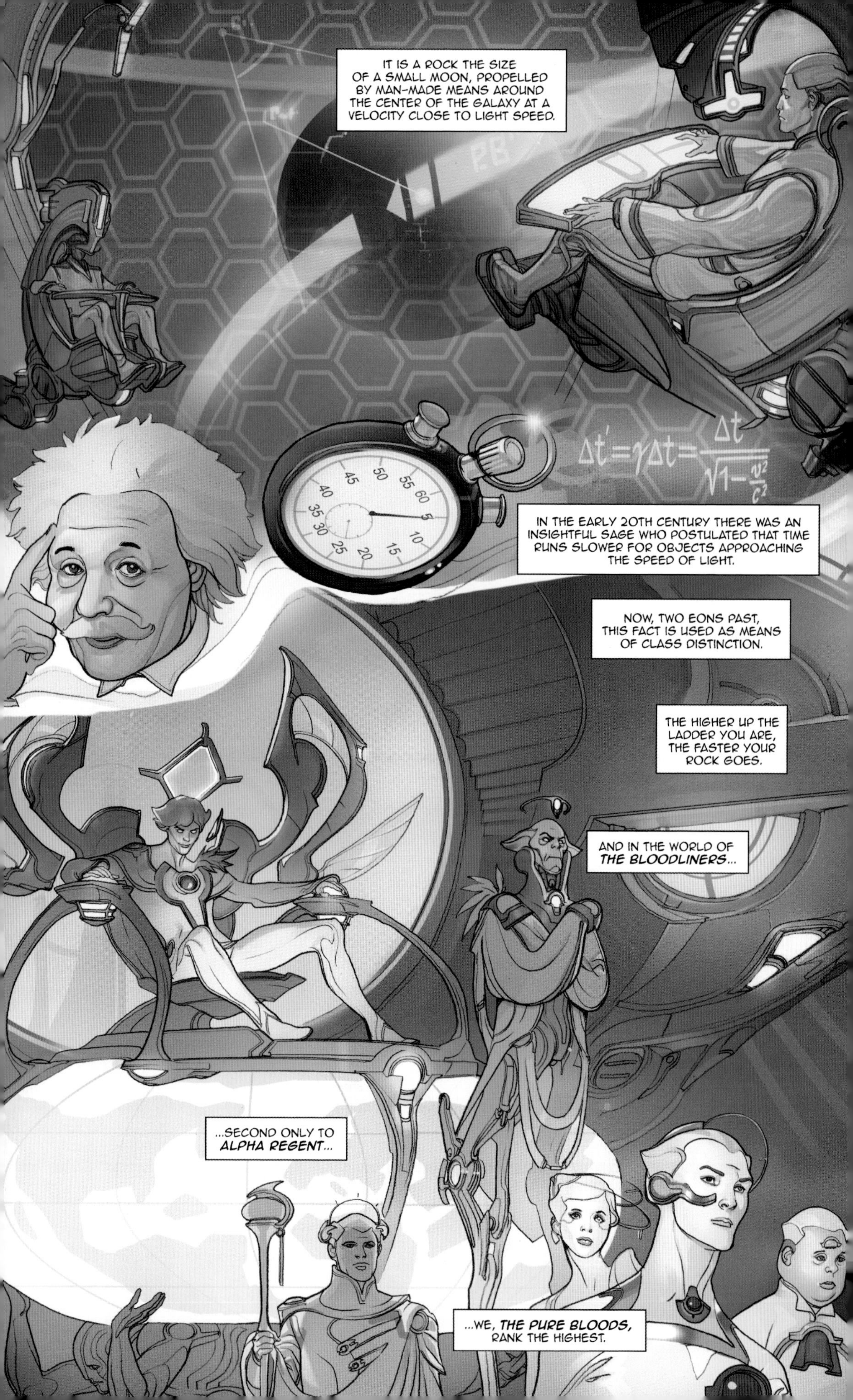
IT IS A ROCK THE SIZE OF A SMALL MOON, PROPELLED BY MAN-MADE MEANS AROUND THE CENTER OF THE GALAXY AT A VELOCITY CLOSE TO LIGHT SPEED.
$\Delta t' = \gamma \Delta t = \frac{\Delta t}{\sqrt{1-\frac{v^2}{c^2}}}$
IN THE EARLY 20TH CENTURY THERE WAS AN INSIGHTFUL SAGE WHO POSTULATED THAT TIME RUNS SLOWER FOR OBJECTS APPROACHING THE SPEED OF LIGHT.
NOW, TWO EONS PAST, THIS FACT IS USED AS MEANS OF CLASS DISTINCTION.
THE HIGHER UP THE LADDER YOU ARE, THE FASTER YOUR ROCK GOES.
AND IN THE WORLD OF *THE BLOODLINERS*...
...SECOND ONLY TO *ALPHA REGENT*...
...WE, *THE PURE BLOODS*, RANK THE HIGHEST.

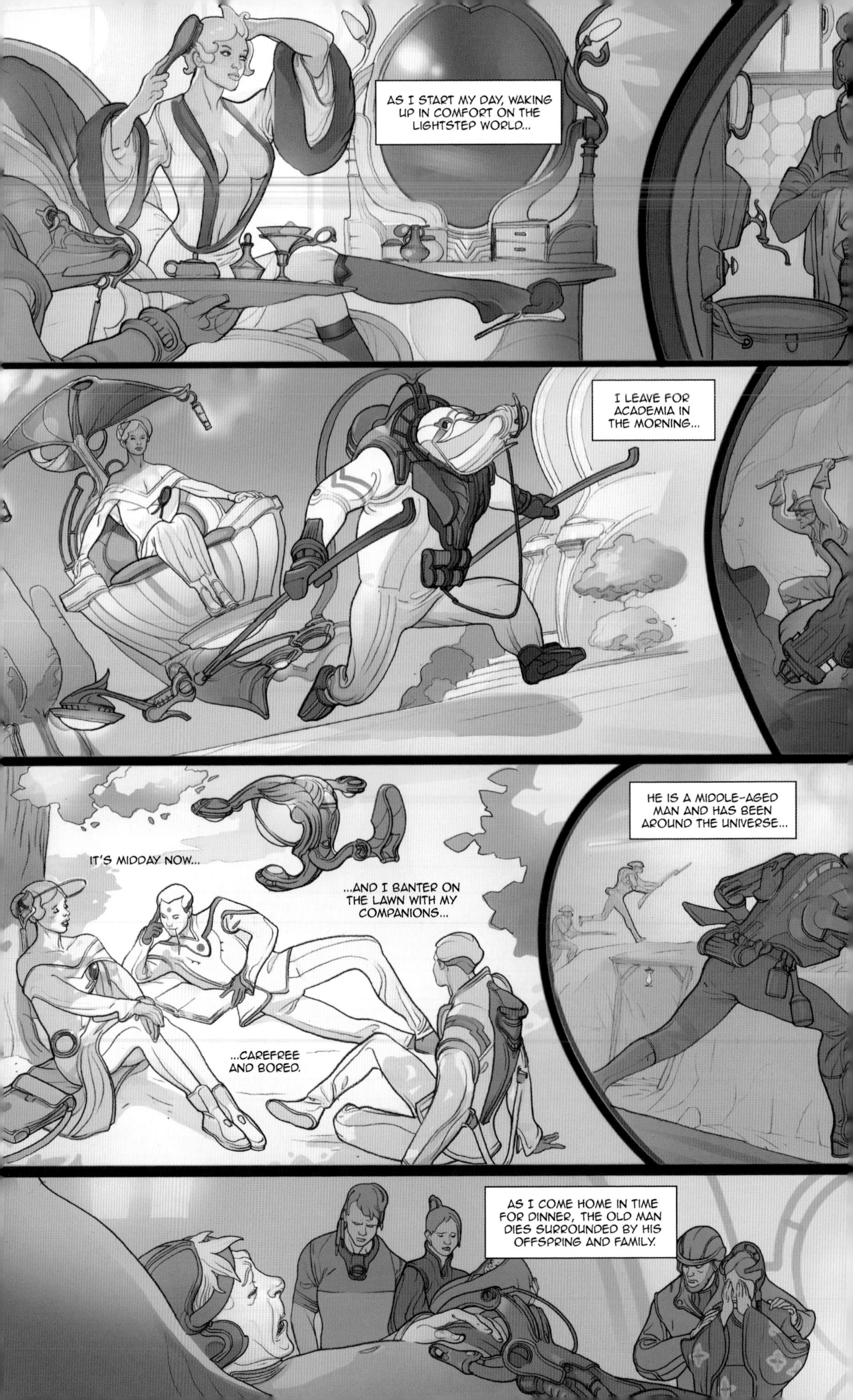
AS I START MY DAY, WAKING UP IN COMFORT ON THE LIGHTSTEP WORLD...
I LEAVE FOR ACADEMIA IN THE MORNING...
IT'S MIDDAY NOW...
...AND I BANTER ON THE LAWN WITH MY COMPANIONS...
...CAREFREE AND BORED.
HE IS A MIDDLE-AGED MAN AND HAS BEEN AROUND THE UNIVERSE...
AS I COME HOME IN TIME FOR DINNER, THE OLD MAN DIES SURROUNDED BY HIS OFFSPRING AND FAMILY.

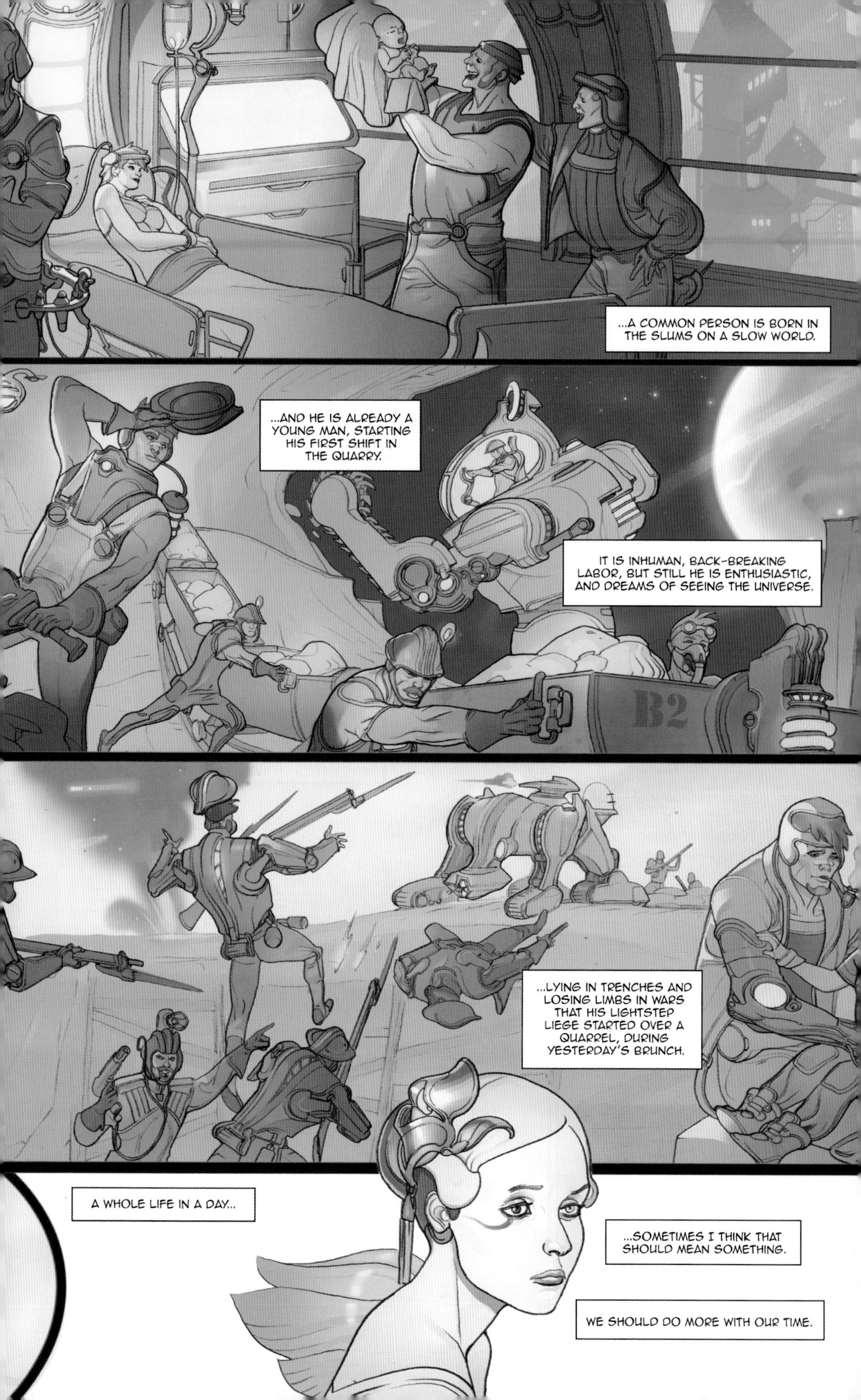
...A COMMON PERSON IS BORN IN THE SLUMS ON A SLOW WORLD.
...AND HE IS ALREADY A YOUNG MAN, STARTING HIS FIRST SHIFT IN THE QUARRY.
IT IS INHUMAN, BACK-BREAKING LABOR, BUT STILL HE IS ENTHUSIASTIC, AND DREAMS OF SEEING THE UNIVERSE.
B2
...LYING IN TRENCHES AND LOSING LIMBS IN WARS THAT HIS LIGHTSTEP LIEGE STARTED OVER A QUARREL, DURING YESTERDAY'S BRUNCH.
A WHOLE LIFE IN A DAY...
...SOMETIMES I THINK THAT SHOULD MEAN SOMETHING.
WE SHOULD DO MORE WITH OUR TIME.

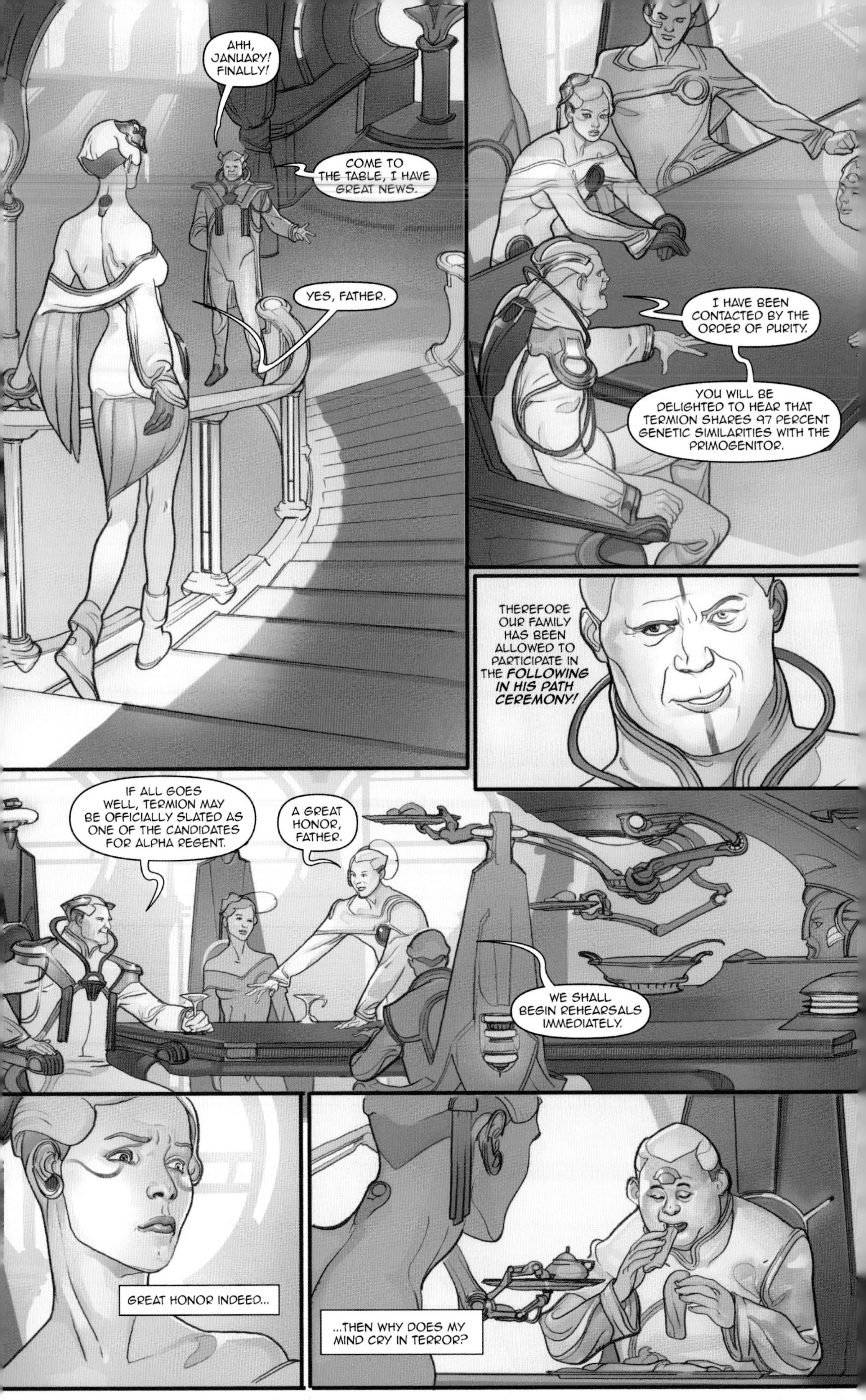
AHH, JANUARY! FINALLY!
COME TO THE TABLE, I HAVE GREAT NEWS.
YES, FATHER.
I HAVE BEEN CONTACTED BY THE ORDER OF PURITY.
YOU WILL BE DELIGHTED TO HEAR THAT TERMION SHARES 97 PERCENT GENETIC SIMILARITIES WITH THE PRIMOGENITOR.
THEREFORE OUR FAMILY HAS BEEN ALLOWED TO PARTICIPATE IN THE *FOLLOWING IN HIS PATH CEREMONY!*
IF ALL GOES WELL, TERMION MAY BE OFFICIALLY SLATED AS ONE OF THE CANDIDATES FOR ALPHA REGENT.
A GREAT HONOR, FATHER.
WE SHALL BEGIN REHEARSALS IMMEDIATELY.
GREAT HONOR INDEED...
...THEN WHY DOES MY MIND CRY IN TERROR?

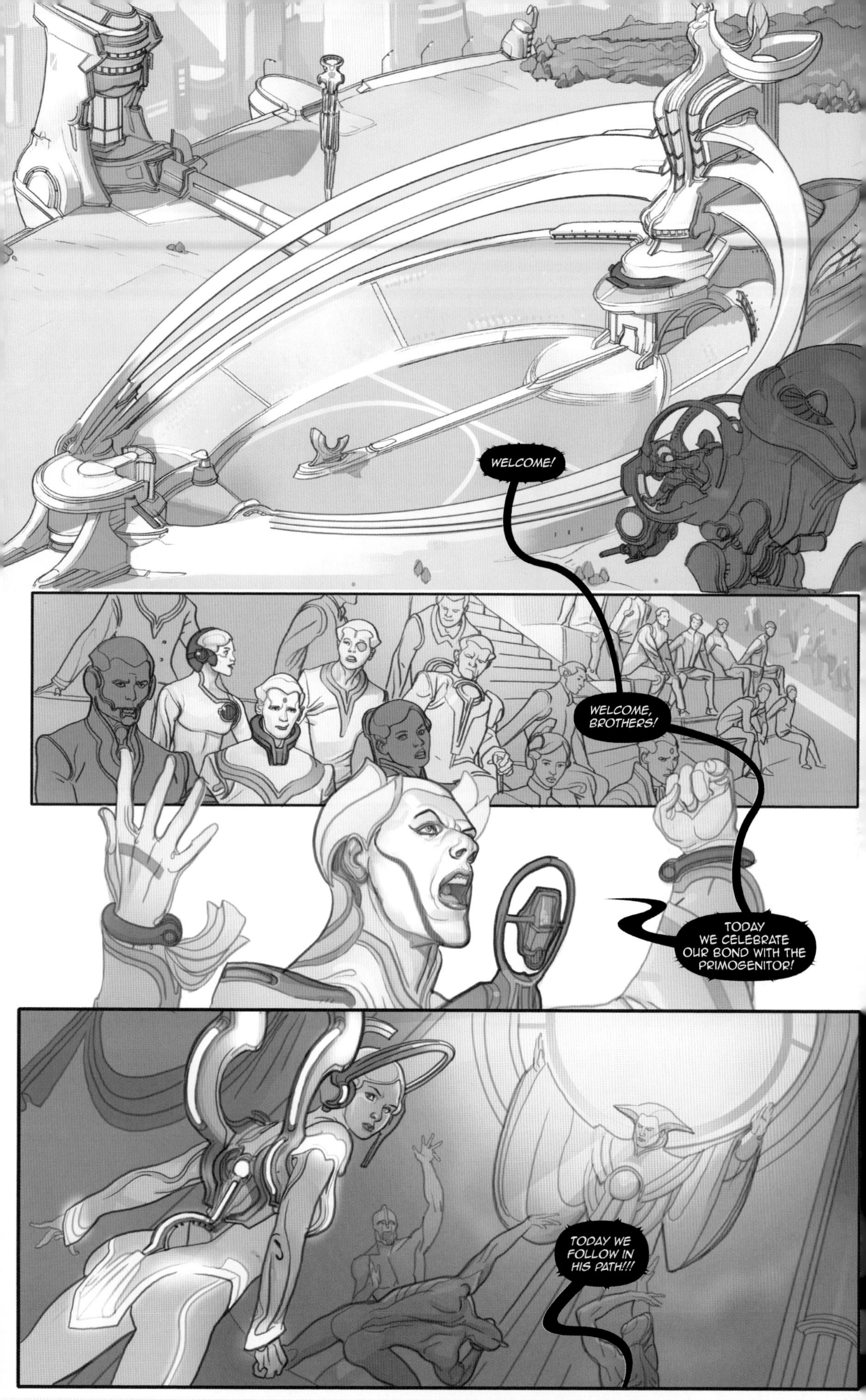
WELCOME!
WELCOME, BROTHERS!
TODAY WE CELEBRATE OUR BOND WITH THE PRIMOGENITOR!
TODAY WE FOLLOW IN HIS PATH!!!

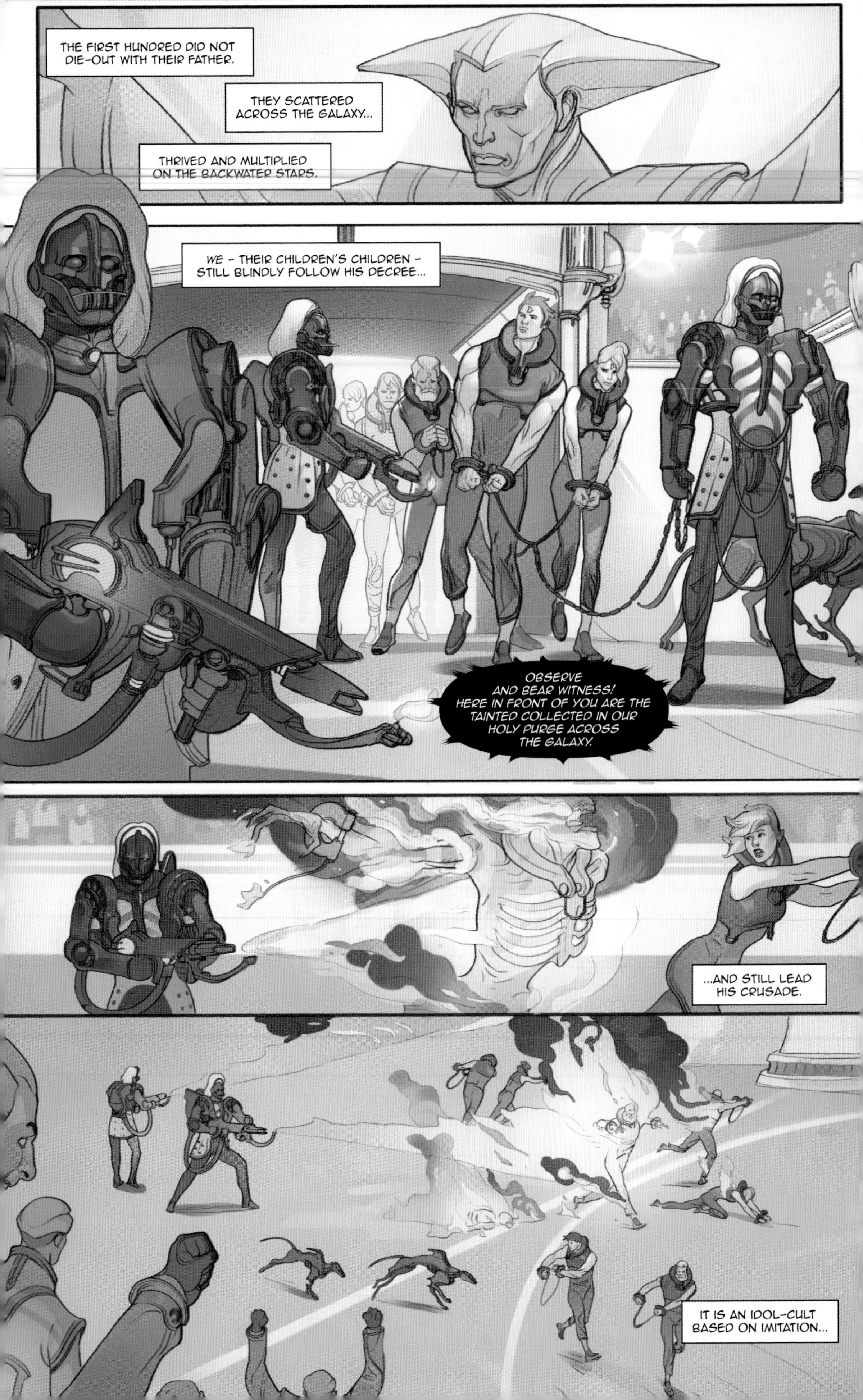
THE FIRST HUNDRED DID NOT DIE-OUT WITH THEIR FATHER.
THEY SCATTERED ACROSS THE GALAXY...
THRIVED AND MULTIPLIED ON THE BACKWATER STARS.
WE - THEIR CHILDREN'S CHILDREN - STILL BLINDLY FOLLOW HIS DECREE...
OBSERVE AND BEAR WITNESS! HERE IN FRONT OF YOU ARE THE TAINTED COLLECTED IN OUR HOLY PURGE ACROSS THE GALAXY.
...AND STILL LEAD HIS CRUSADE.
IT IS AN IDOL-CULT BASED ON IMITATION...

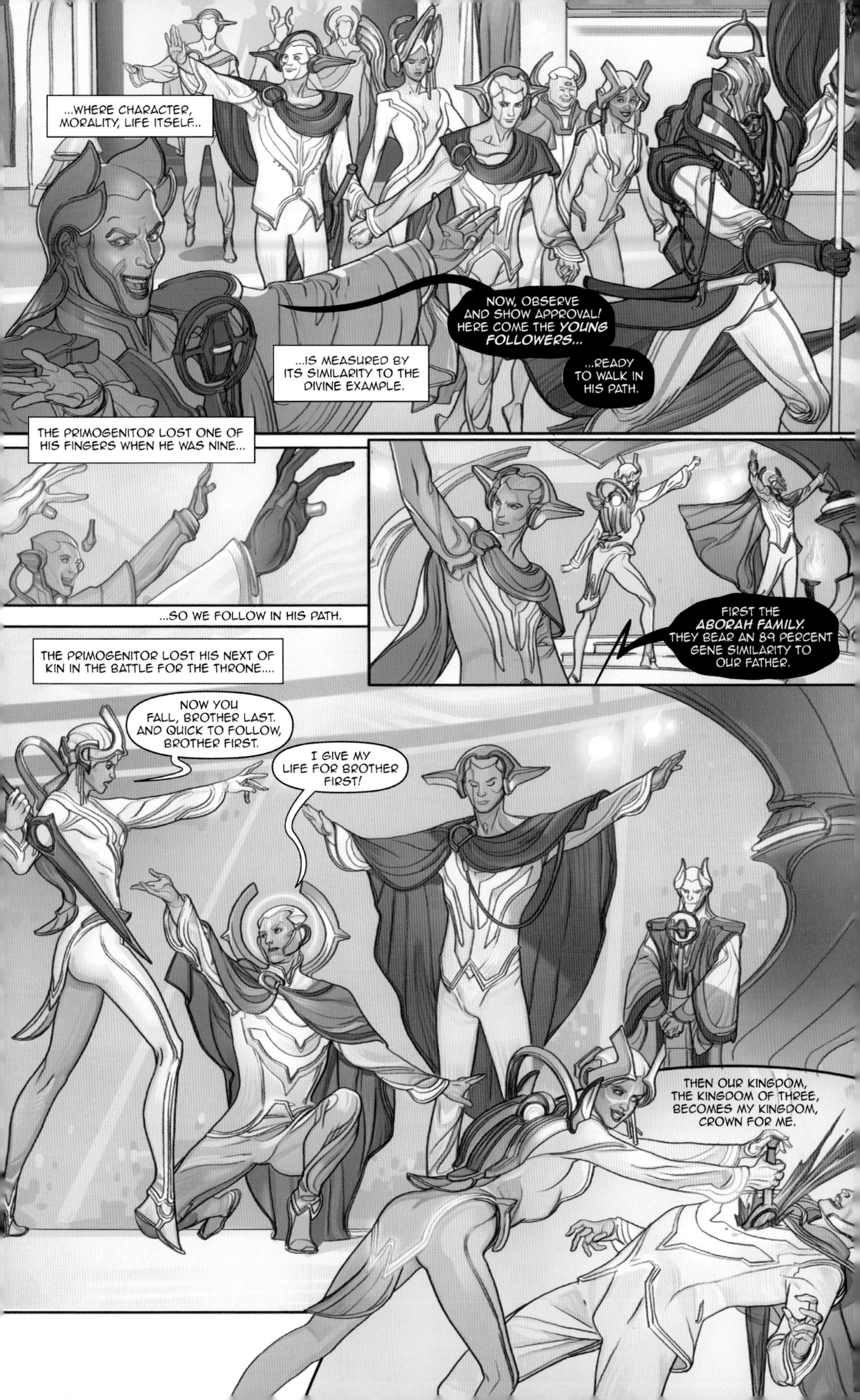
...WHERE CHARACTER, MORALITY, LIFE ITSELF...
NOW, OBSERVE AND SHOW APPROVAL! HERE COME THE *YOUNG FOLLOWERS...*
...IS MEASURED BY ITS SIMILARITY TO THE DIVINE EXAMPLE.
...READY TO WALK IN HIS PATH.
THE PRIMOGENITOR LOST ONE OF HIS FINGERS WHEN HE WAS NINE...
...SO WE FOLLOW IN HIS PATH.
FIRST THE *ABORAH FAMILY.* THEY BEAR AN 89 PERCENT GENE SIMILARITY TO OUR FATHER.
THE PRIMOGENITOR LOST HIS NEXT OF KIN IN THE BATTLE FOR THE THRONE....
NOW YOU FALL, BROTHER LAST. AND QUICK TO FOLLOW, BROTHER FIRST.
I GIVE MY LIFE FOR BROTHER FIRST!
THEN OUR KINGDOM, THE KINGDOM OF THREE, BECOMES MY KINGDOM, CROWN FOR ME.

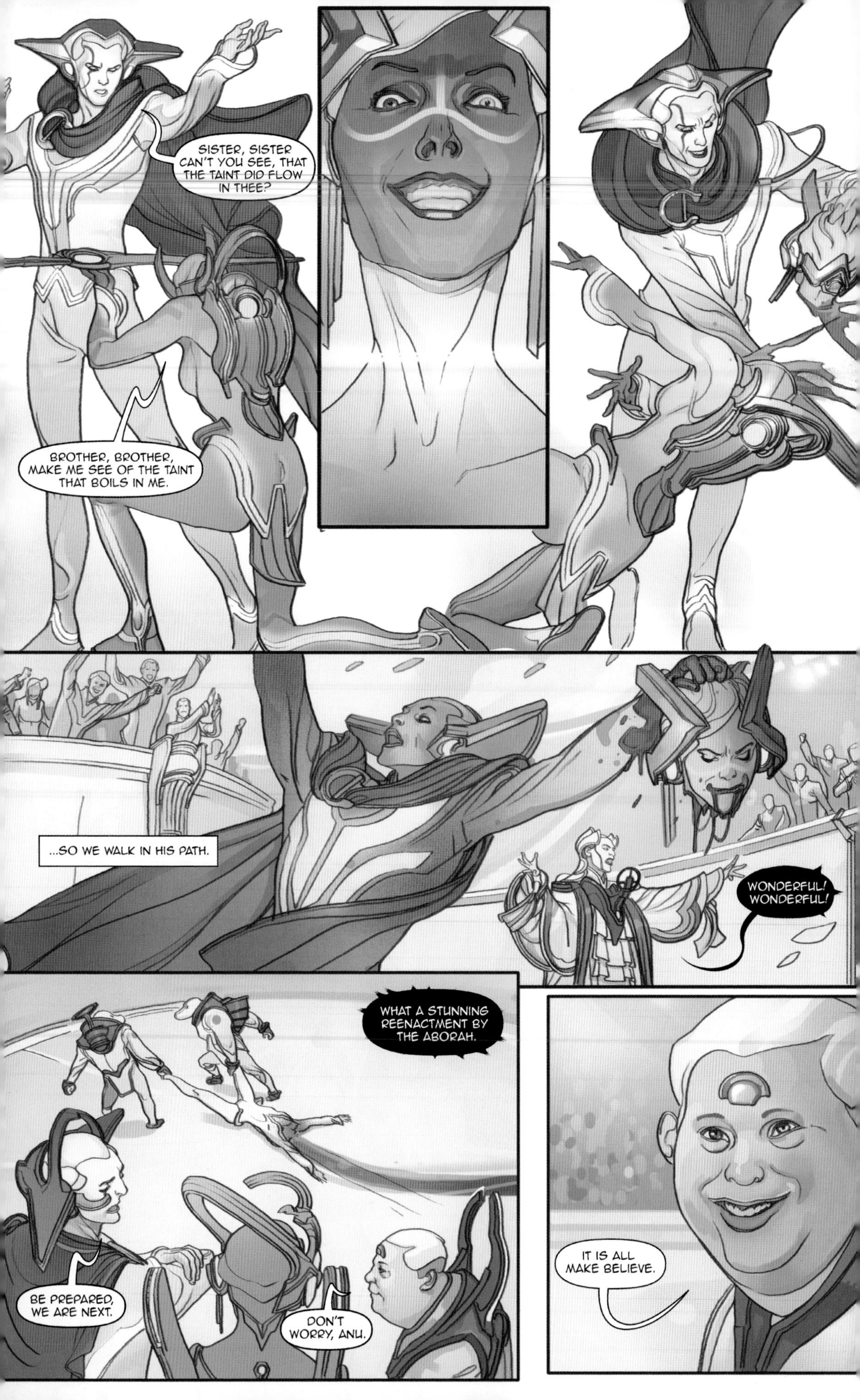
SISTER, SISTER CAN'T YOU SEE, THAT THE TAINT DID FLOW IN THEE?
BROTHER, BROTHER, MAKE ME SEE OF THE TAINT THAT BOILS IN ME.
...SO WE WALK IN HIS PATH.
WONDERFUL! WONDERFUL!
WHAT A STUNNING REENACTMENT BY THE ABORAH.
BE PREPARED, WE ARE NEXT.
DON'T WORRY, ANU.
IT IS ALL MAKE BELIEVE.

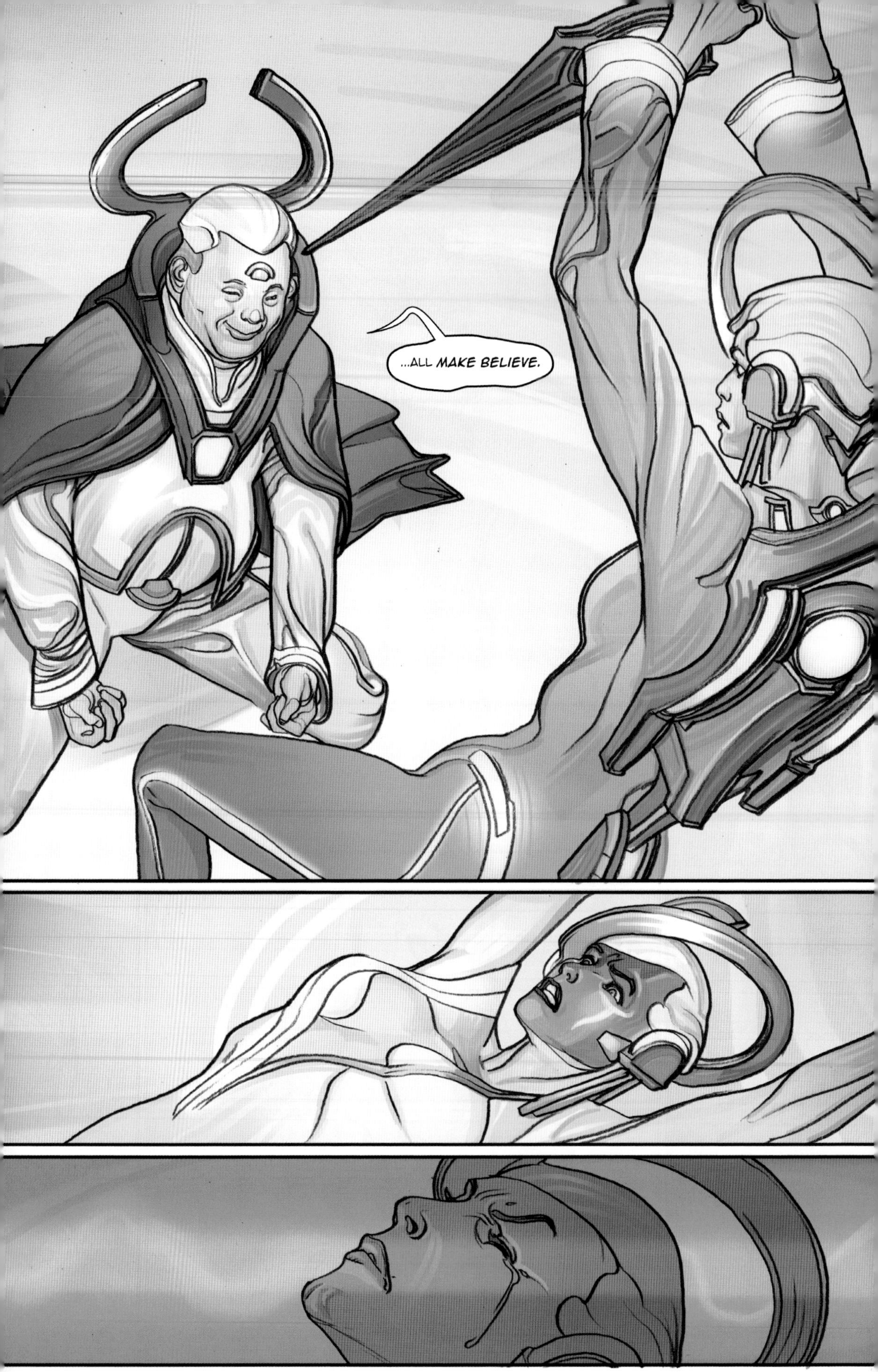
...ALL MAKE BELIEVE.

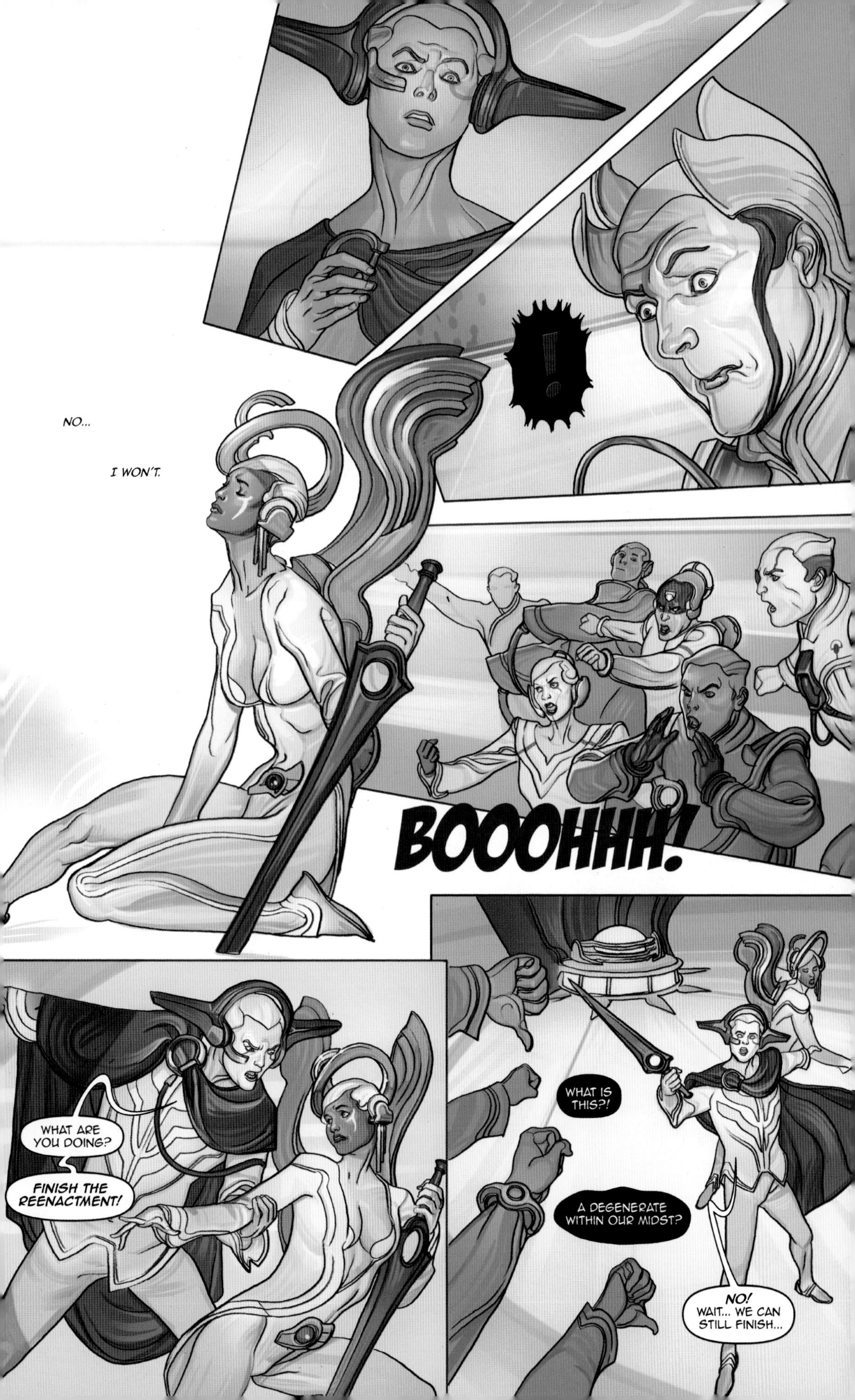
!
NO...
I WON'T.
BOOOHHH!
WHAT ARE YOU DOING?
FINISH THE REENACTMENT!
WHAT IS THIS?!
A DEGENERATE WITHIN OUR MIDST?
NO! WAIT... WE CAN STILL FINISH...

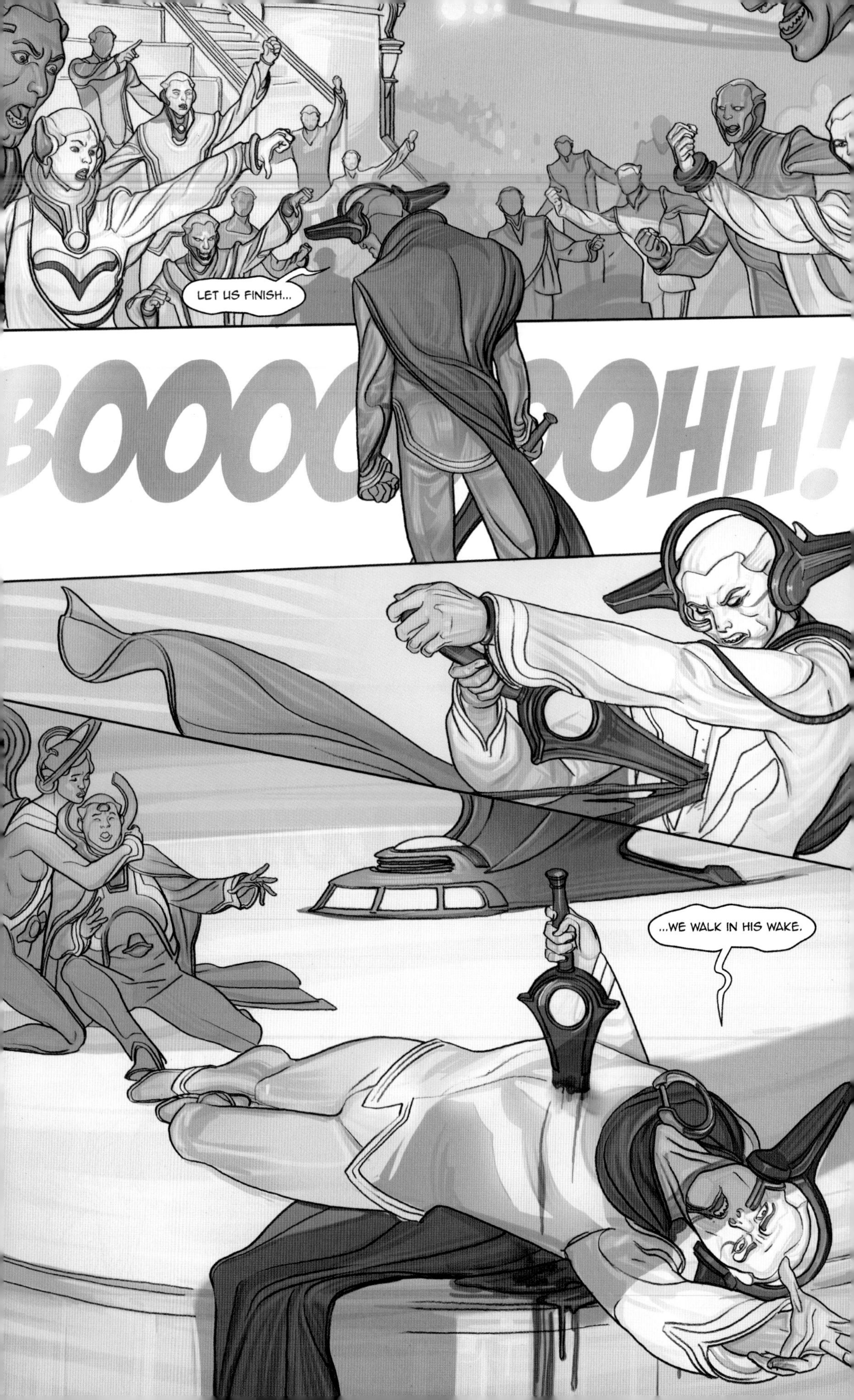
LET US FINISH...
BOOOOOOOHH!
...WE WALK IN HIS WAKE.

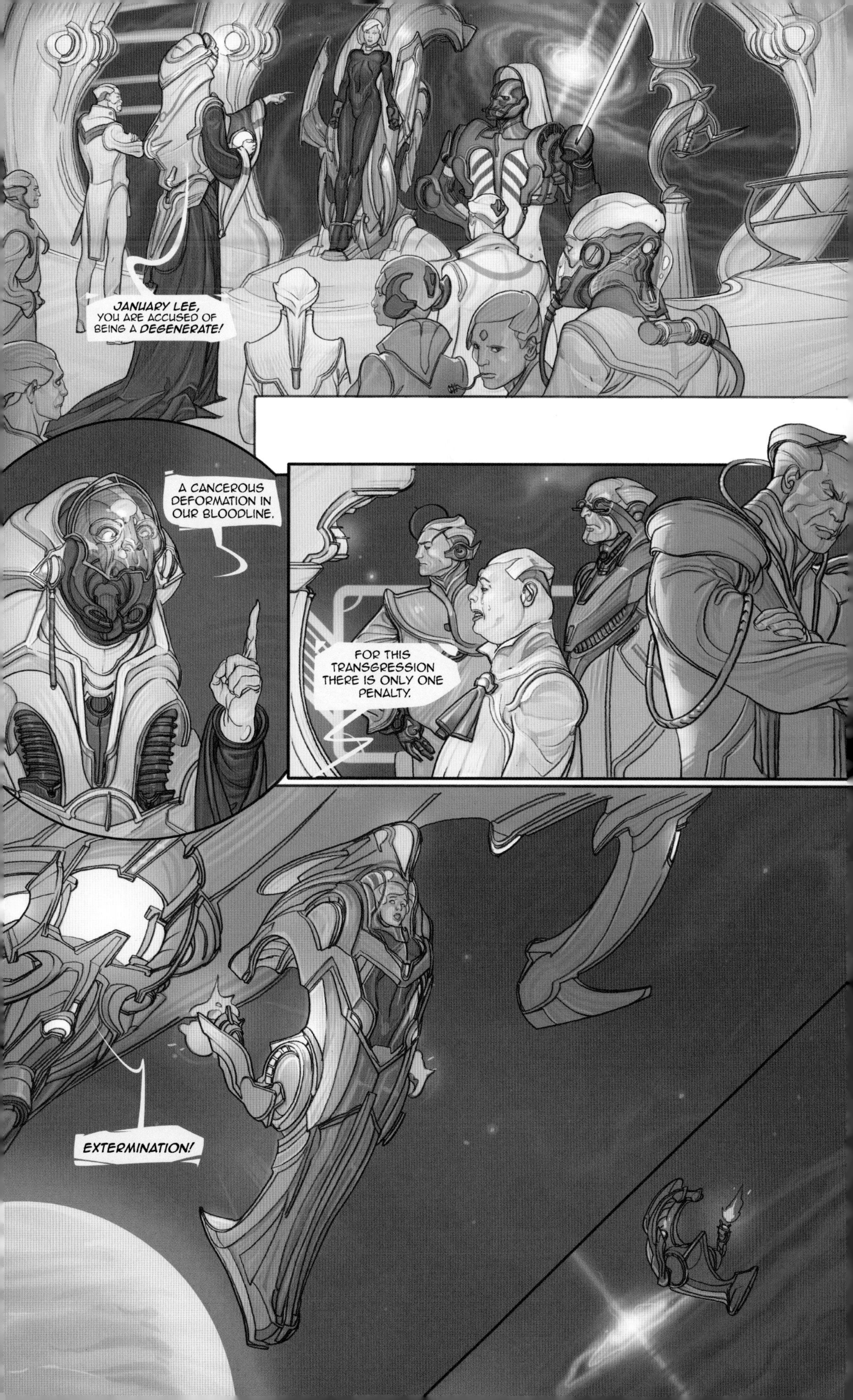
JANUARY LEE, YOU ARE ACCUSED OF BEING A DEGENERATE!
A CANCEROUS DEFORMATION IN OUR BLOODLINE.
FOR THIS TRANSGRESSION THERE IS ONLY ONE PENALTY.
EXTERMINATION!

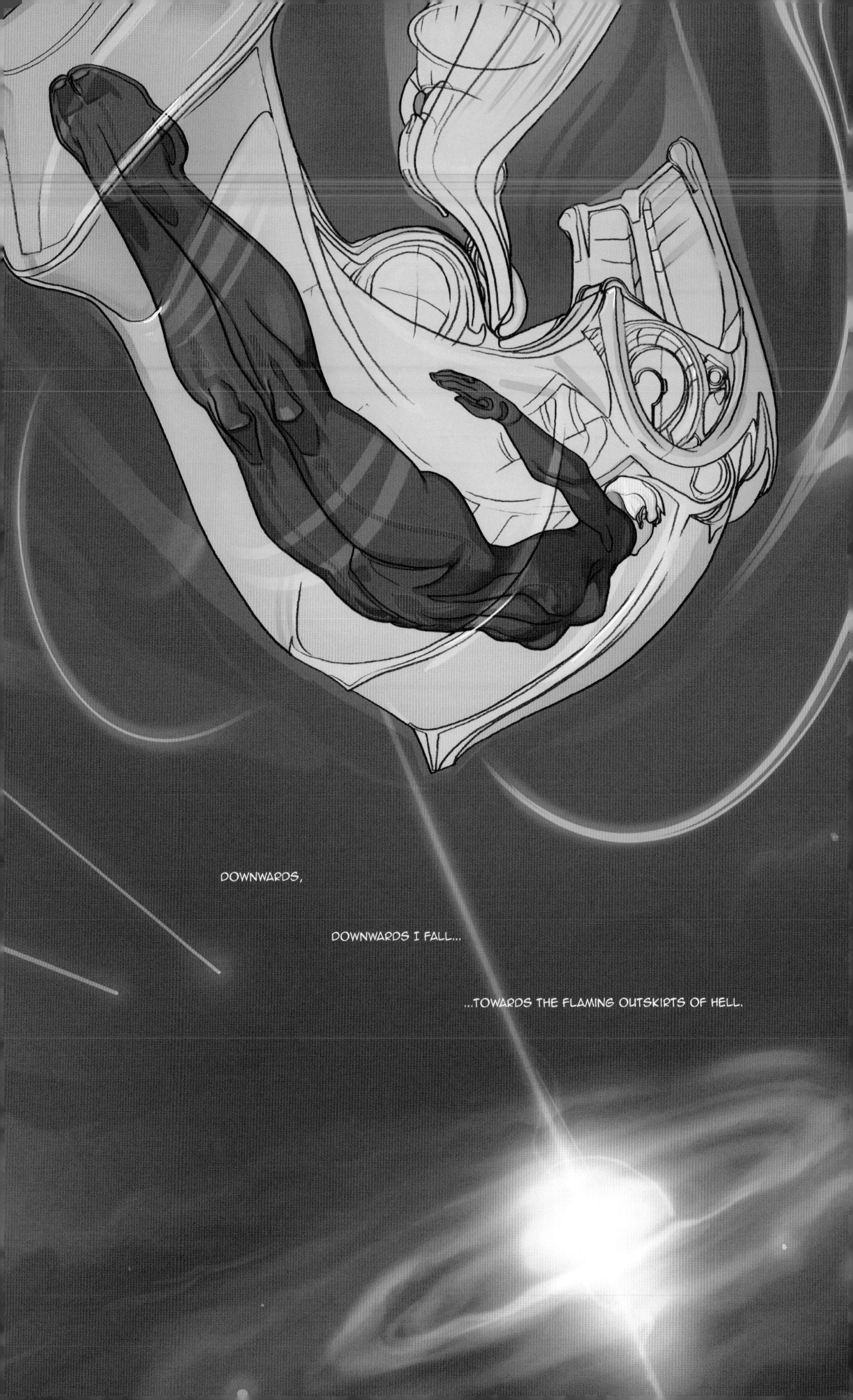
DOWNWARDS,
DOWNWARDS I FALL...
...TOWARDS THE FLAMING OUTSKIRTS OF HELL.

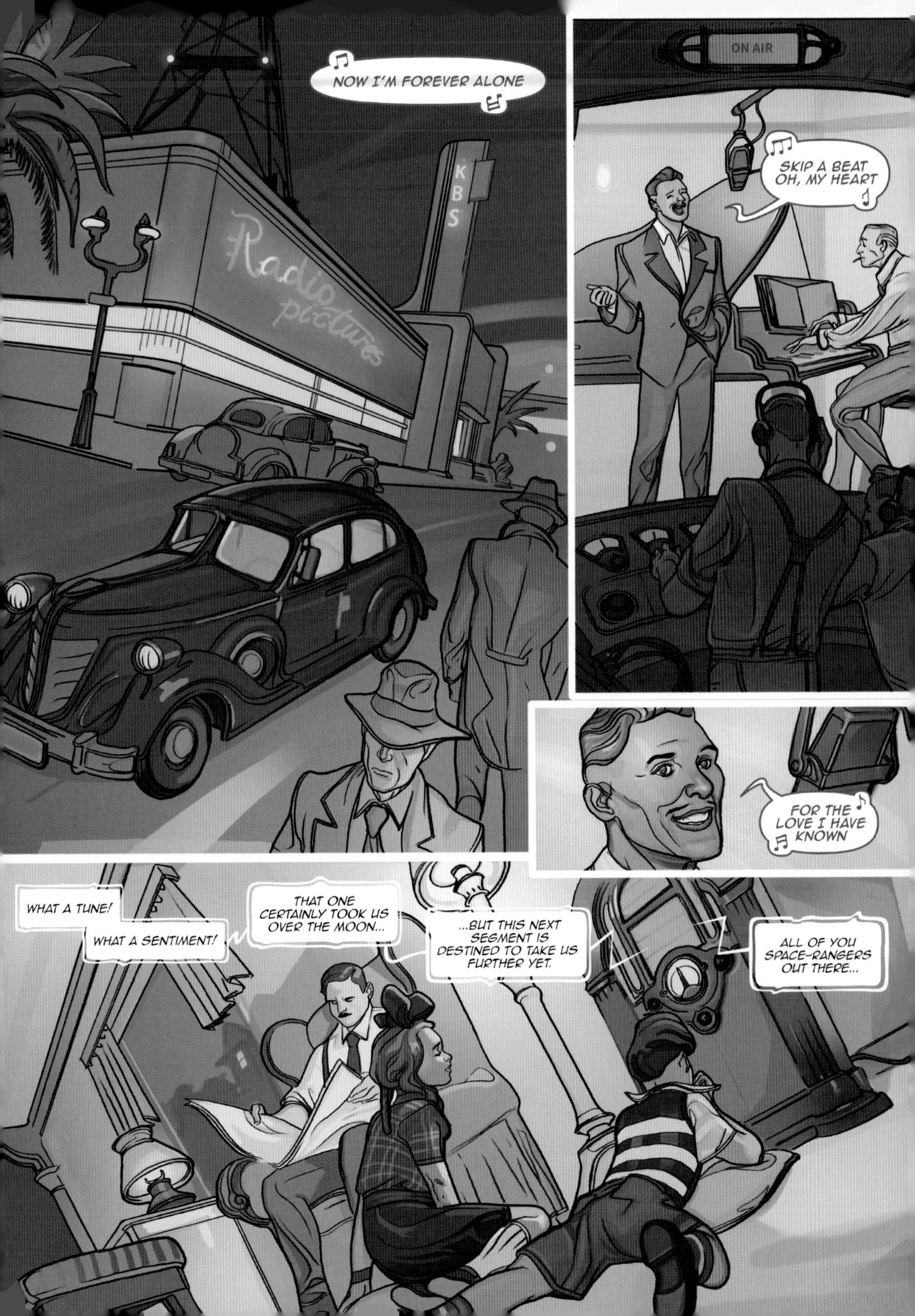
NOW I'M FOREVER ALONE
Radio pictures
KBS
ON AIR
SKIP A BEAT OH, MY HEART
FOR THE LOVE I HAVE KNOWN
WHAT A TUNE!
WHAT A SENTIMENT!
THAT ONE CERTAINLY TOOK US OVER THE MOON...
...BUT THIS NEXT SEGMENT IS DESTINED TO TAKE US FURTHER YET.
ALL OF YOU SPACE-RANGERS OUT THERE...

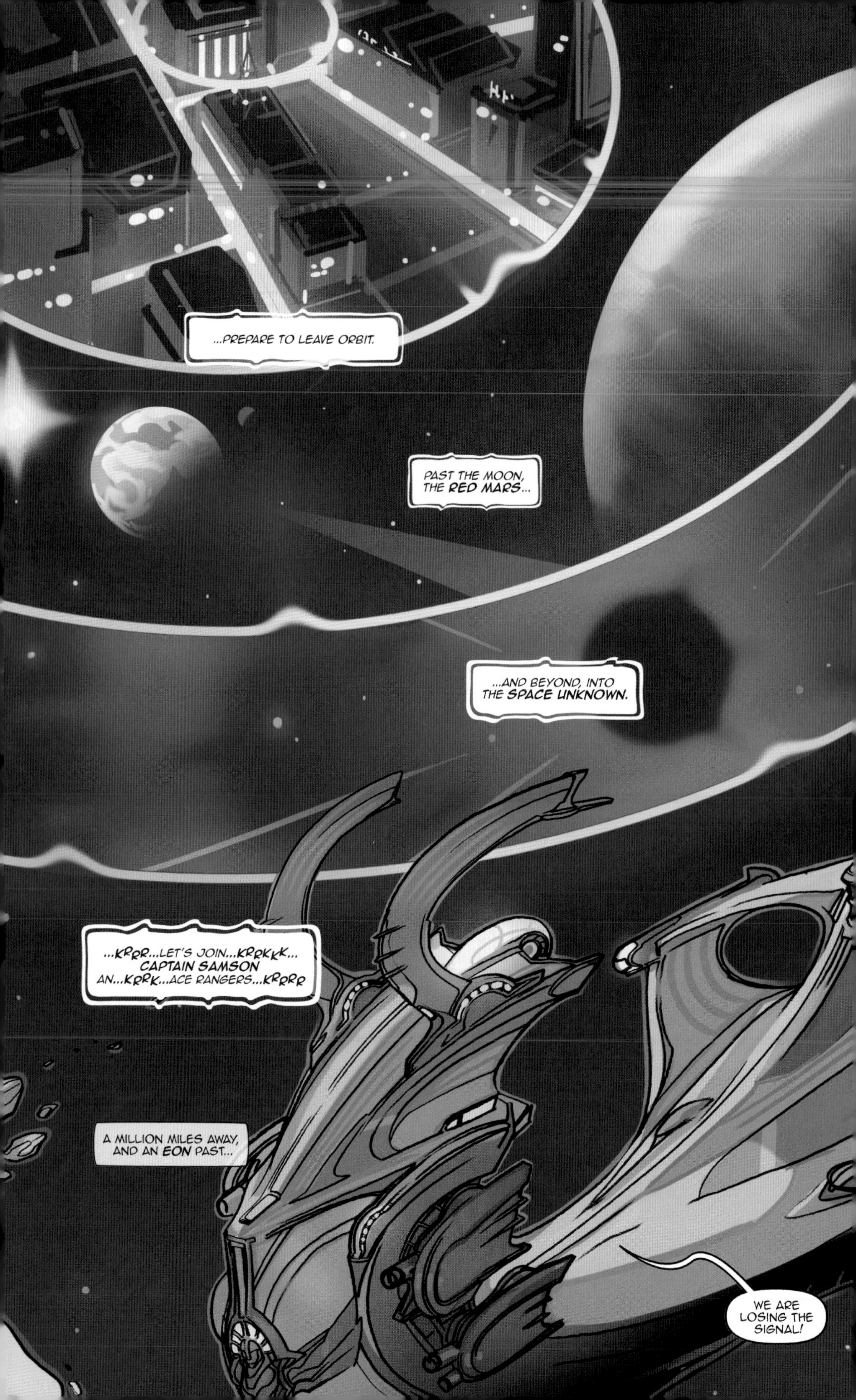
...PREPARE TO LEAVE ORBIT.
PAST THE MOON, THE RED MARS...
...AND BEYOND, INTO THE SPACE UNKNOWN.
...KRRR...LET'S JOIN...KRRKKK... CAPTAIN SAMSON AN...KRRK...ACE RANGERS...KRRRR
A MILLION MILES AWAY, AND AN EON PAST...
WE ARE LOSING THE SIGNAL!

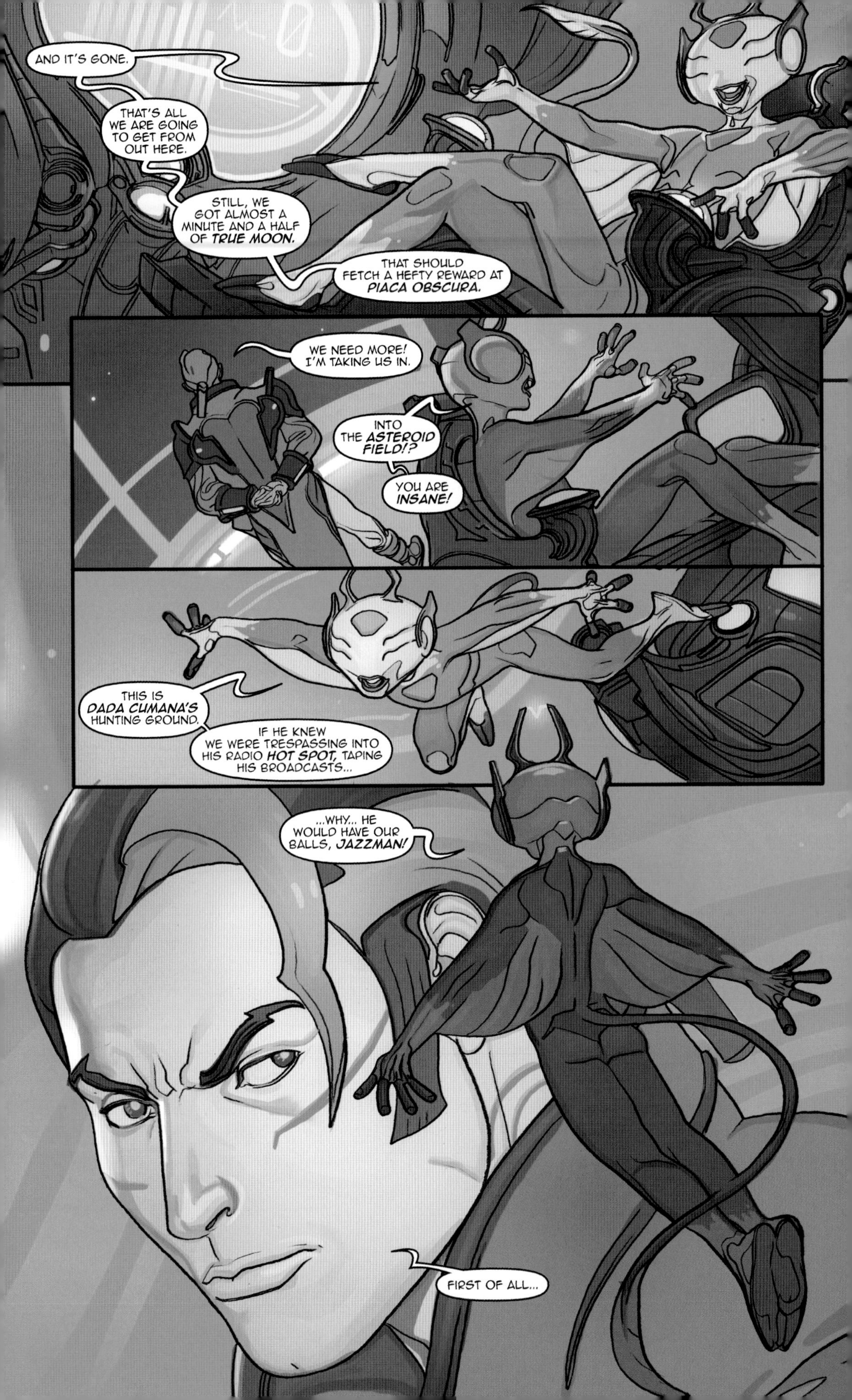
AND IT'S GONE.
THAT'S ALL WE ARE GOING TO GET FROM OUT HERE.
STILL, WE GOT ALMOST A MINUTE AND A HALF OF TRUE MOON.
THAT SHOULD FETCH A HEFTY REWARD AT PIACA OBSCURA.
WE NEED MORE! I'M TAKING US IN.
INTO THE ASTEROID FIELD!?
YOU ARE INSANE!
THIS IS DADA CUMANA'S HUNTING GROUND.
IF HE KNEW WE WERE TRESPASSING INTO HIS RADIO HOT SPOT, TAPING HIS BROADCASTS...
...WHY... HE WOULD HAVE OUR BALLS, JAZZMAN!
FIRST OF ALL...

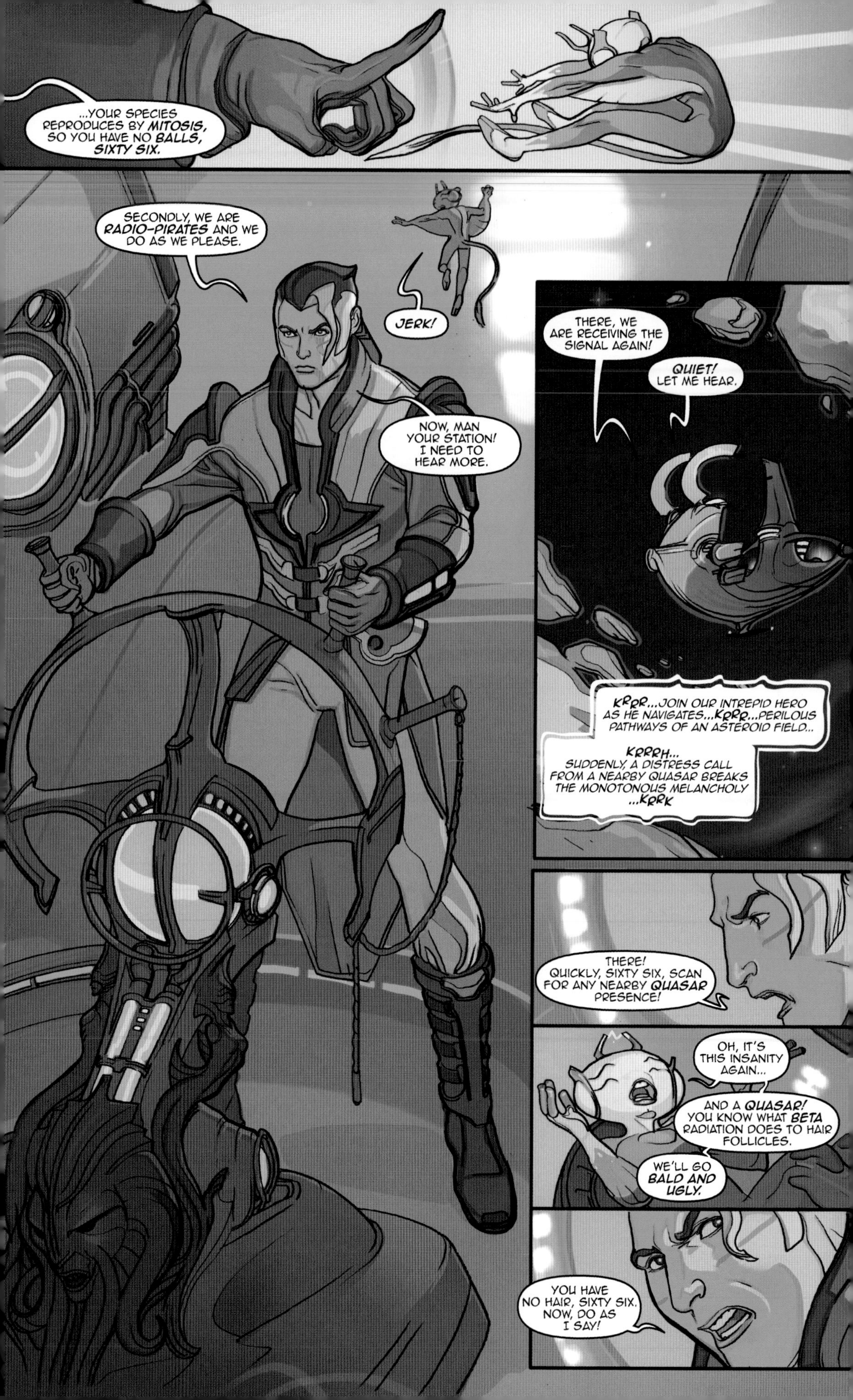

...YOUR SPECIES REPRODUCES BY MITOSIS, SO YOU HAVE NO BALLS, SIXTY SIX.
SECONDLY, WE ARE RADIO-PIRATES AND WE DO AS WE PLEASE.
JERK!
NOW, MAN YOUR STATION! I NEED TO HEAR MORE.
THERE, WE ARE RECEIVING THE SIGNAL AGAIN!
QUIET! LET ME HEAR.
KRRR...JOIN OUR INTREPID HERO AS HE NAVIGATES...KRRR...PERILOUS PATHWAYS OF AN ASTEROID FIELD...
KRRRH... SUDDENLY, A DISTRESS CALL FROM A NEARBY QUASAR BREAKS THE MONOTONOUS MELANCHOLY ...KRRK
THERE! QUICKLY, SIXTY SIX, SCAN FOR ANY NEARBY QUASAR PRESENCE!
OH, IT'S THIS INSANITY AGAIN...
AND A QUASAR! YOU KNOW WHAT BETA RADIATION DOES TO HAIR FOLLICLES.
WE'LL GO BALD AND UGLY.
YOU HAVE NO HAIR, SIXTY SIX. NOW, DO AS I SAY!

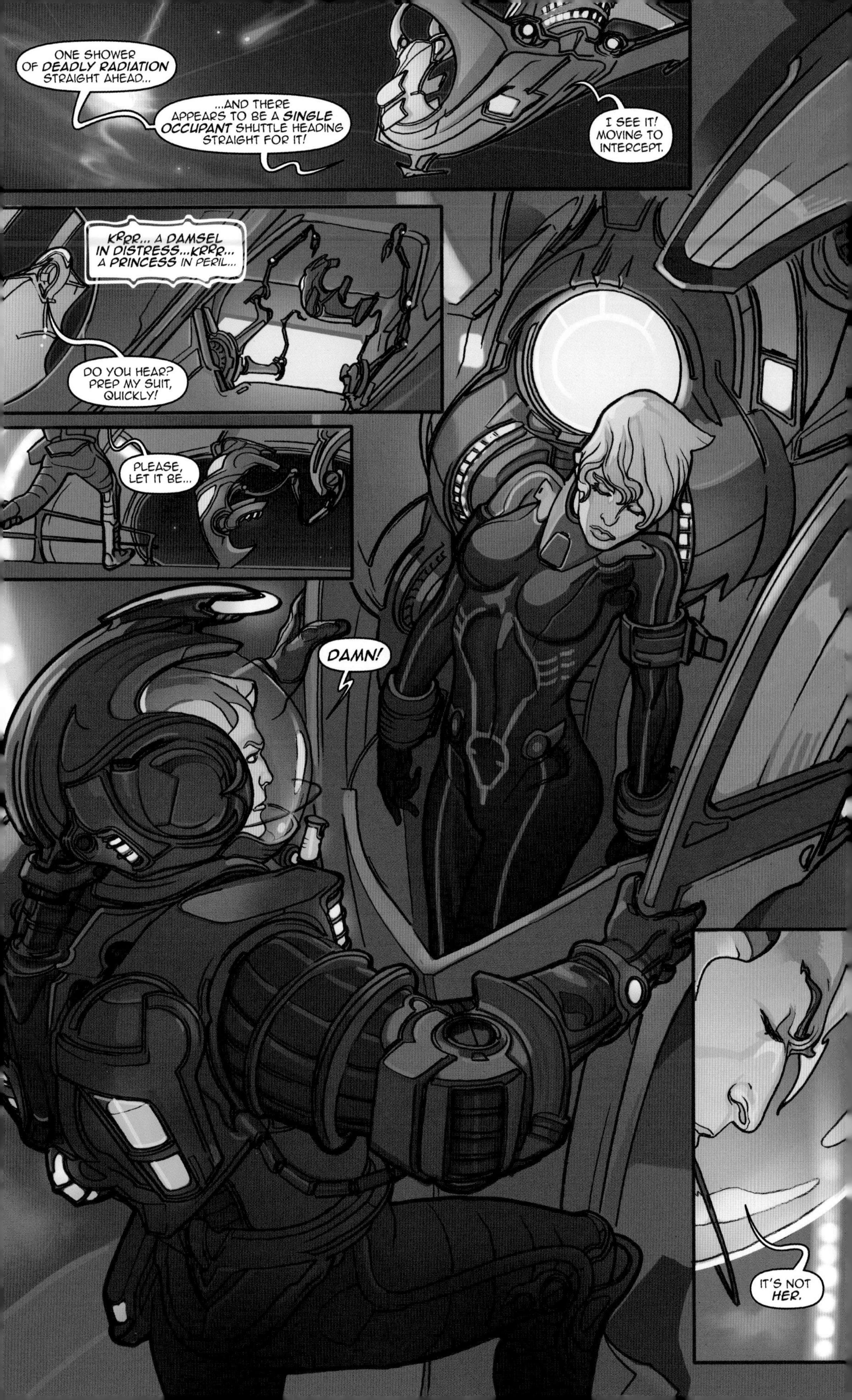
ONE SHOWER OF DEADLY RADIATION STRAIGHT AHEAD...
...AND THERE APPEARS TO BE A SINGLE OCCUPANT SHUTTLE HEADING STRAIGHT FOR IT!
I SEE IT! MOVING TO INTERCEPT.
KRRR... A DAMSEL IN DISTRESS...KRRR... A PRINCESS IN PERIL...
DO YOU HEAR? PREP MY SUIT, QUICKLY!
PLEASE, LET IT BE...
DAMN!
IT'S NOT HER.

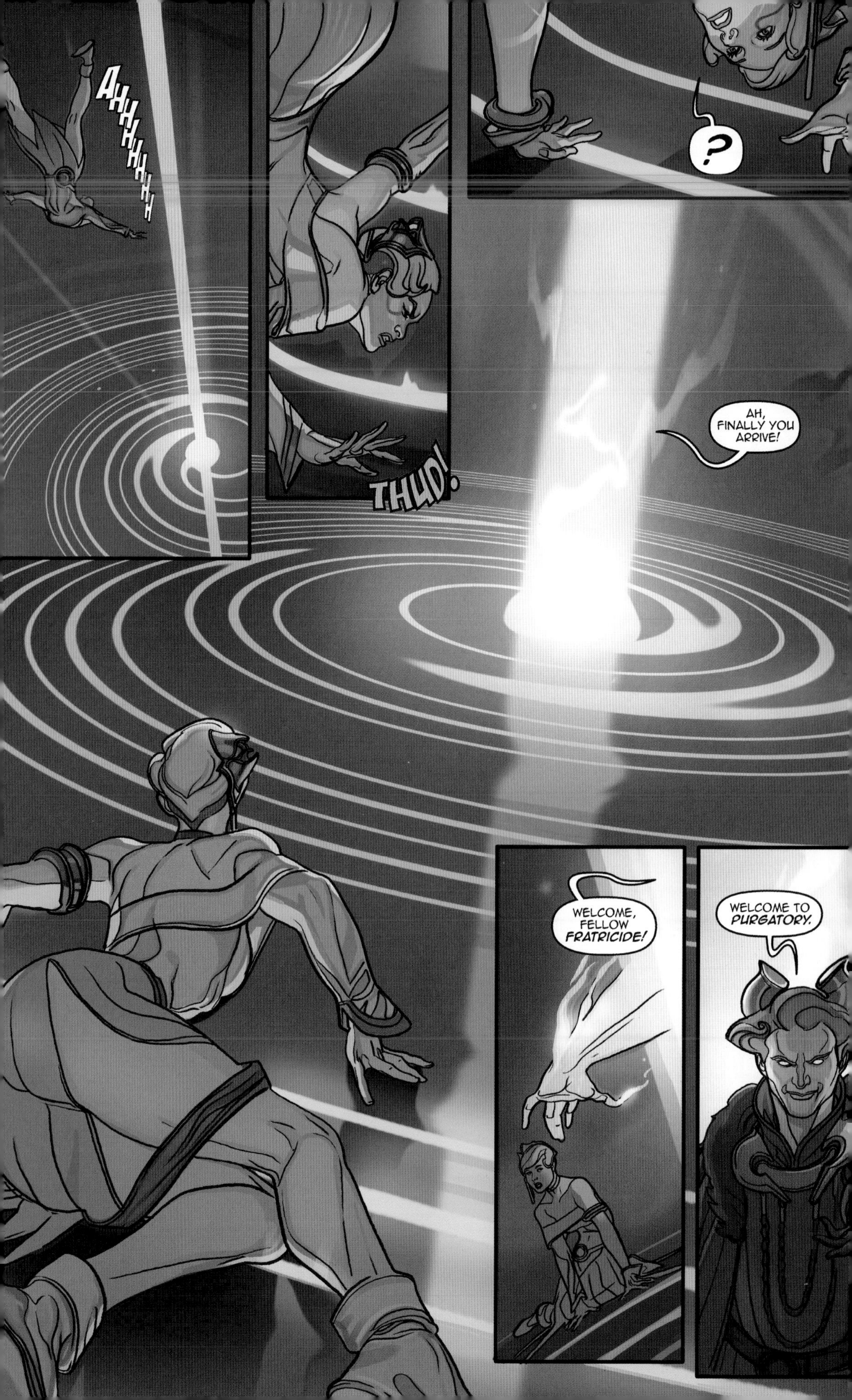
AHHHHHHHH
THUD!
?
AH, FINALLY YOU ARRIVE!
WELCOME, FELLOW FRATRICIDE!
WELCOME TO PURGATORY.

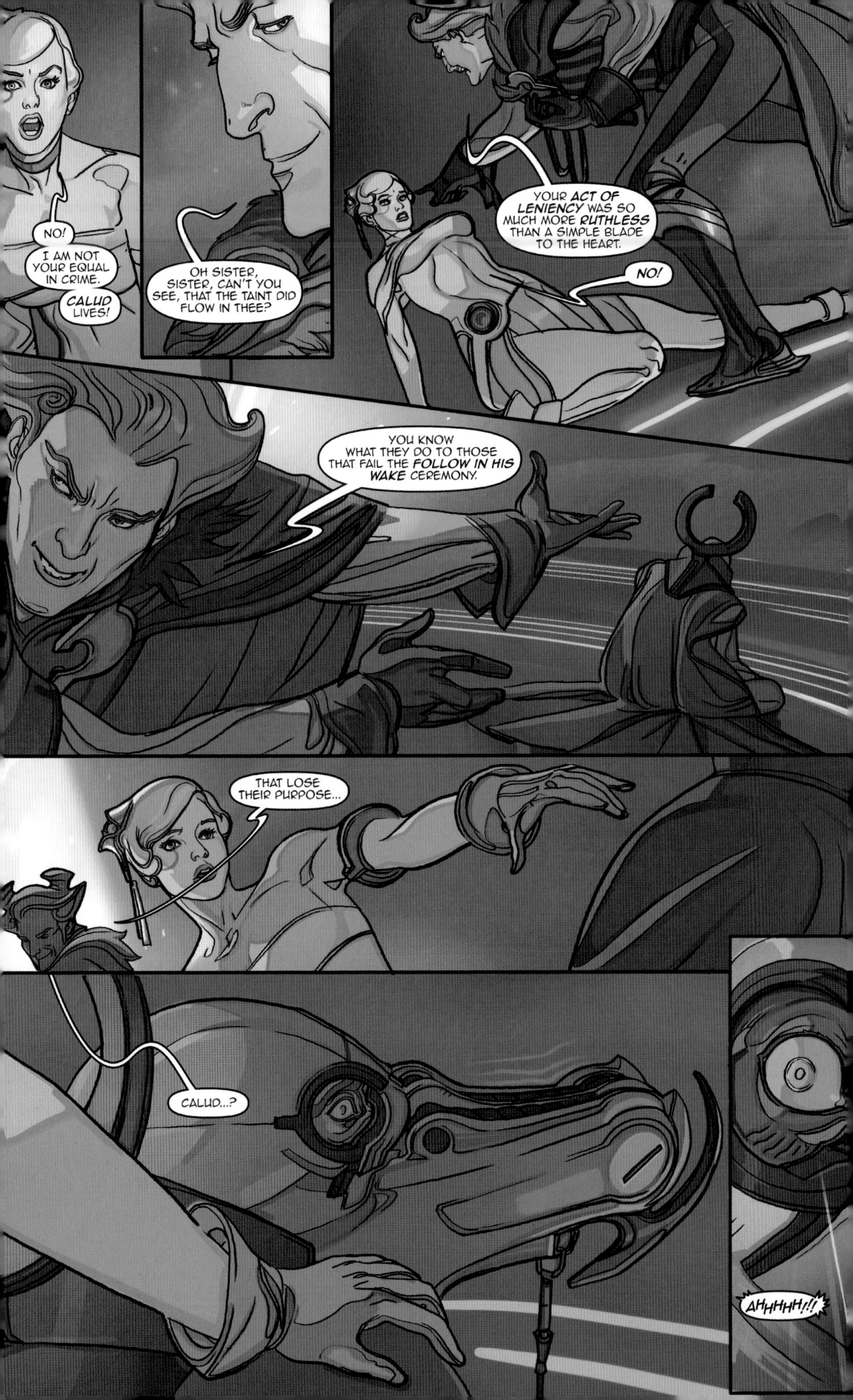
NO!
I AM NOT YOUR EQUAL IN CRIME.
CALUD LIVES!
OH SISTER, SISTER, CAN'T YOU SEE, THAT THE TAINT DID FLOW IN THEE?
YOUR ACT OF LENIENCY WAS SO MUCH MORE RUTHLESS THAN A SIMPLE BLADE TO THE HEART.
NO!
YOU KNOW WHAT THEY DO TO THOSE THAT FAIL THE FOLLOW IN HIS WAKE CEREMONY.
THAT LOSE THEIR PURPOSE...
CALUD...?
AHHHHH!!!

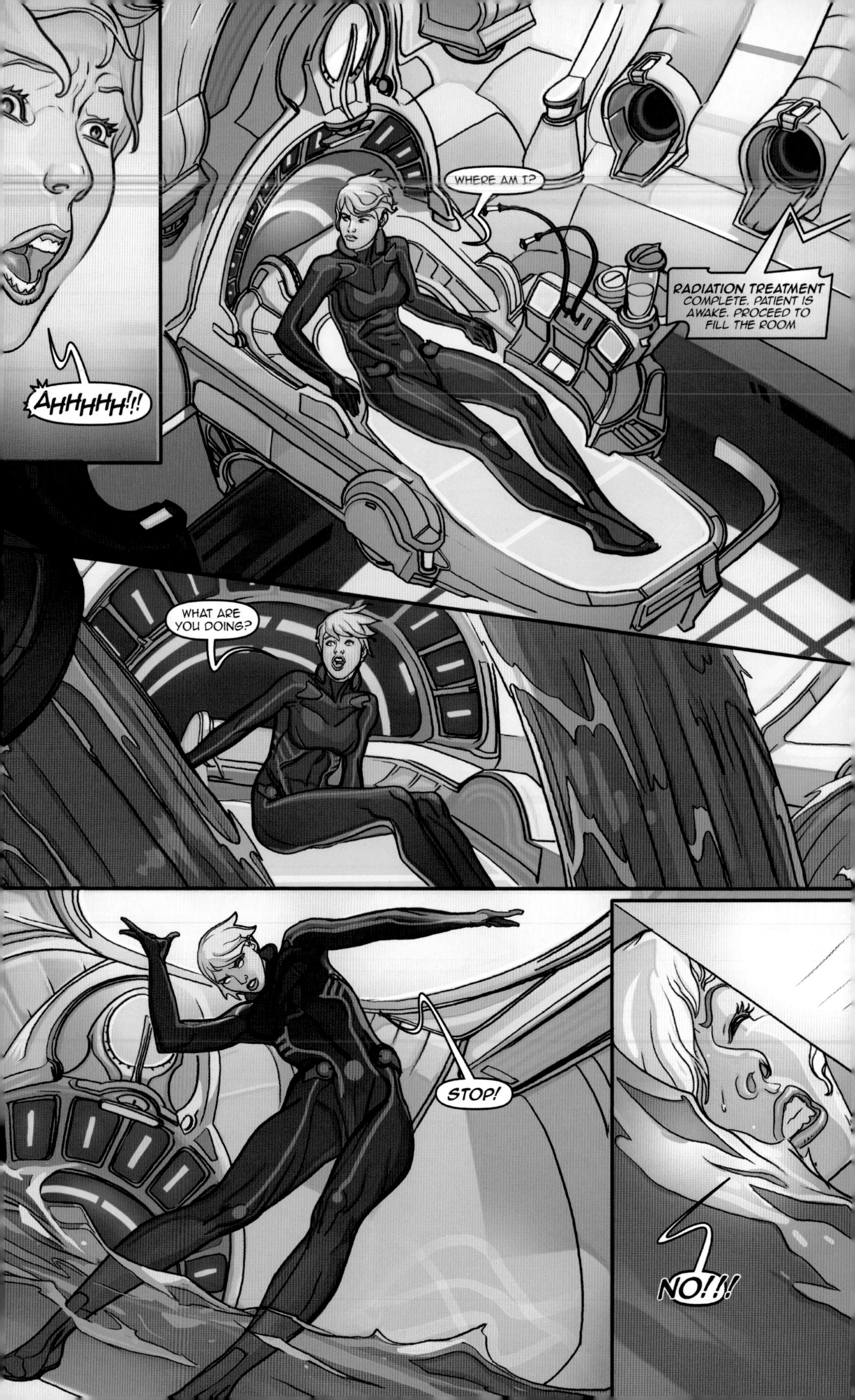
AHHHHH!!!
WHERE AM I?
RADIATION TREATMENT COMPLETE. PATIENT IS AWAKE. PROCEED TO FILL THE ROOM
WHAT ARE YOU DOING?
STOP!
NO!!!

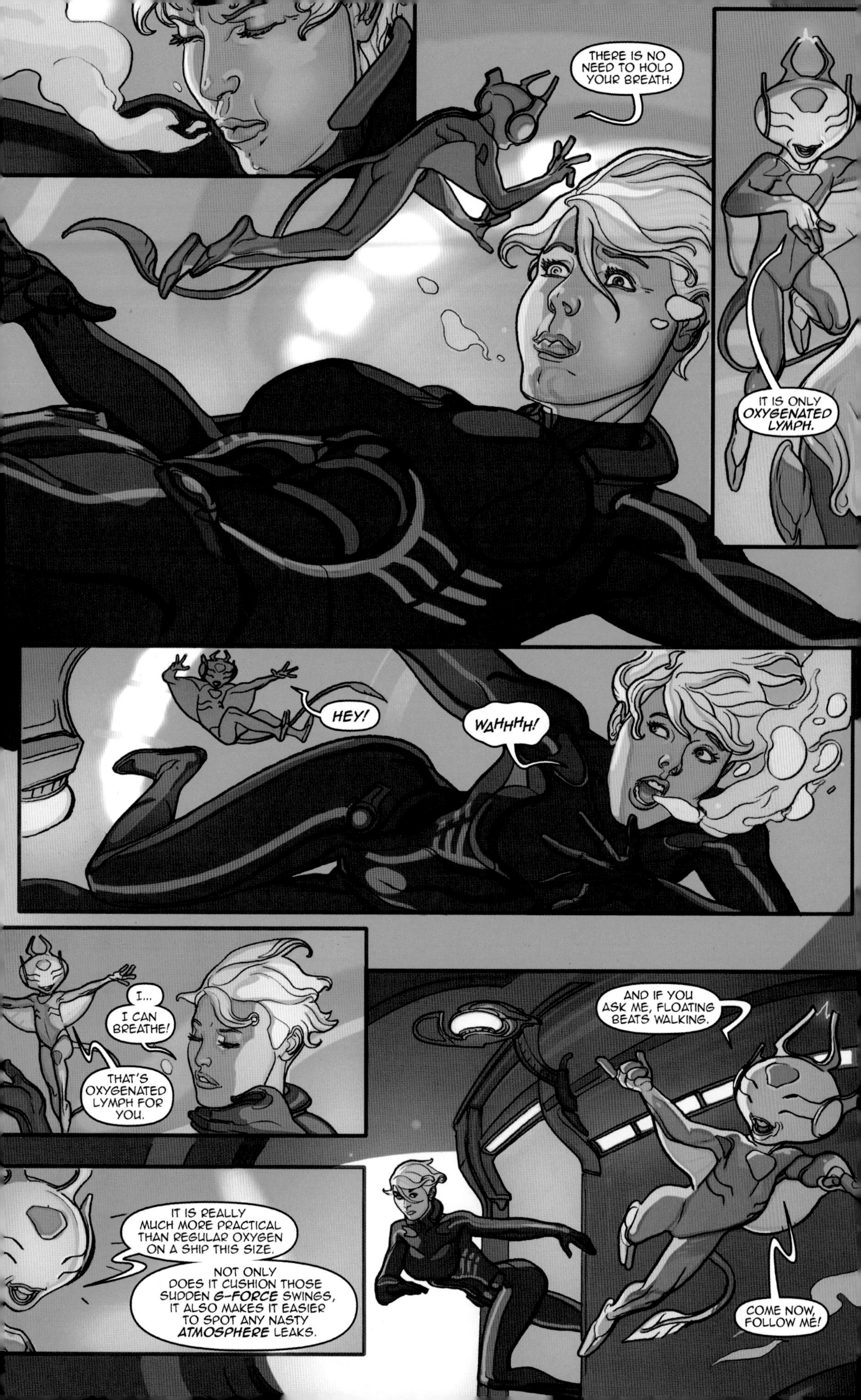
THERE IS NO NEED TO HOLD YOUR BREATH.
IT IS ONLY OXYGENATED LYMPH.
HEY!
WAHHHH!
I... I CAN BREATHE!
THAT'S OXYGENATED LYMPH FOR YOU.
AND IF YOU ASK ME, FLOATING BEATS WALKING.
IT IS REALLY MUCH MORE PRACTICAL THAN REGULAR OXYGEN ON A SHIP THIS SIZE.
NOT ONLY DOES IT CUSHION THOSE SUDDEN G-FORCE SWINGS, IT ALSO MAKES IT EASIER TO SPOT ANY NASTY ATMOSPHERE LEAKS.
COME NOW, FOLLOW ME!

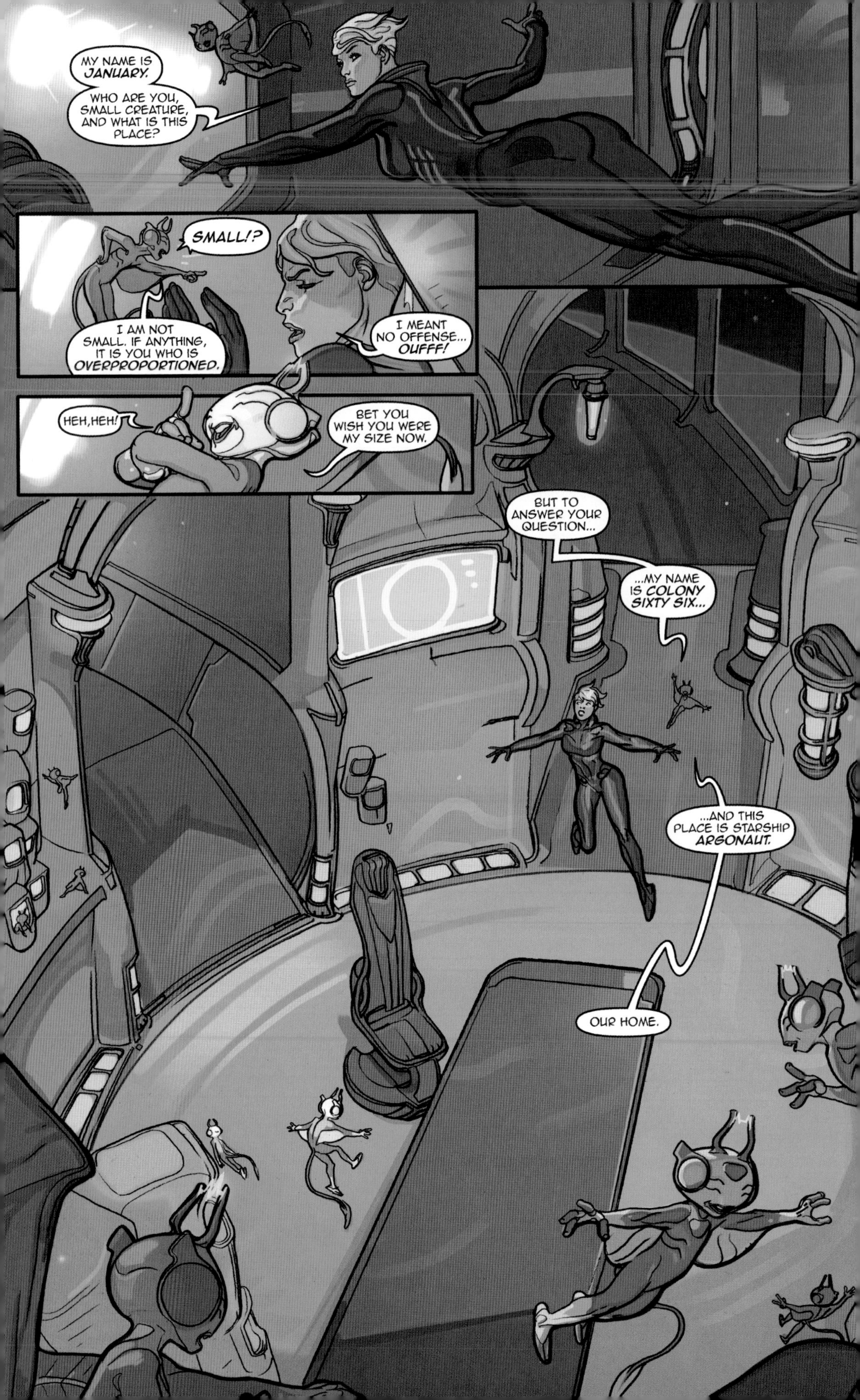
MY NAME IS JANUARY.
WHO ARE YOU, SMALL CREATURE, AND WHAT IS THIS PLACE?
SMALL!?
I AM NOT SMALL. IF ANYTHING, IT IS YOU WHO IS OVERPROPORTIONED.
I MEANT NO OFFENSE... OUFFF!
HEH,HEH!
BET YOU WISH YOU WERE MY SIZE NOW.
BUT TO ANSWER YOUR QUESTION...
...MY NAME IS COLONY SIXTY SIX...
...AND THIS PLACE IS STARSHIP ARGONAUT.
OUR HOME.

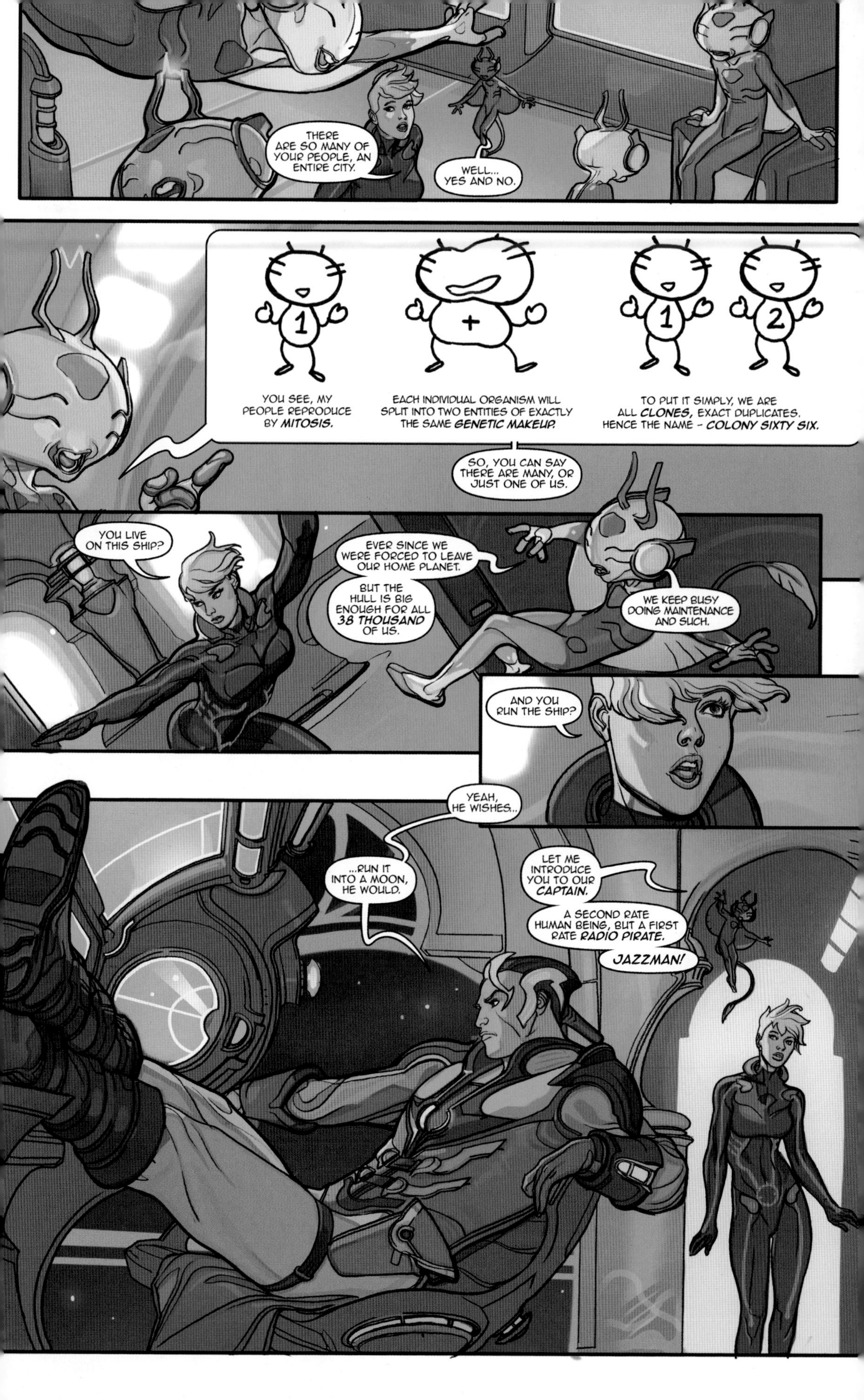
THERE ARE SO MANY OF YOUR PEOPLE, AN ENTIRE CITY.
WELL... YES AND NO.
1
+
1
2
YOU SEE, MY PEOPLE REPRODUCE BY MITOSIS.
EACH INDIVIDUAL ORGANISM WILL SPLIT INTO TWO ENTITIES OF EXACTLY THE SAME GENETIC MAKEUP.
TO PUT IT SIMPLY, WE ARE ALL CLONES, EXACT DUPLICATES. HENCE THE NAME - COLONY SIXTY SIX.
SO, YOU CAN SAY THERE ARE MANY, OR JUST ONE OF US.
YOU LIVE ON THIS SHIP?
EVER SINCE WE WERE FORCED TO LEAVE OUR HOME PLANET.
BUT THE HULL IS BIG ENOUGH FOR ALL 38 THOUSAND OF US.
WE KEEP BUSY DOING MAINTENANCE AND SUCH.
AND YOU RUN THE SHIP?
YEAH, HE WISHES...
...RUN IT INTO A MOON, HE WOULD.
LET ME INTRODUCE YOU TO OUR CAPTAIN.
A SECOND RATE HUMAN BEING, BUT A FIRST RATE RADIO PIRATE.
JAZZMAN!

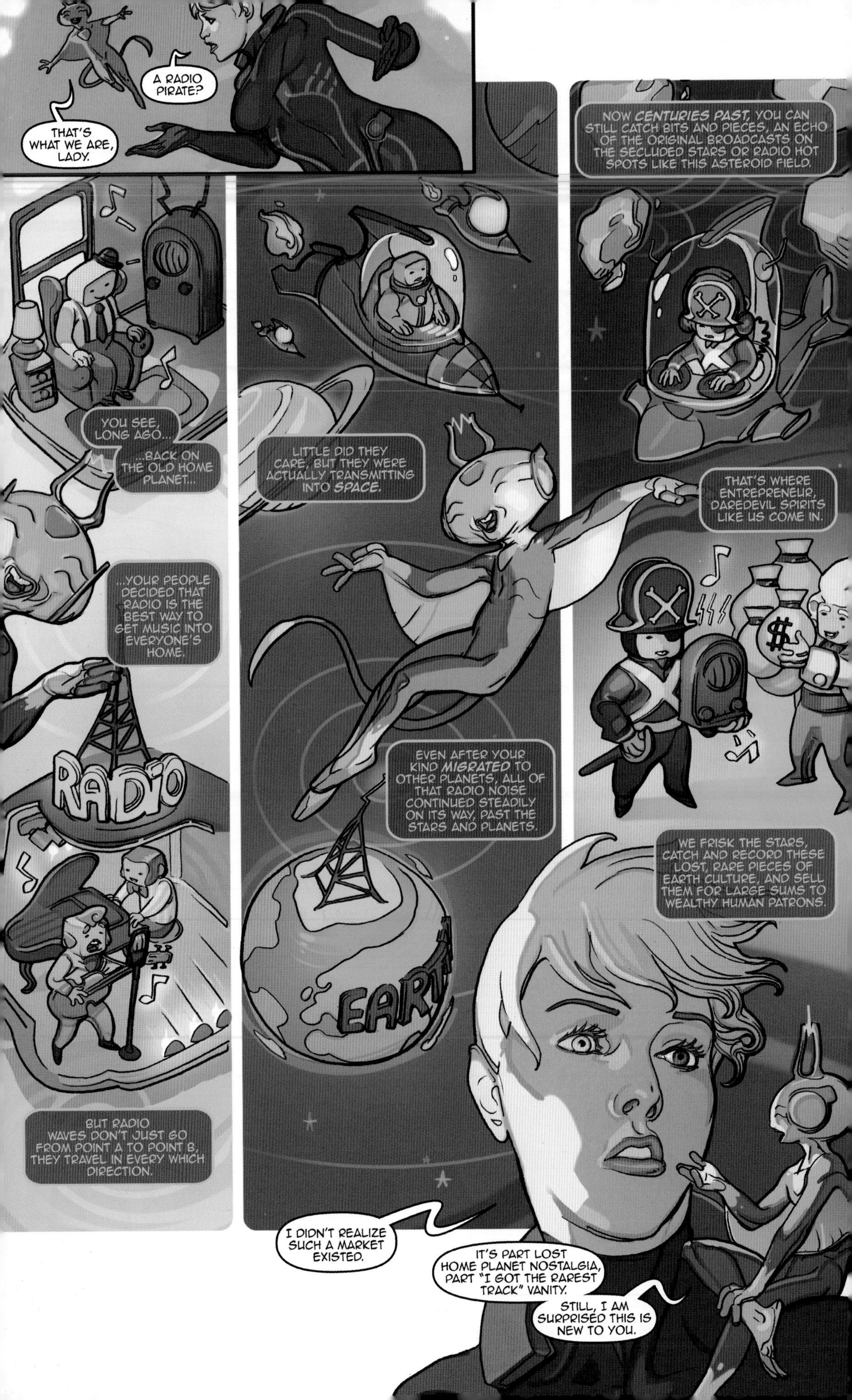

A RADIO PIRATE?
THAT'S WHAT WE ARE, LADY.
YOU SEE, LONG AGO...
...BACK ON THE OLD HOME PLANET...
...YOUR PEOPLE DECIDED THAT RADIO IS THE BEST WAY TO GET MUSIC INTO EVERYONE'S HOME.
RADIO
BUT RADIO WAVES DON'T JUST GO FROM POINT A TO POINT B, THEY TRAVEL IN EVERY WHICH DIRECTION.
LITTLE DID THEY CARE, BUT THEY WERE ACTUALLY TRANSMITTING INTO *SPACE*.
EVEN AFTER YOUR KIND *MIGRATED* TO OTHER PLANETS, ALL OF THAT RADIO NOISE CONTINUED STEADILY ON ITS WAY, PAST THE STARS AND PLANETS.
NOW *CENTURIES PAST*, YOU CAN STILL CATCH BITS AND PIECES, AN ECHO OF THE ORIGINAL BROADCASTS ON THE SECLUDED STARS OR RADIO HOT SPOTS LIKE THIS ASTEROID FIELD.
THAT'S WHERE ENTREPRENEUR, DAREDEVIL SPIRITS LIKE US COME IN.
WE FRISK THE STARS, CATCH AND RECORD THESE LOST, RARE PIECES OF EARTH CULTURE, AND SELL THEM FOR LARGE SUMS TO WEALTHY HUMAN PATRONS.
I DIDN'T REALIZE SUCH A MARKET EXISTED.
IT'S PART LOST HOME PLANET NOSTALGIA, PART "I GOT THE RAREST TRACK" VANITY.
STILL, I AM SURPRISED THIS IS NEW TO YOU.

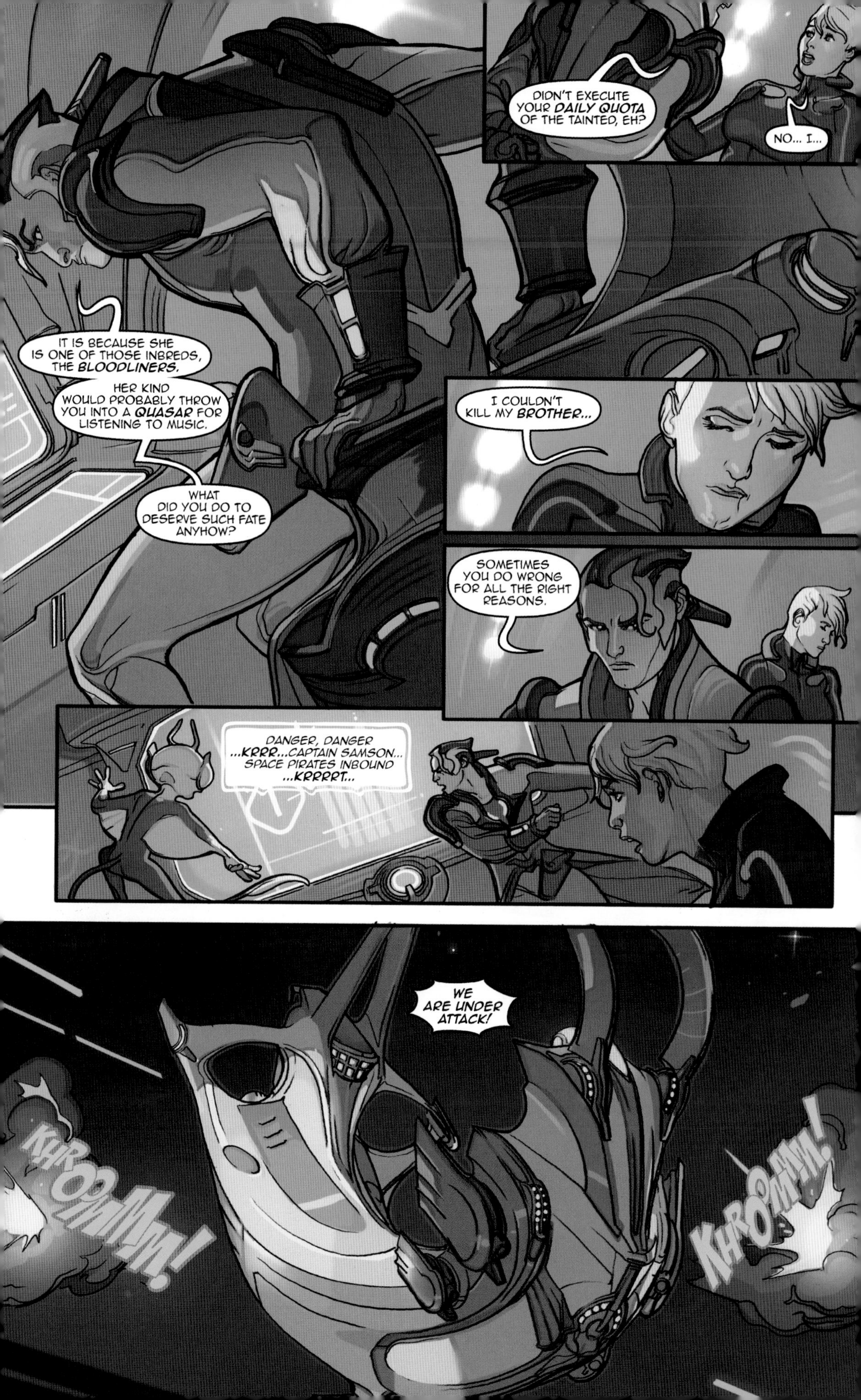
DIDN'T EXECUTE YOUR DAILY QUOTA OF THE TAINTED, EH?
NO... I...
IT IS BECAUSE SHE IS ONE OF THOSE INBREDS, THE BLOODLINERS.
HER KIND WOULD PROBABLY THROW YOU INTO A QUASAR FOR LISTENING TO MUSIC.
WHAT DID YOU DO TO DESERVE SUCH FATE ANYHOW?
I COULDN'T KILL MY BROTHER...
SOMETIMES YOU DO WRONG FOR ALL THE RIGHT REASONS.
DANGER, DANGER ...KRRR...CAPTAIN SAMSON... SPACE PIRATES INBOUND ...KRRRRT...
WE ARE UNDER ATTACK!
KHROOMMM!
KHROOMMM!

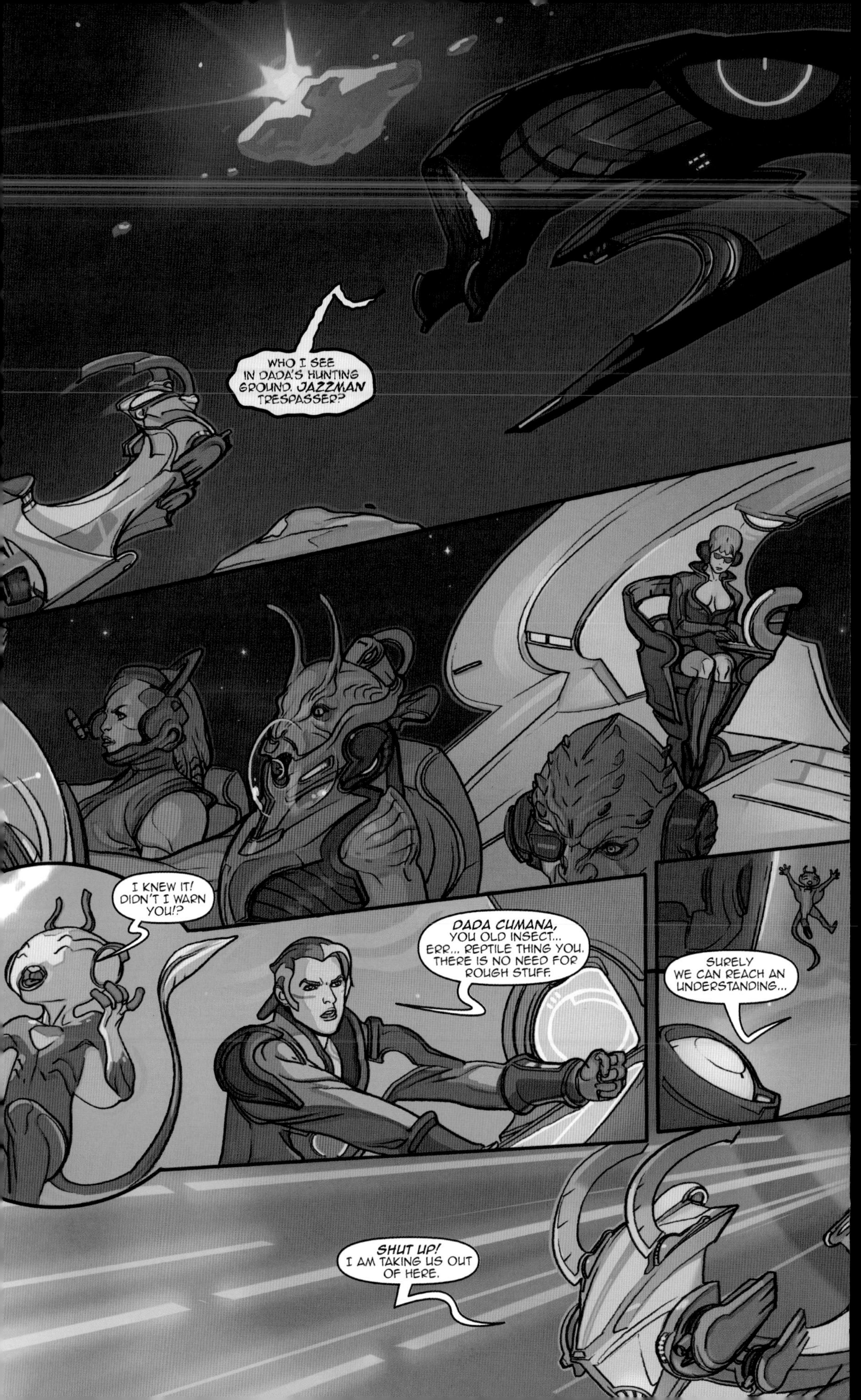
WHO I SEE IN DADA'S HUNTING GROUND, JAZZMAN TRESPASSER?
I KNEW IT! DIDN'T I WARN YOU!?
DADA CUMANA, YOU OLD INSECT... ERR... REPTILE THING YOU. THERE IS NO NEED FOR ROUGH STUFF.
SURELY WE CAN REACH AN UNDERSTANDING...
SHUT UP! I AM TAKING US OUT OF HERE.

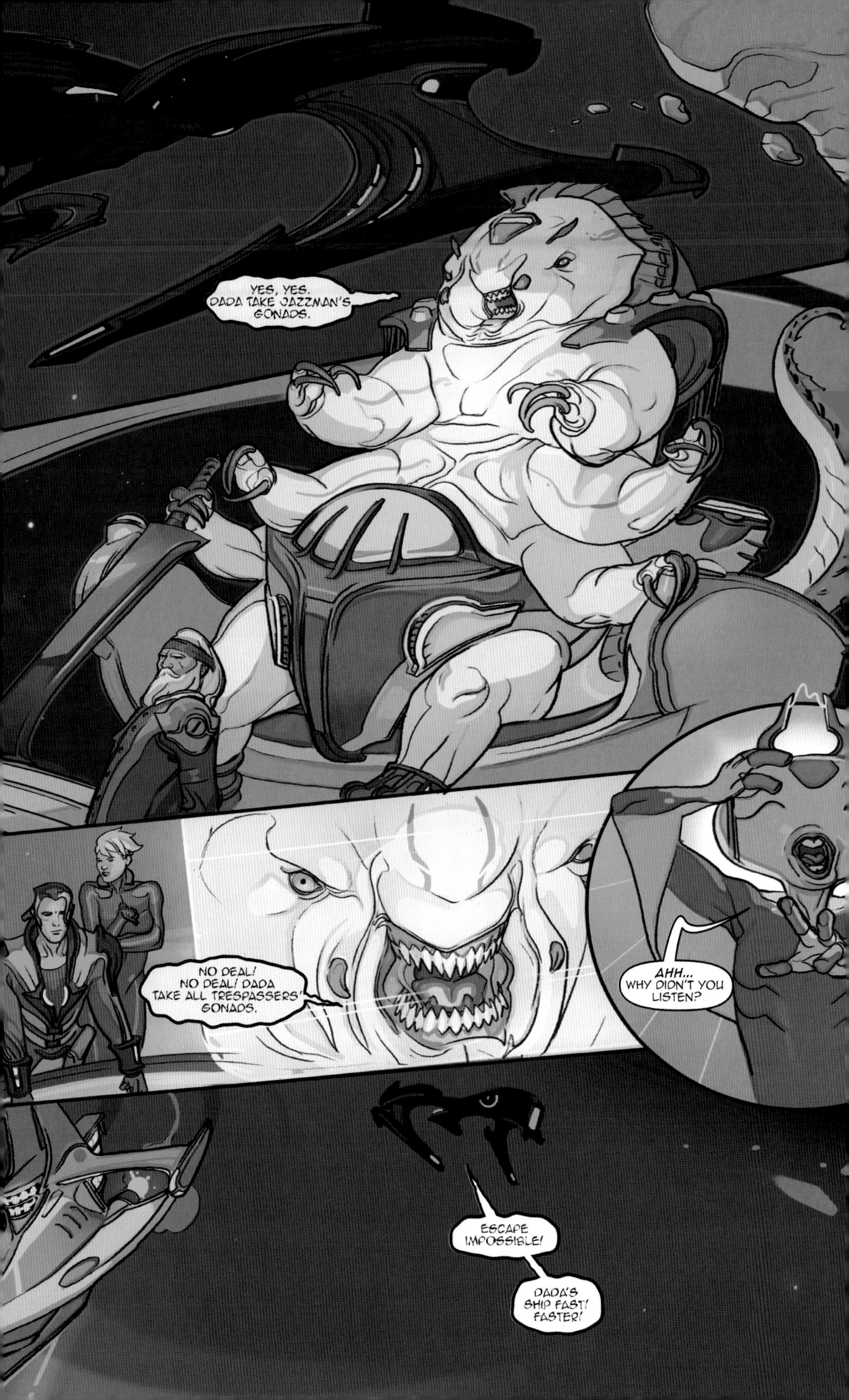
YES, YES. DADA TAKE JAZZMAN'S GONADS.
NO DEAL! NO DEAL! DADA TAKE ALL TRESPASSERS' GONADS.
AHH... WHY DIDN'T YOU LISTEN?
ESCAPE IMPOSSIBLE!
DADA'S SHIP FAST! FASTER!

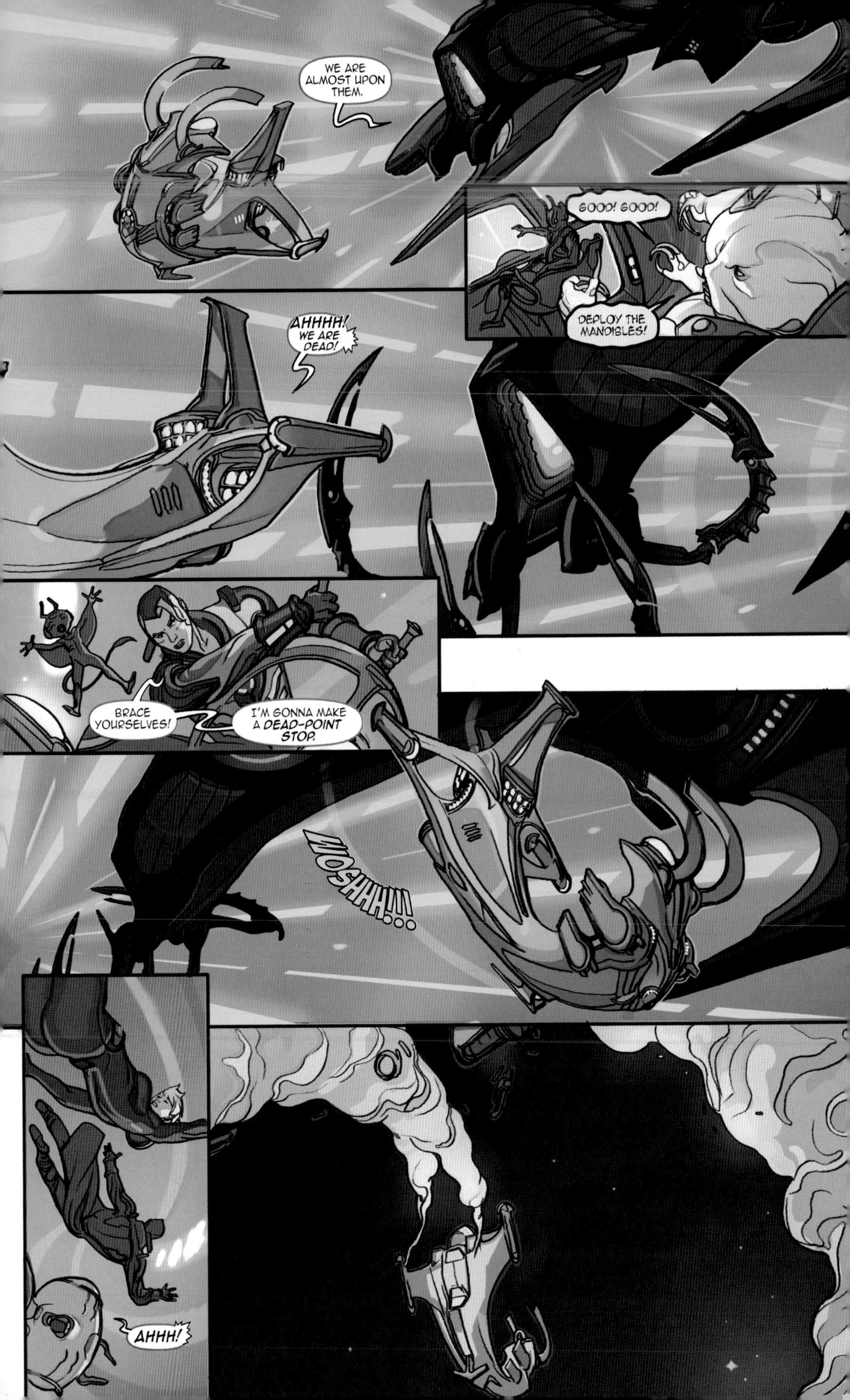
WE ARE ALMOST UPON THEM.
GOOD! GOOD!
DEPLOY THE MANDIBLES!
AHHHH! WE ARE DEAD!
BRACE YOURSELVES!
I'M GONNA MAKE A DEAD-POINT STOP.
WOOSHHH!!!
AHHH!

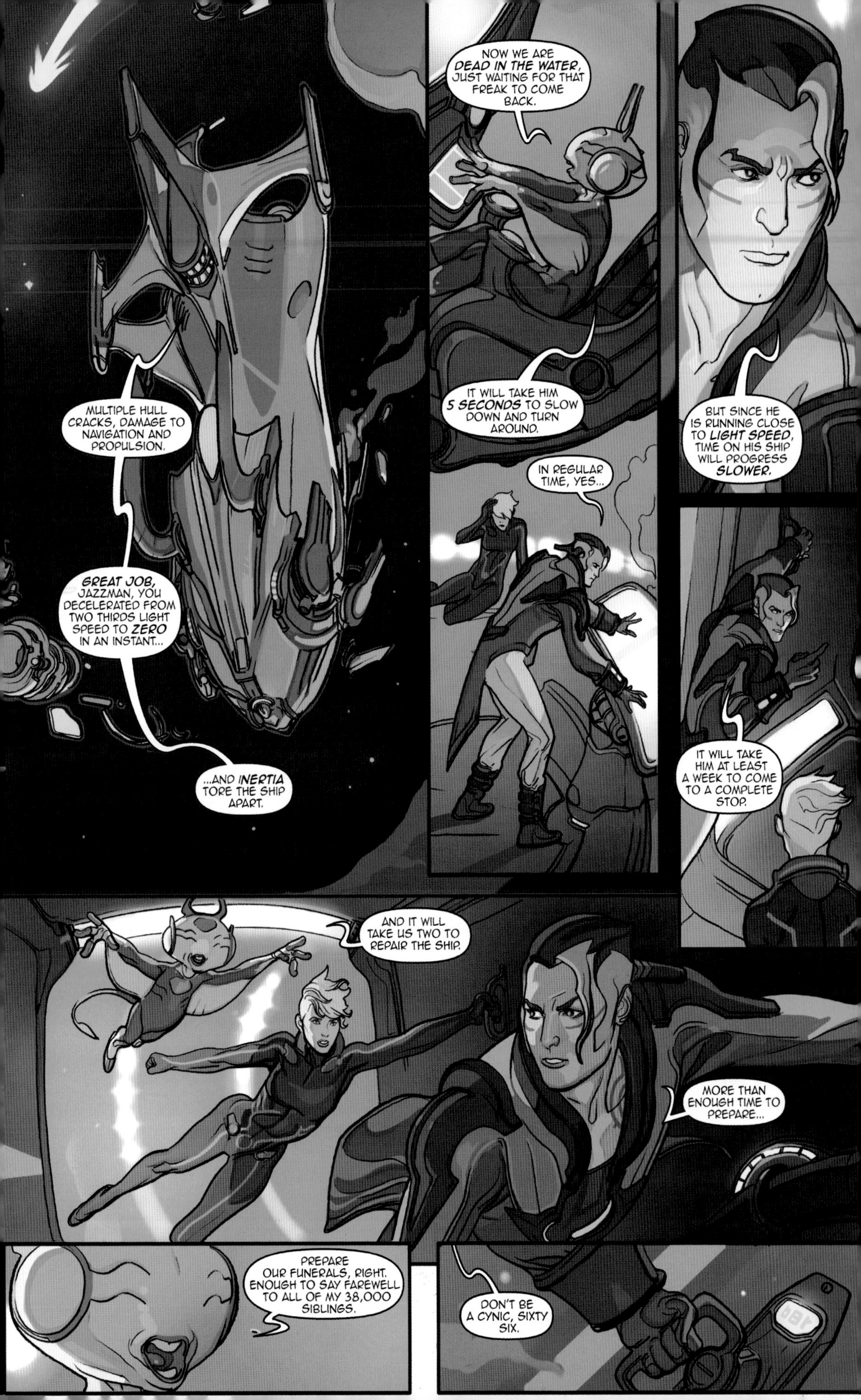
MULTIPLE HULL CRACKS, DAMAGE TO NAVIGATION AND PROPULSION.
GREAT JOB, JAZZMAN, YOU DECELERATED FROM TWO THIRDS LIGHT SPEED TO ZERO IN AN INSTANT...
...AND INERTIA TORE THE SHIP APART.
NOW WE ARE DEAD IN THE WATER, JUST WAITING FOR THAT FREAK TO COME BACK.
IT WILL TAKE HIM 5 SECONDS TO SLOW DOWN AND TURN AROUND.
IN REGULAR TIME, YES...
BUT SINCE HE IS RUNNING CLOSE TO LIGHT SPEED, TIME ON HIS SHIP WILL PROGRESS SLOWER.
IT WILL TAKE HIM AT LEAST A WEEK TO COME TO A COMPLETE STOP.
AND IT WILL TAKE US TWO TO REPAIR THE SHIP.
MORE THAN ENOUGH TIME TO PREPARE...
PREPARE OUR FUNERALS, RIGHT. ENOUGH TO SAY FAREWELL TO ALL OF MY 38,000 SIBLINGS.
DON'T BE A CYNIC, SIXTY SIX.

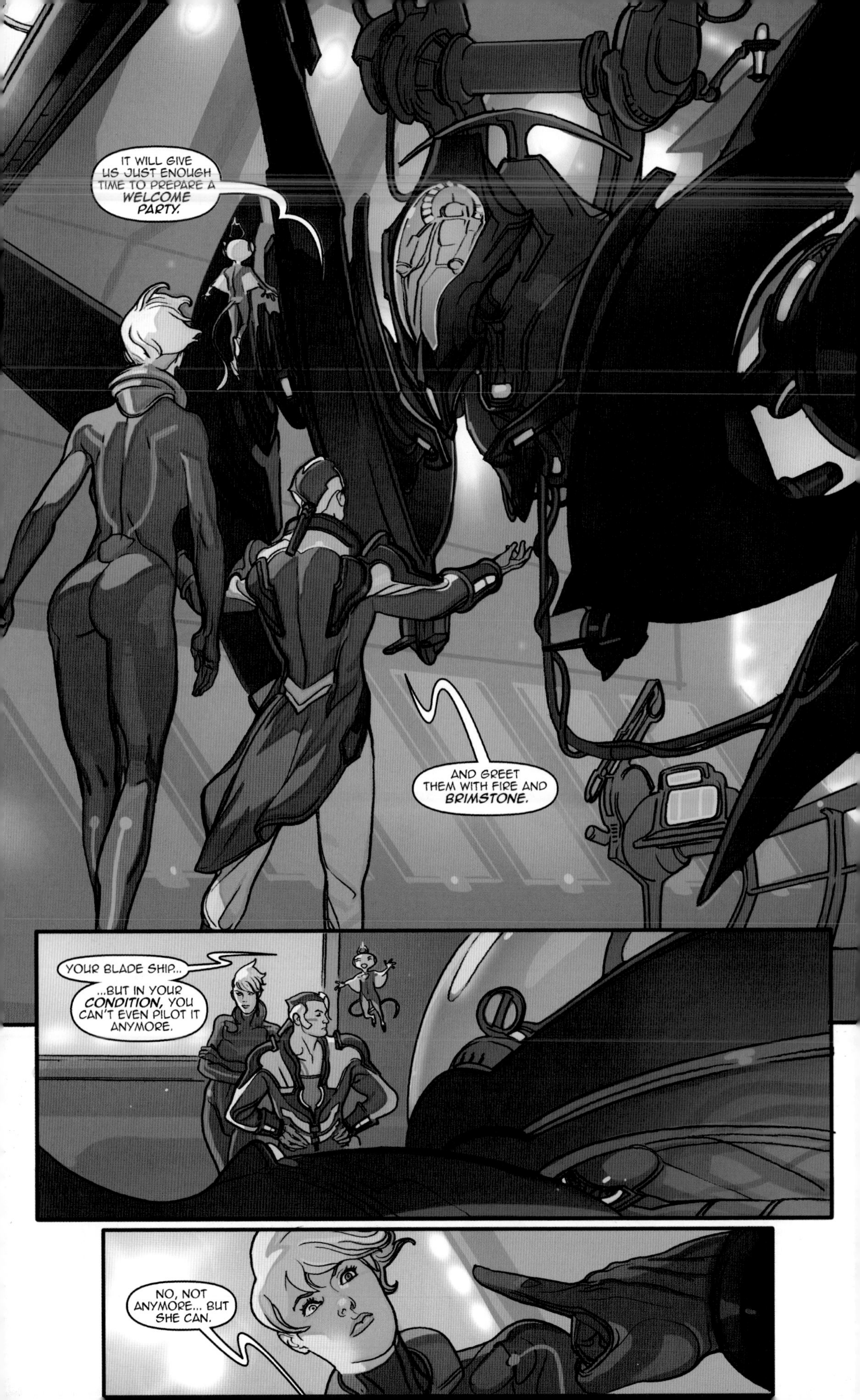
IT WILL GIVE US JUST ENOUGH TIME TO PREPARE A *WELCOME PARTY.*
AND GREET THEM WITH FIRE AND *BRIMSTONE.*
YOUR BLADE SHIP...
...BUT IN YOUR *CONDITION,* YOU CAN'T EVEN PILOT IT ANYMORE.
NO, NOT ANYMORE... BUT SHE CAN.

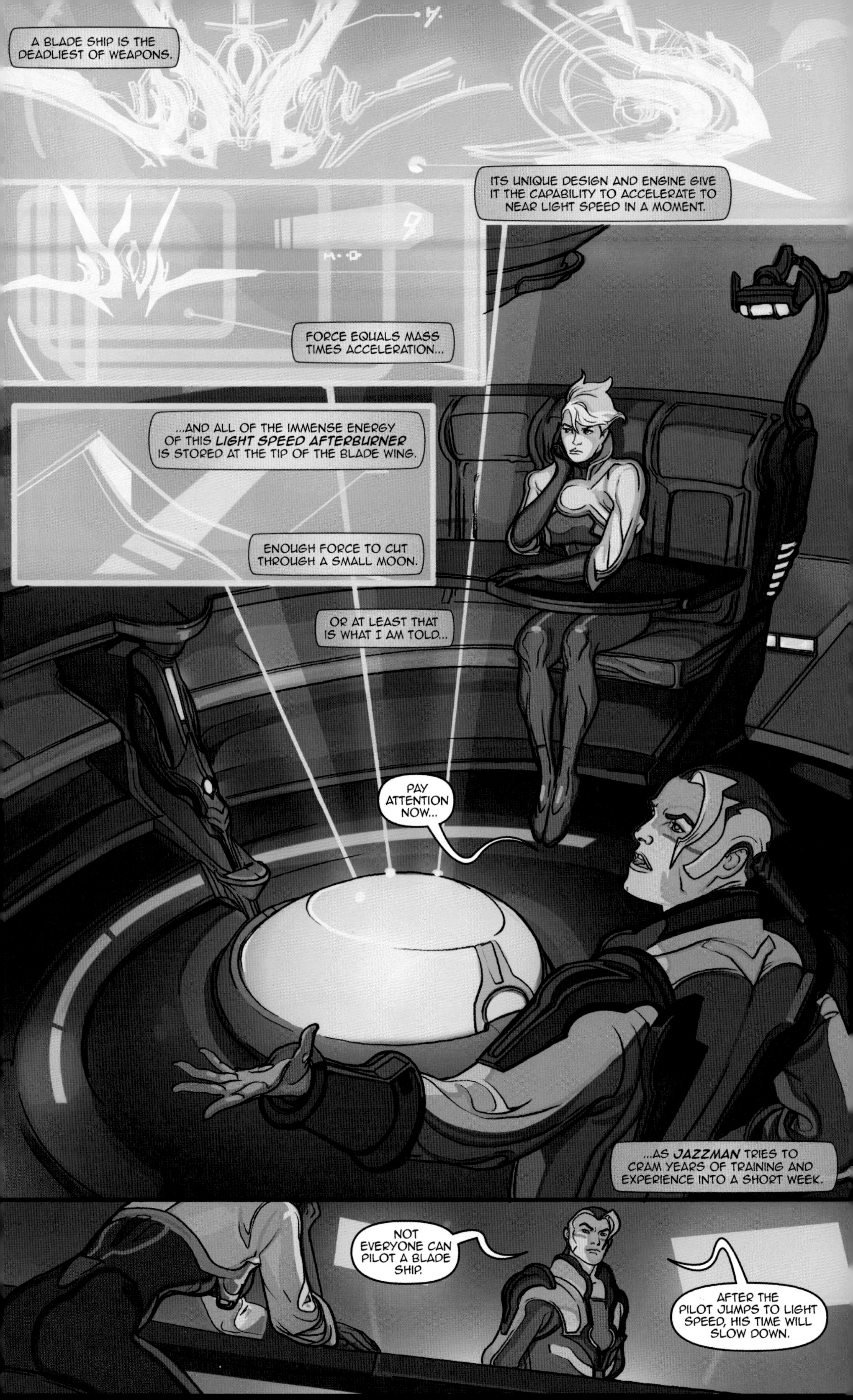
A BLADE SHIP IS THE DEADLIEST OF WEAPONS.
ITS UNIQUE DESIGN AND ENGINE GIVE IT THE CAPABILITY TO ACCELERATE TO NEAR LIGHT SPEED IN A MOMENT.
FORCE EQUALS MASS TIMES ACCELERATION...
...AND ALL OF THE IMMENSE ENERGY OF THIS LIGHT SPEED AFTERBURNER IS STORED AT THE TIP OF THE BLADE WING.
ENOUGH FORCE TO CUT THROUGH A SMALL MOON.
OR AT LEAST THAT IS WHAT I AM TOLD...
PAY ATTENTION NOW...
...AS JAZZMAN TRIES TO CRAM YEARS OF TRAINING AND EXPERIENCE INTO A SHORT WEEK.
NOT EVERYONE CAN PILOT A BLADE SHIP.
AFTER THE PILOT JUMPS TO LIGHT SPEED, HIS TIME WILL SLOW DOWN.

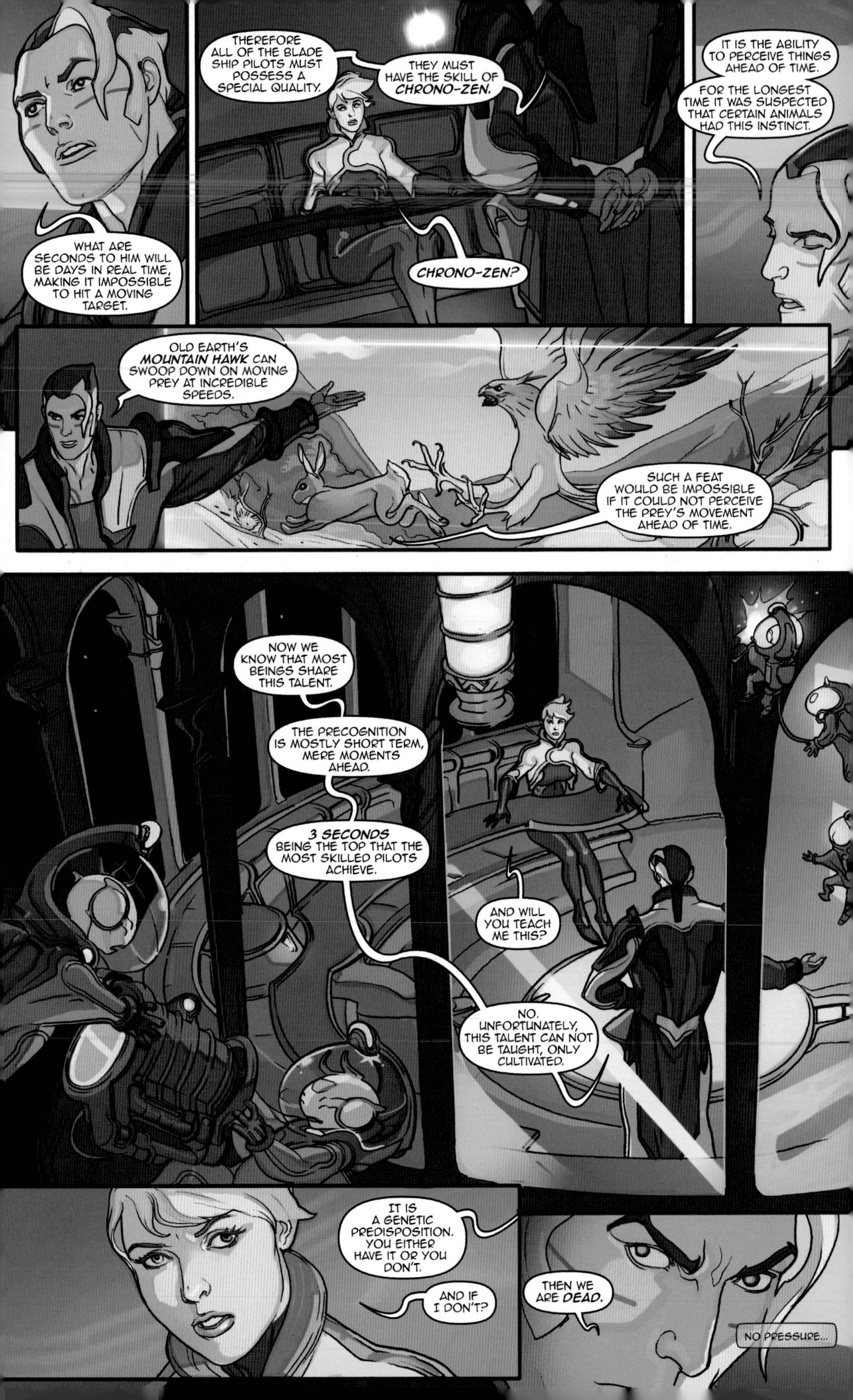
WHAT ARE SECONDS TO HIM WILL BE DAYS IN REAL TIME, MAKING IT IMPOSSIBLE TO HIT A MOVING TARGET.
THEREFORE ALL OF THE BLADE SHIP PILOTS MUST POSSESS A SPECIAL QUALITY.
THEY MUST HAVE THE SKILL OF CHRONO-ZEN.
CHRONO-ZEN?
IT IS THE ABILITY TO PERCEIVE THINGS AHEAD OF TIME.
FOR THE LONGEST TIME IT WAS SUSPECTED THAT CERTAIN ANIMALS HAD THIS INSTINCT.
OLD EARTH'S MOUNTAIN HAWK CAN SWOOP DOWN ON MOVING PREY AT INCREDIBLE SPEEDS.
SUCH A FEAT WOULD BE IMPOSSIBLE IF IT COULD NOT PERCEIVE THE PREY'S MOVEMENT AHEAD OF TIME.
NOW WE KNOW THAT MOST BEINGS SHARE THIS TALENT.
THE PRECOGNITION IS MOSTLY SHORT TERM, MERE MOMENTS AHEAD.
3 SECONDS BEING THE TOP THAT THE MOST SKILLED PILOTS ACHIEVE.
AND WILL YOU TEACH ME THIS?
NO. UNFORTUNATELY, THIS TALENT CAN NOT BE TAUGHT, ONLY CULTIVATED.
IT IS A GENETIC PREDISPOSITION. YOU EITHER HAVE IT OR YOU DON'T.
AND IF I DON'T?
THEN WE ARE DEAD.
NO PRESSURE...

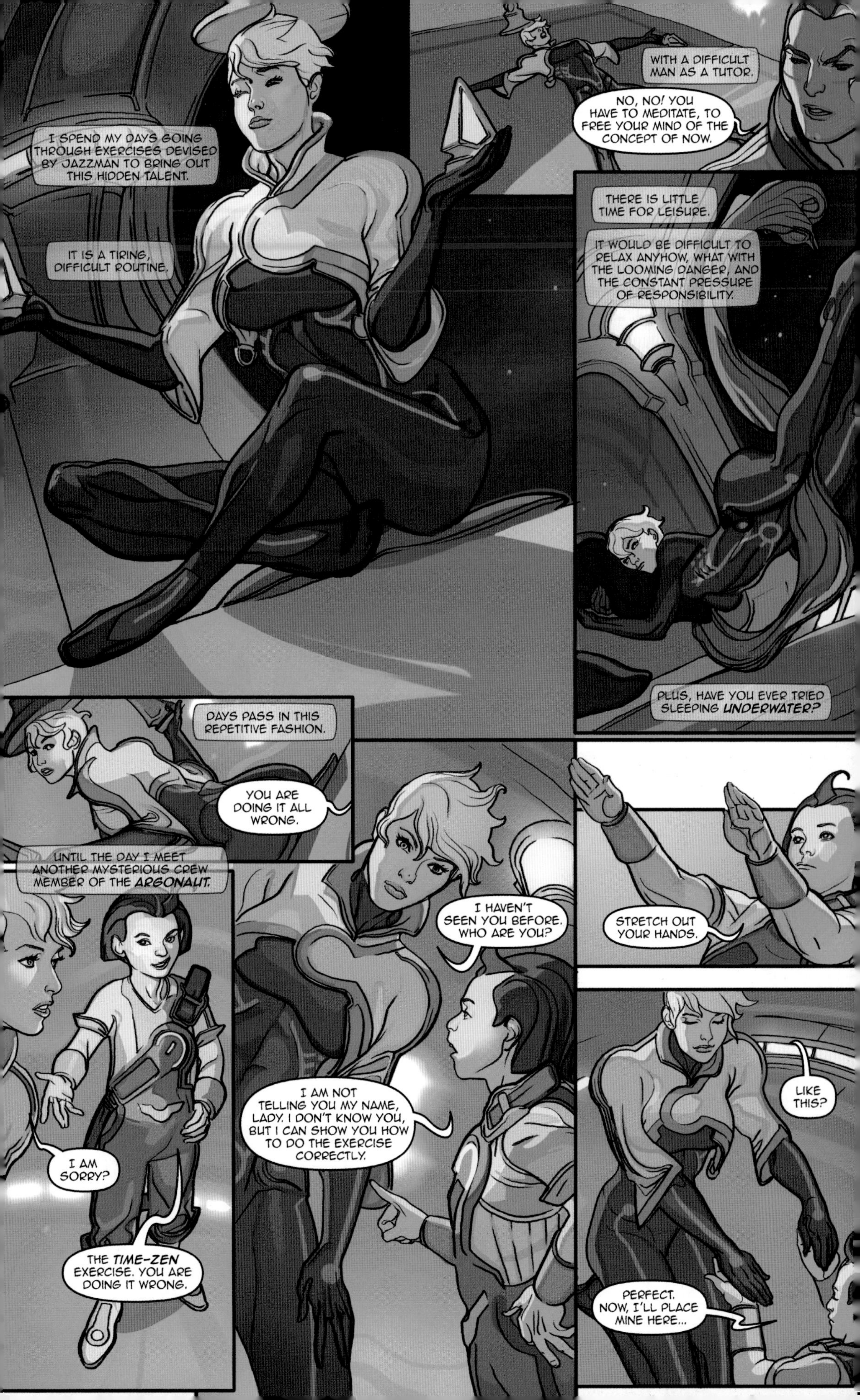
I SPEND MY DAYS GOING THROUGH EXERCISES DEVISED BY JAZZMAN TO BRING OUT THIS HIDDEN TALENT.
IT IS A TIRING, DIFFICULT ROUTINE.
WITH A DIFFICULT MAN AS A TUTOR.
NO, NO! YOU HAVE TO MEDITATE, TO FREE YOUR MIND OF THE CONCEPT OF NOW.
THERE IS LITTLE TIME FOR LEISURE.
IT WOULD BE DIFFICULT TO RELAX ANYHOW, WHAT WITH THE LOOMING DANGER, AND THE CONSTANT PRESSURE OF RESPONSIBILITY.
PLUS, HAVE YOU EVER TRIED SLEEPING *UNDERWATER?*
DAYS PASS IN THIS REPETITIVE FASHION.
YOU ARE DOING IT ALL WRONG.
UNTIL THE DAY I MEET ANOTHER MYSTERIOUS CREW MEMBER OF THE *ARGONAUT.*
I AM SORRY?
THE *TIME-ZEN* EXERCISE. YOU ARE DOING IT WRONG.
I HAVEN'T SEEN YOU BEFORE. WHO ARE YOU?
I AM NOT TELLING YOU MY NAME, LADY. I DON'T KNOW YOU, BUT I CAN SHOW YOU HOW TO DO THE EXERCISE CORRECTLY.
STRETCH OUT YOUR HANDS.
LIKE THIS?
PERFECT. NOW, I'LL PLACE MINE HERE...

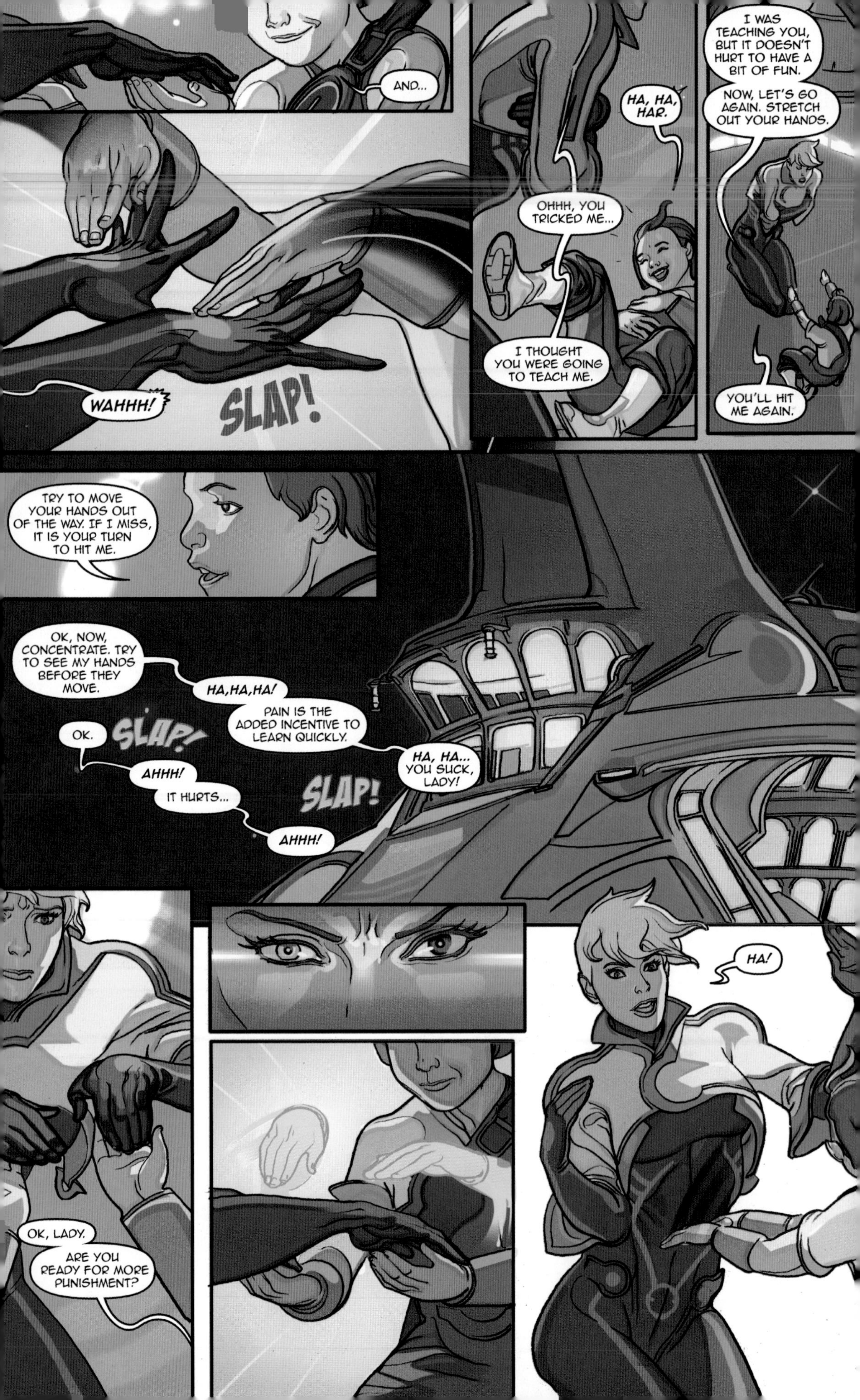
AND...
WAHHH!
SLAP!
HA, HA, HAR.
OHHH, YOU TRICKED ME...
I THOUGHT YOU WERE GOING TO TEACH ME.
I WAS TEACHING YOU, BUT IT DOESN'T HURT TO HAVE A BIT OF FUN.
NOW, LET'S GO AGAIN. STRETCH OUT YOUR HANDS.
YOU'LL HIT ME AGAIN.
TRY TO MOVE YOUR HANDS OUT OF THE WAY. IF I MISS, IT IS YOUR TURN TO HIT ME.
OK, NOW, CONCENTRATE. TRY TO SEE MY HANDS BEFORE THEY MOVE.
HA,HA,HA!
PAIN IS THE ADDED INCENTIVE TO LEARN QUICKLY.
OK.
SLAP!
AHHH!
IT HURTS...
HA, HA... YOU SUCK, LADY!
SLAP!
AHHH!
OK, LADY.
ARE YOU READY FOR MORE PUNISHMENT?
HA!

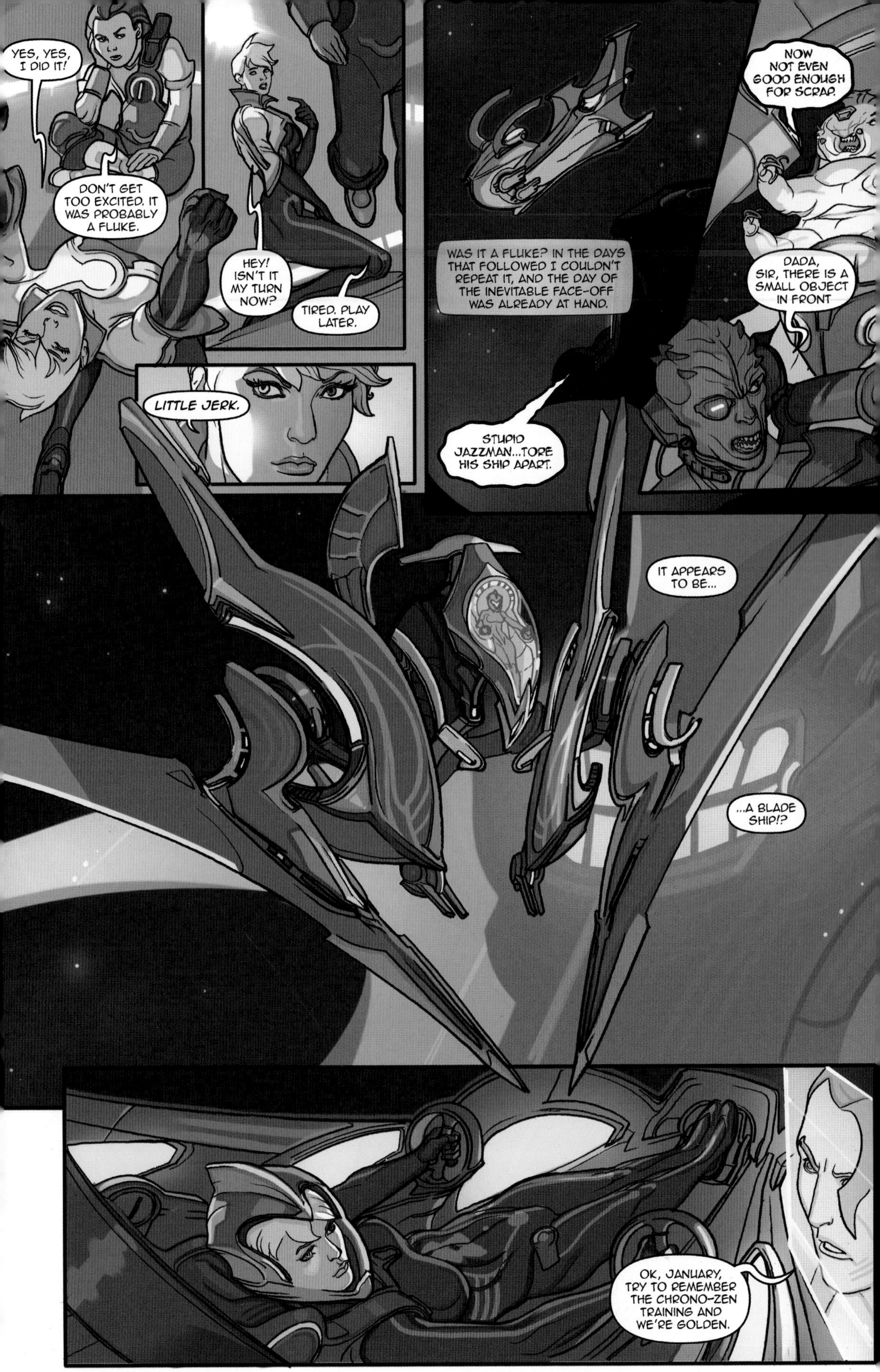
YES, YES, I DID IT!
DON'T GET TOO EXCITED. IT WAS PROBABLY A FLUKE.
HEY! ISN'T IT MY TURN NOW?
TIRED. PLAY LATER.
LITTLE JERK.
WAS IT A FLUKE? IN THE DAYS THAT FOLLOWED I COULDN'T REPEAT IT, AND THE DAY OF THE INEVITABLE FACE-OFF WAS ALREADY AT HAND.
NOW NOT EVEN GOOD ENOUGH FOR SCRAP.
DADA, SIR, THERE IS A SMALL OBJECT IN FRONT
STUPID JAZZMAN...TORE HIS SHIP APART.
IT APPEARS TO BE...
...A BLADE SHIP!?
OK, JANUARY, TRY TO REMEMBER THE CHRONO-ZEN TRAINING AND WE'RE GOLDEN.

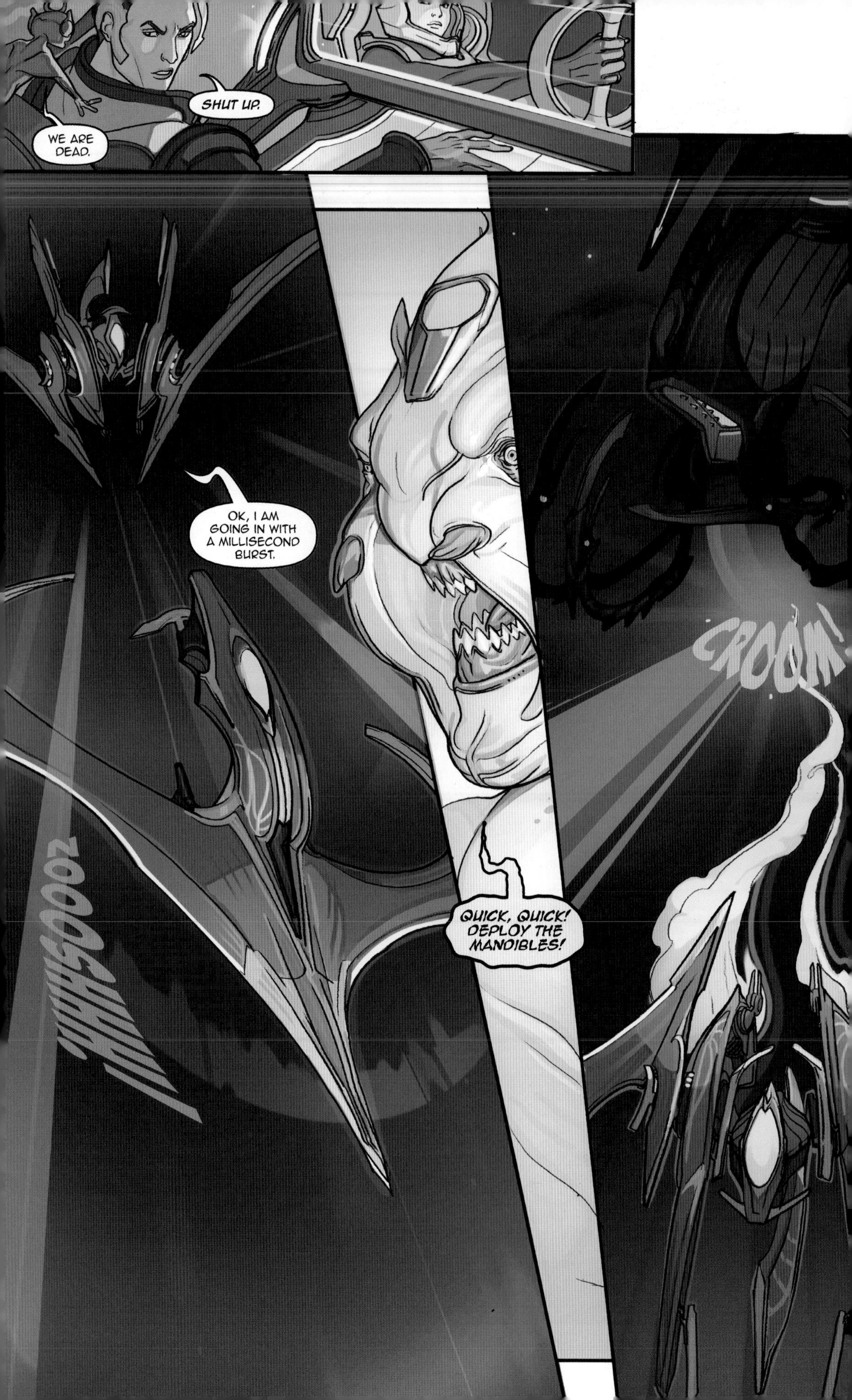
WE ARE DEAD.
SHUT UP.
OK, I AM GOING IN WITH A MILLISECOND BURST.
CROOM!
ZOOOSHHH!
QUICK, QUICK! DEPLOY THE MANDIBLES!

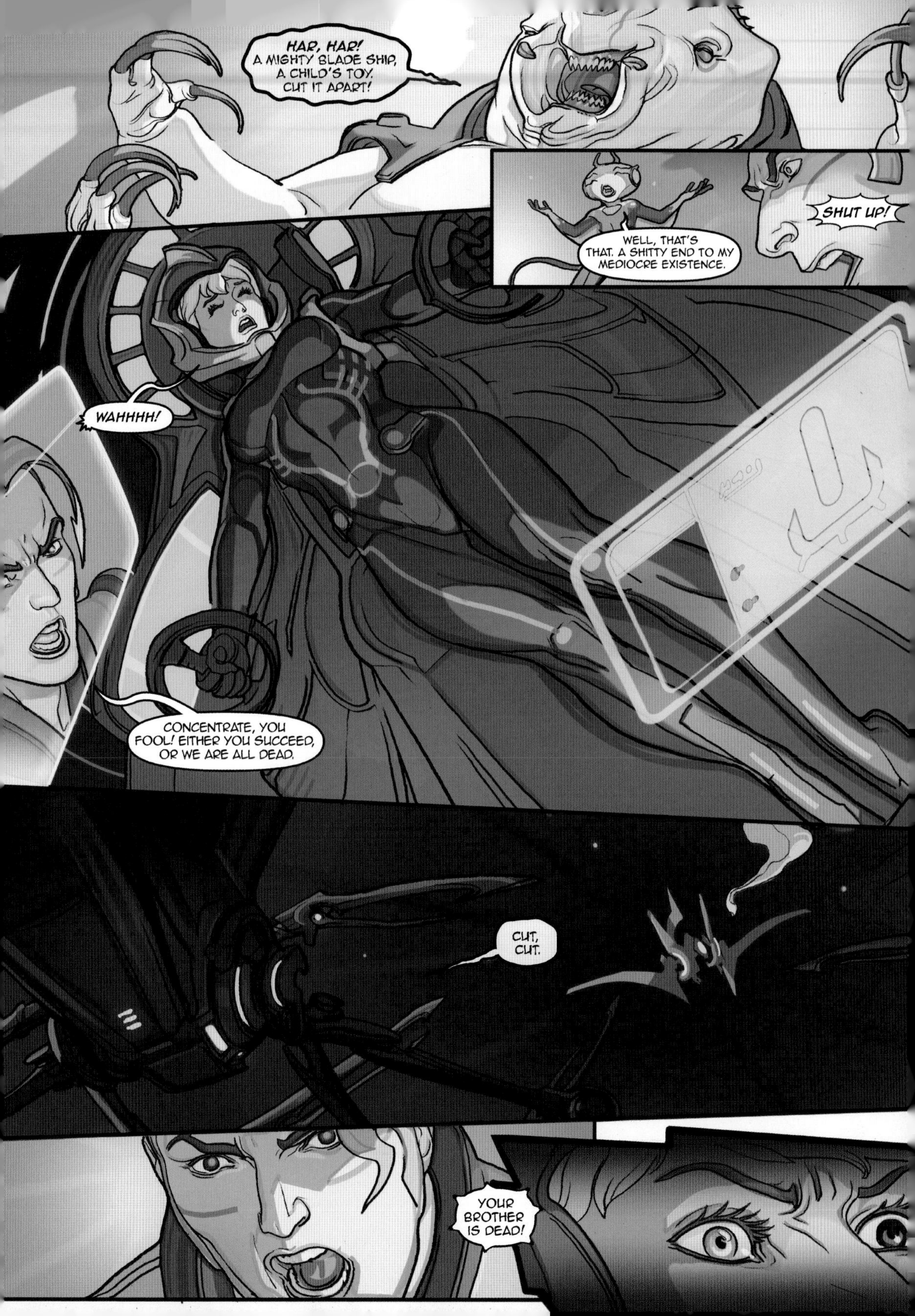
HAR, HAR!
A MIGHTY BLADE SHIP, A CHILD'S TOY. CUT IT APART!
WELL, THAT'S THAT. A SHITTY END TO MY MEDIOCRE EXISTENCE.
SHUT UP!
WAHHHH!
CONCENTRATE, YOU FOOL! EITHER YOU SUCCEED, OR WE ARE ALL DEAD.
CUT, CUT.
YOUR BROTHER IS DEAD!

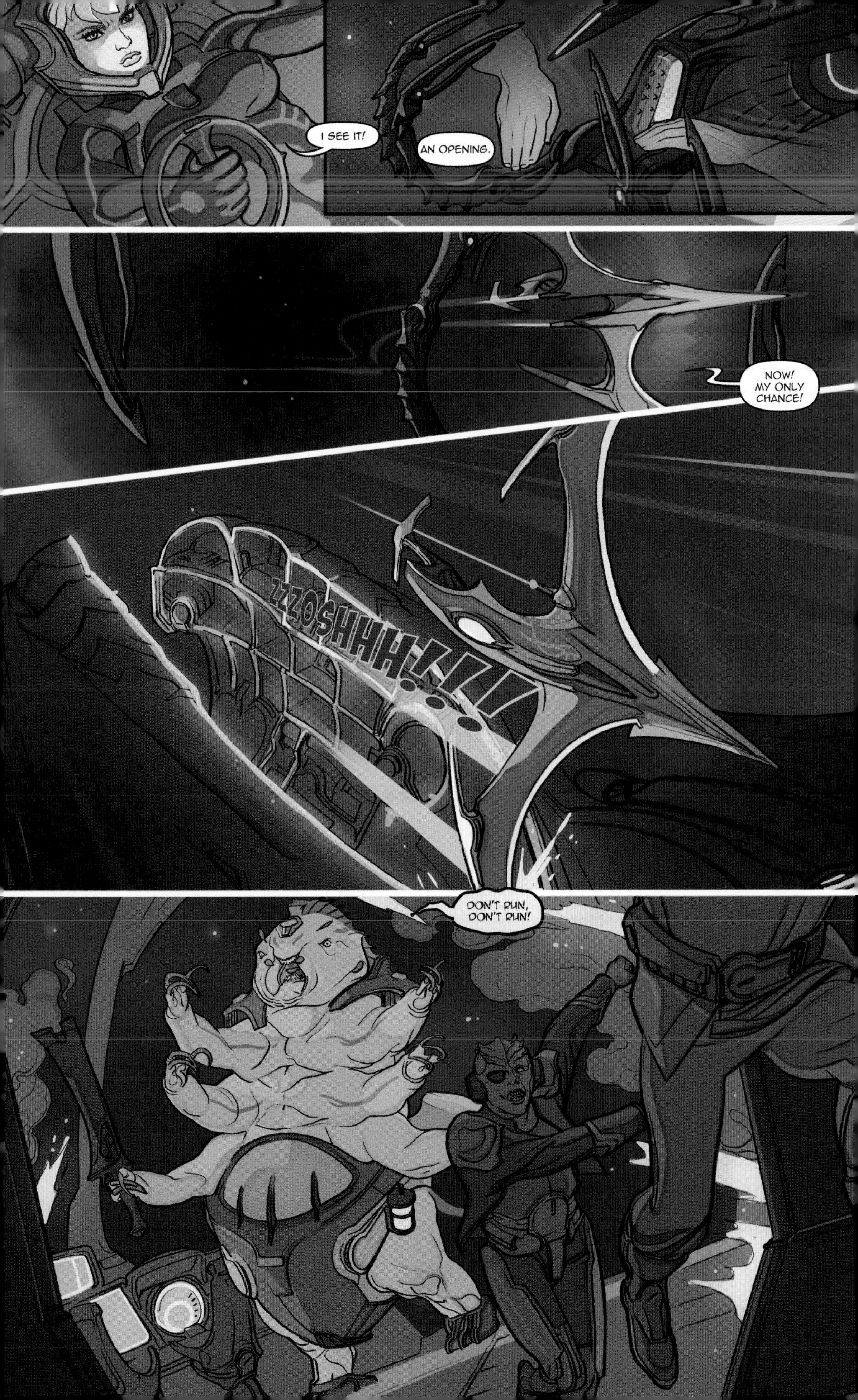
I SEE IT!
AN OPENING.
NOW! MY ONLY CHANCE!
ZZZOSHHHH!!!!!
DON'T RUN, DON'T RUN!

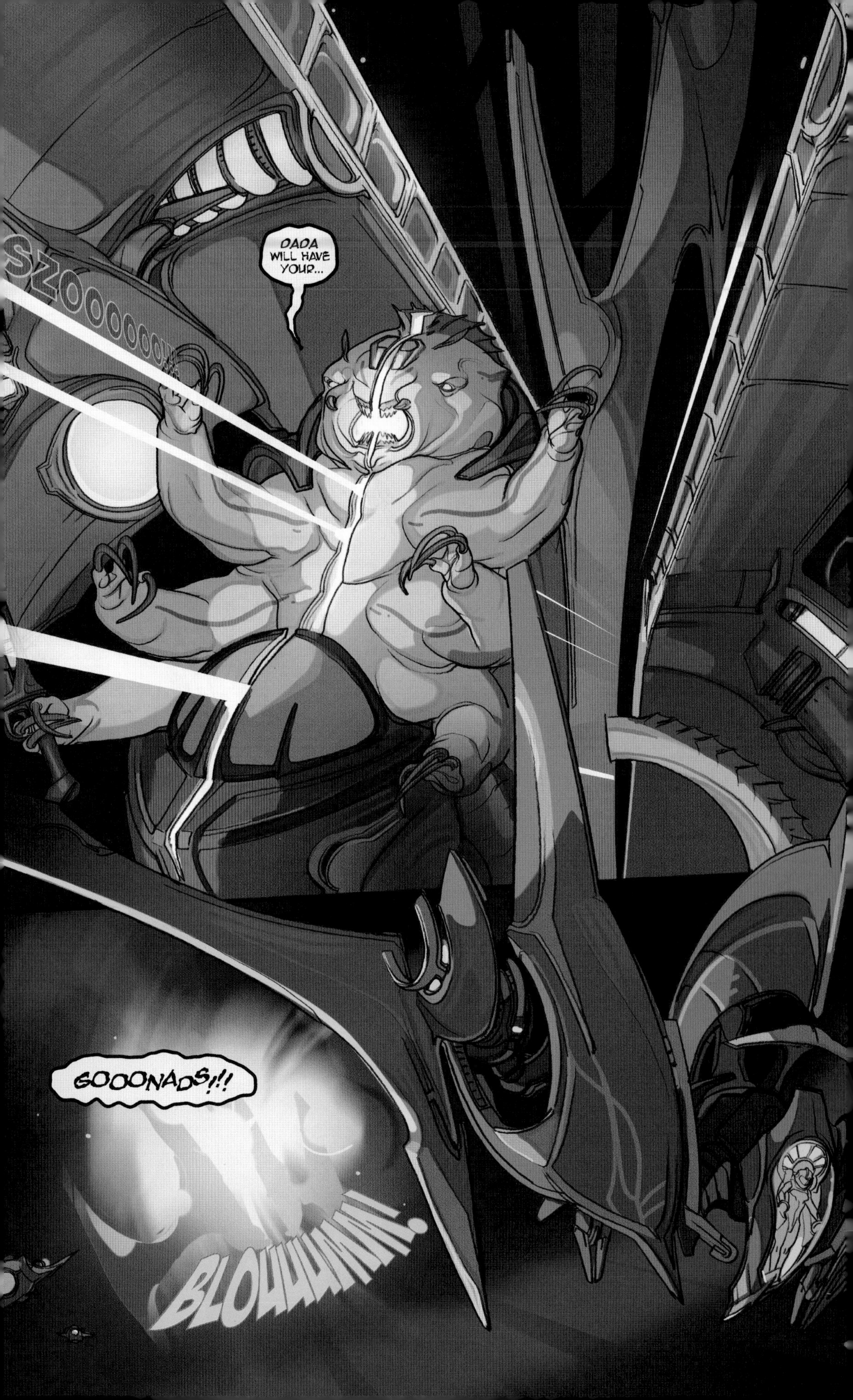
DADA WILL HAVE YOUR...
SZOOOOOOO!!
GOOOONADS!!!
BLOUUUMMM!

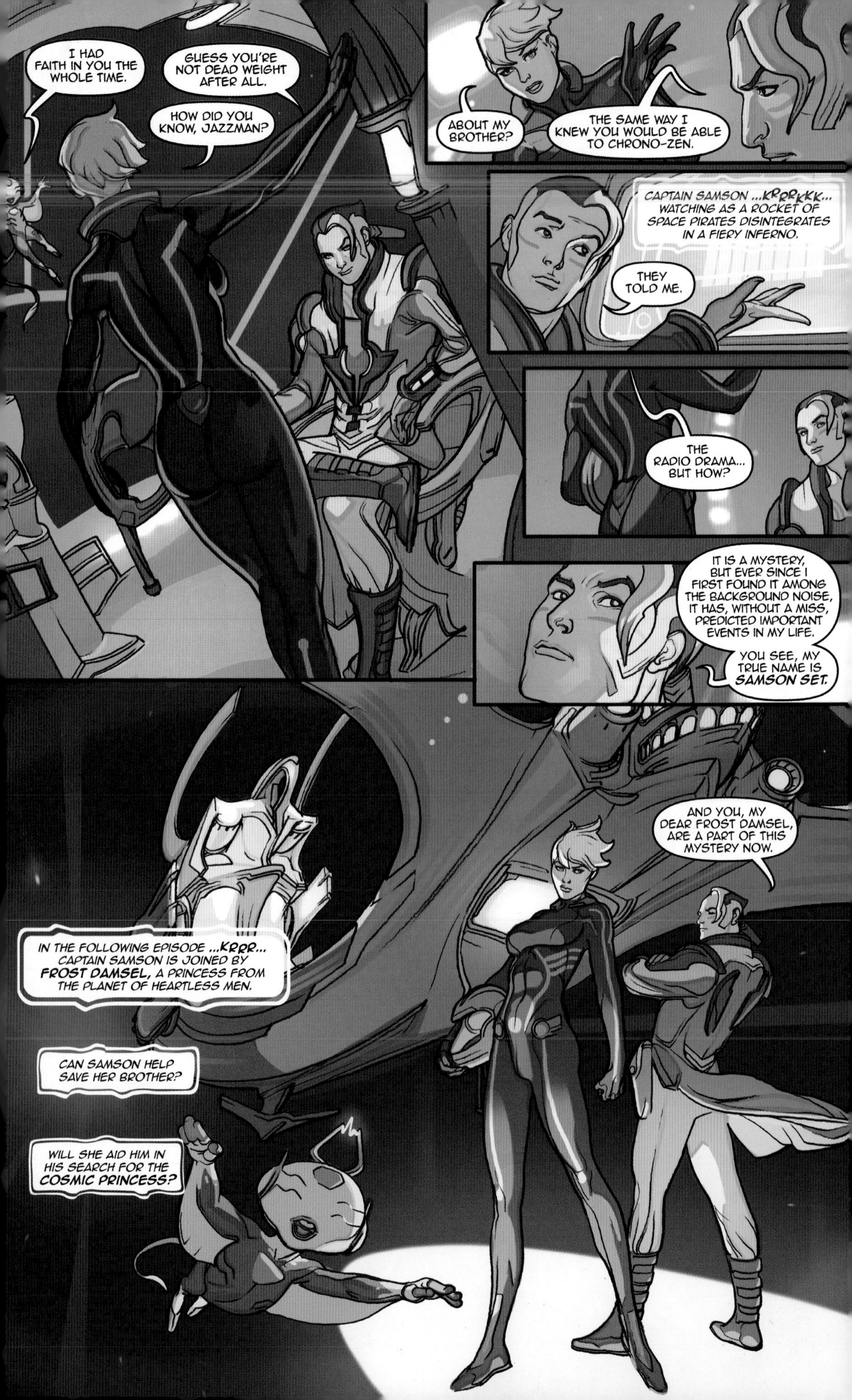
I HAD FAITH IN YOU THE WHOLE TIME.
GUESS YOU'RE NOT DEAD WEIGHT AFTER ALL.
HOW DID YOU KNOW, JAZZMAN?
ABOUT MY BROTHER?
THE SAME WAY I KNEW YOU WOULD BE ABLE TO CHRONO-ZEN.
CAPTAIN SAMSON ...KRRRKKK... WATCHING AS A ROCKET OF SPACE PIRATES DISINTEGRATES IN A FIERY INFERNO.
THEY TOLD ME.
THE RADIO DRAMA... BUT HOW?
IT IS A MYSTERY, BUT EVER SINCE I FIRST FOUND IT AMONG THE BACKGROUND NOISE, IT HAS, WITHOUT A MISS, PREDICTED IMPORTANT EVENTS IN MY LIFE.
YOU SEE, MY TRUE NAME IS SAMSON SET.
AND YOU, MY DEAR FROST DAMSEL, ARE A PART OF THIS MYSTERY NOW.
IN THE FOLLOWING EPISODE ...KRRR... CAPTAIN SAMSON IS JOINED BY FROST DAMSEL, A PRINCESS FROM THE PLANET OF HEARTLESS MEN.
CAN SAMSON HELP SAVE HER BROTHER?
WILL SHE AID HIM IN HIS SEARCH FOR THE COSMIC PRINCESS?

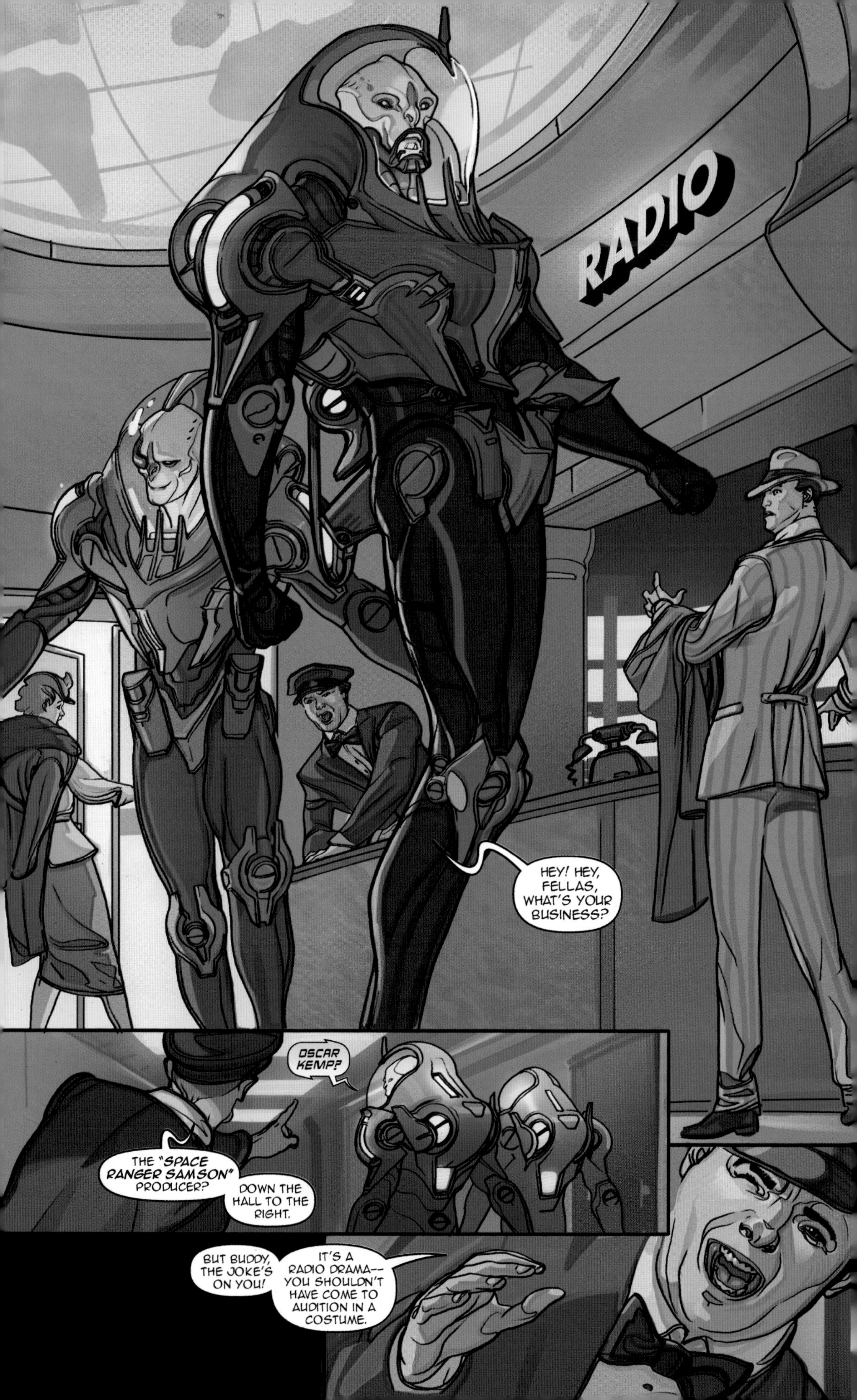
RADIO
HEY! HEY, FELLAS, WHAT'S YOUR BUSINESS?
OSCAR KEMP?
THE "SPACE RANGER SAMSON" PRODUCER?
DOWN THE HALL TO THE RIGHT.
BUT BUDDY, THE JOKE'S ON YOU!
IT'S A RADIO DRAMA-- YOU SHOULDN'T HAVE COME TO AUDITION IN A COSTUME.

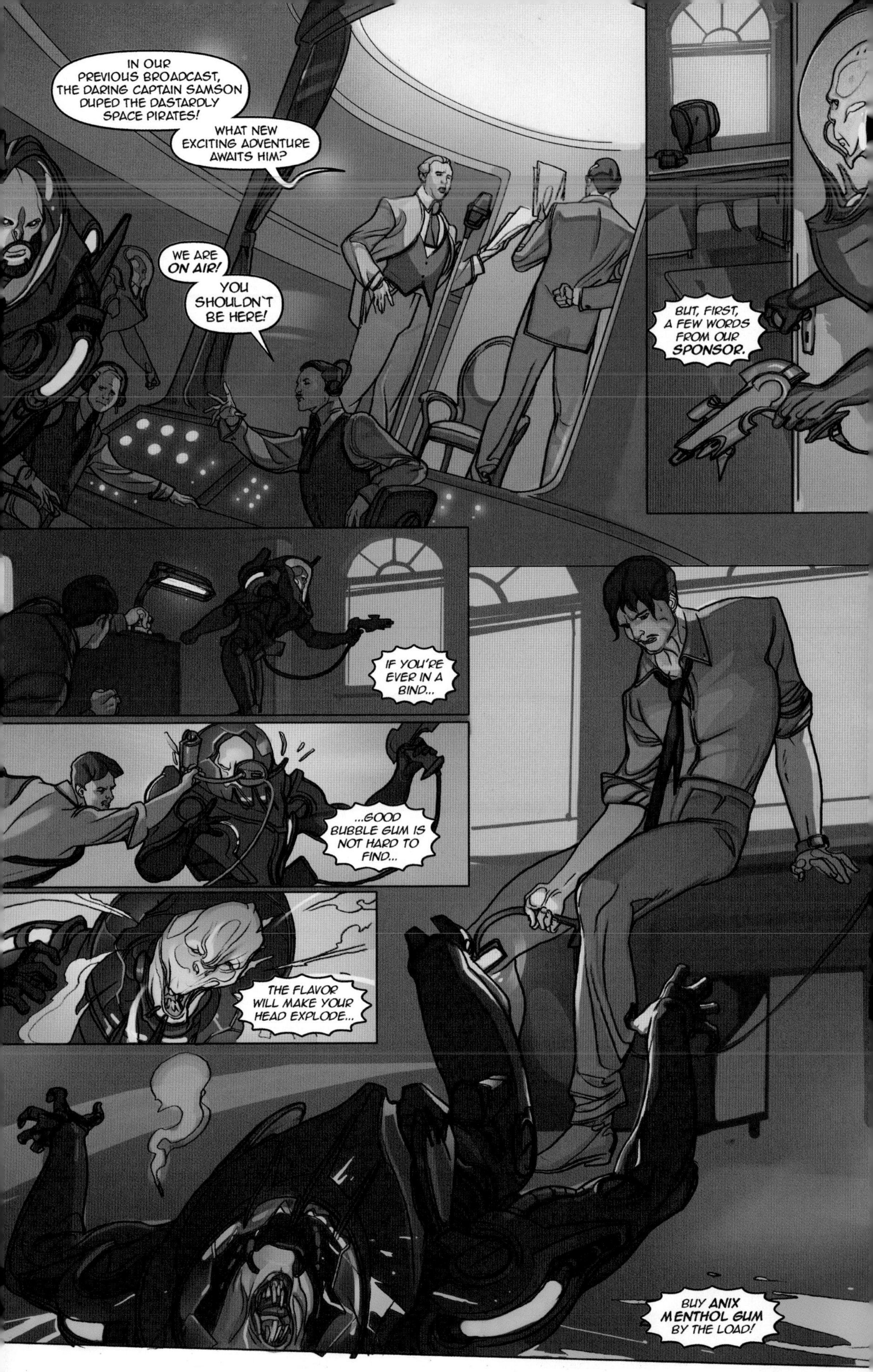
IN OUR PREVIOUS BROADCAST, THE DARING CAPTAIN SAMSON DUPED THE DASTARDLY SPACE PIRATES!
WHAT NEW EXCITING ADVENTURE AWAITS HIM?
WE ARE ON AIR!
YOU SHOULDN'T BE HERE!
BUT, FIRST, A FEW WORDS FROM OUR SPONSOR.
IF YOU'RE EVER IN A BIND...
...GOOD BUBBLE GUM IS NOT HARD TO FIND...
THE FLAVOR WILL MAKE YOUR HEAD EXPLODE...
BUY ANIX MENTHOL GUM BY THE LOAD!

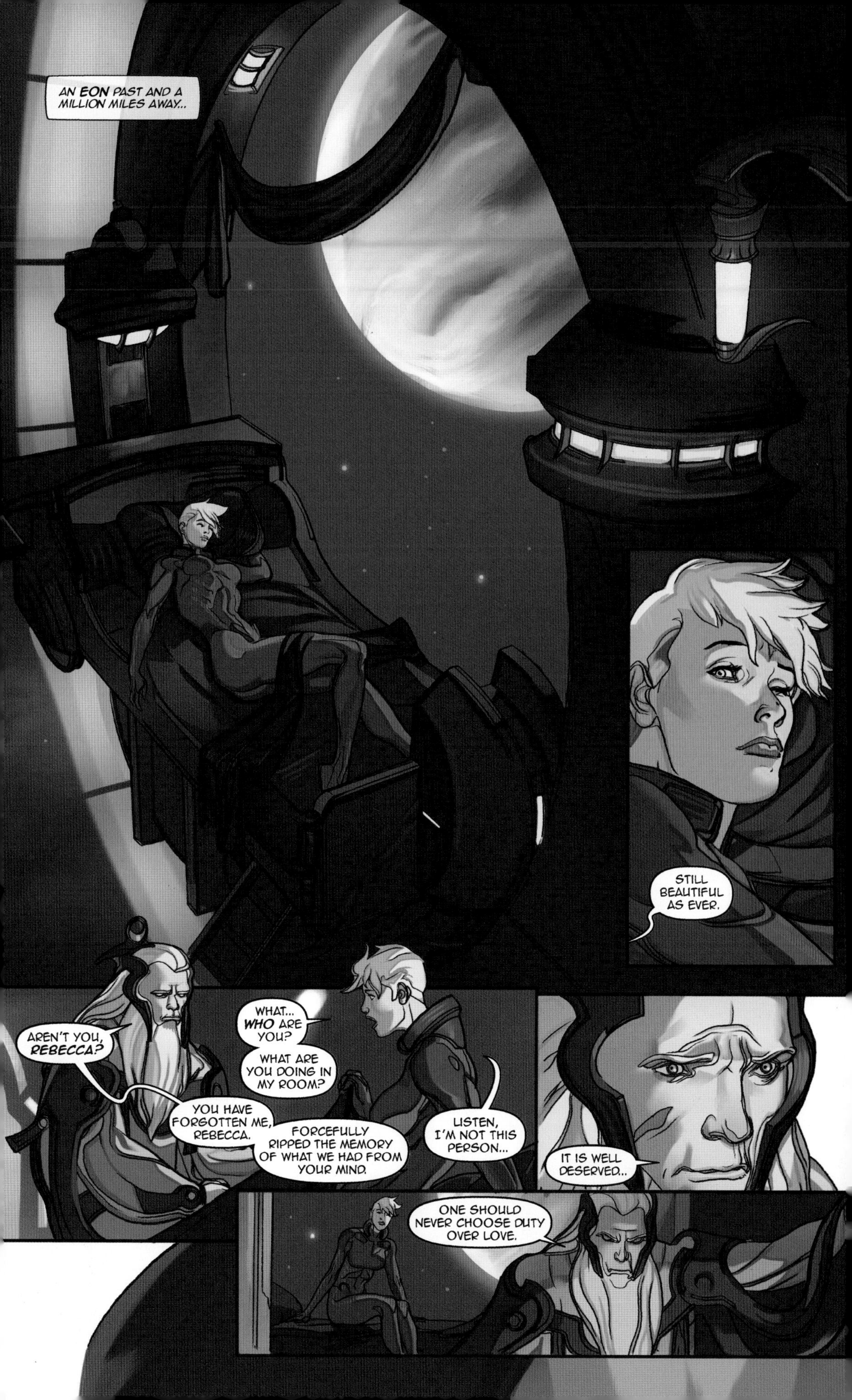
AN EON PAST AND A MILLION MILES AWAY...
STILL BEAUTIFUL AS EVER.
AREN'T YOU, REBECCA?
WHAT... WHO ARE YOU?
WHAT ARE YOU DOING IN MY ROOM?
YOU HAVE FORGOTTEN ME, REBECCA.
FORCEFULLY RIPPED THE MEMORY OF WHAT WE HAD FROM YOUR MIND.
LISTEN, I'M NOT THIS PERSON...
IT IS WELL DESERVED...
ONE SHOULD NEVER CHOOSE DUTY OVER LOVE.

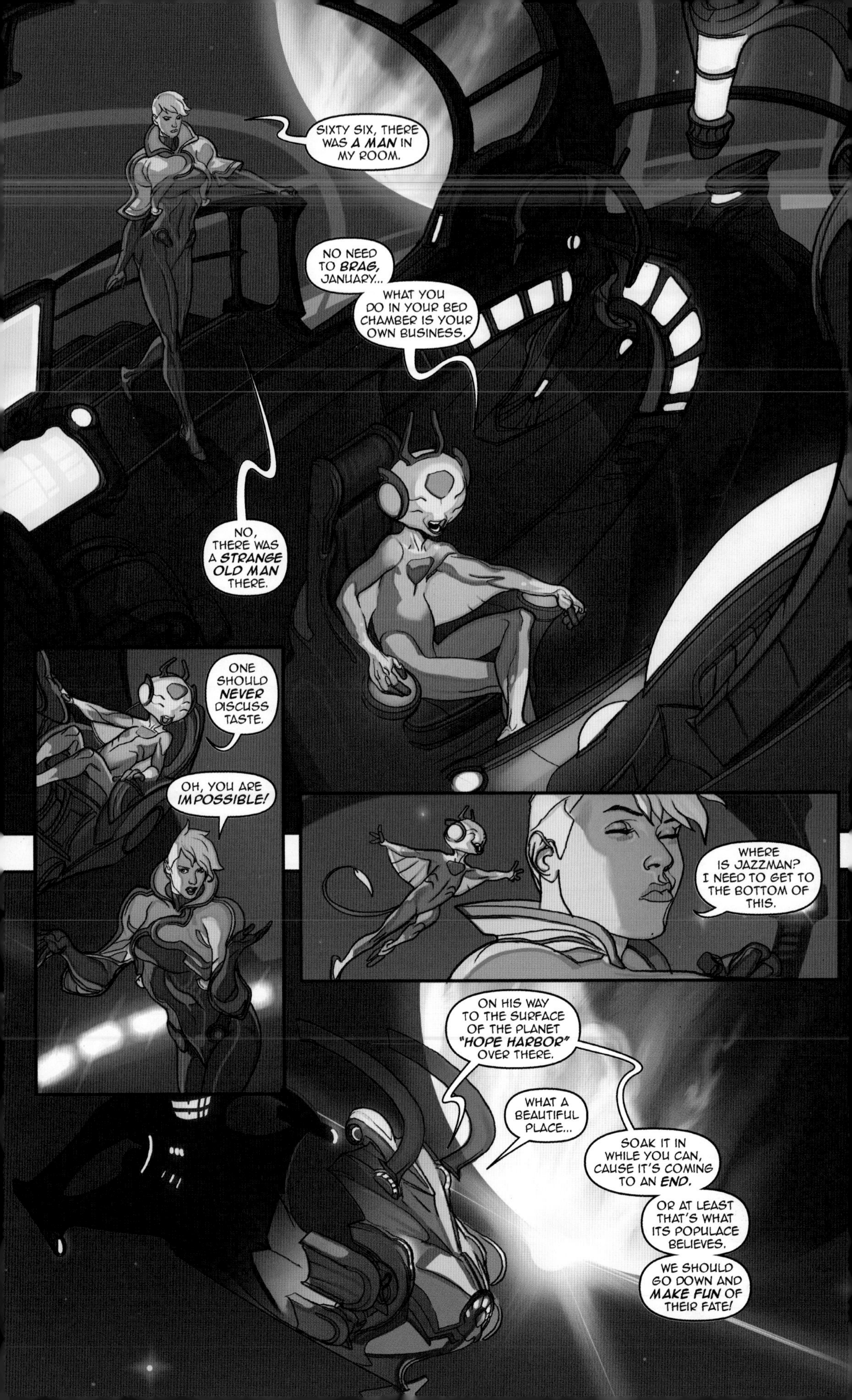
SIXTY SIX, THERE WAS A MAN IN MY ROOM.
NO NEED TO BRAG, JANUARY...
WHAT YOU DO IN YOUR BED CHAMBER IS YOUR OWN BUSINESS.
NO, THERE WAS A STRANGE OLD MAN THERE.
ONE SHOULD NEVER DISCUSS TASTE.
OH, YOU ARE IMPOSSIBLE!
WHERE IS JAZZMAN? I NEED TO GET TO THE BOTTOM OF THIS.
ON HIS WAY TO THE SURFACE OF THE PLANET "HOPE HARBOR" OVER THERE.
WHAT A BEAUTIFUL PLACE...
SOAK IT IN WHILE YOU CAN, CAUSE IT'S COMING TO AN END.
OR AT LEAST THAT'S WHAT ITS POPULACE BELIEVES.
WE SHOULD GO DOWN AND MAKE FUN OF THEIR FATE!

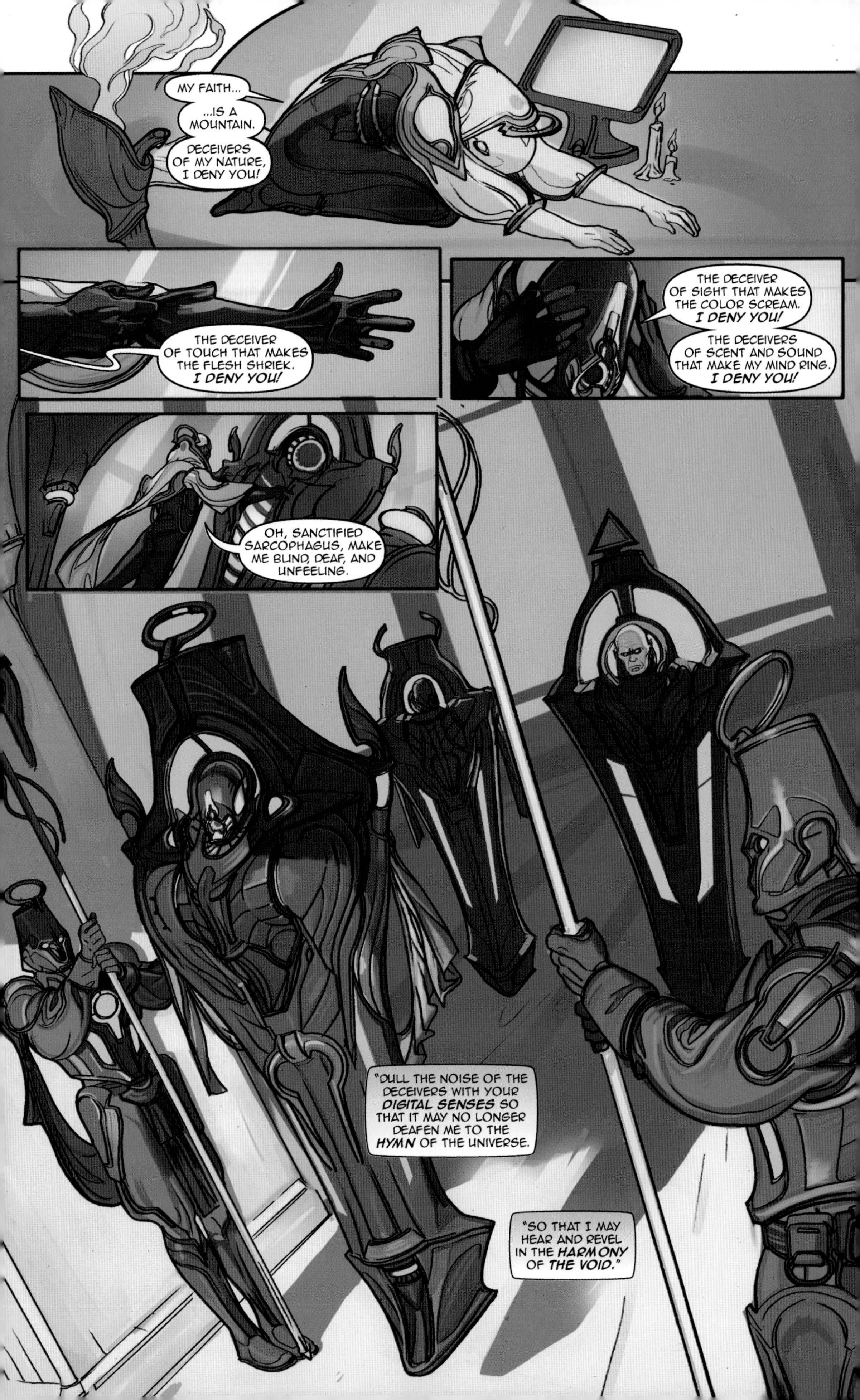
MY FAITH...
...IS A MOUNTAIN.
DECEIVERS OF MY NATURE, I DENY YOU!
THE DECEIVER OF TOUCH THAT MAKES THE FLESH SHRIEK. I DENY YOU!
THE DECEIVER OF SIGHT THAT MAKES THE COLOR SCREAM. I DENY YOU!
THE DECEIVERS OF SCENT AND SOUND THAT MAKE MY MIND RING. I DENY YOU!
OH, SANCTIFIED SARCOPHAGUS, MAKE ME BLIND, DEAF, AND UNFEELING.
"DULL THE NOISE OF THE DECEIVERS WITH YOUR DIGITAL SENSES SO THAT IT MAY NO LONGER DEAFEN ME TO THE HYMN OF THE UNIVERSE.
"SO THAT I MAY HEAR AND REVEL IN THE HARMONY OF THE VOID."

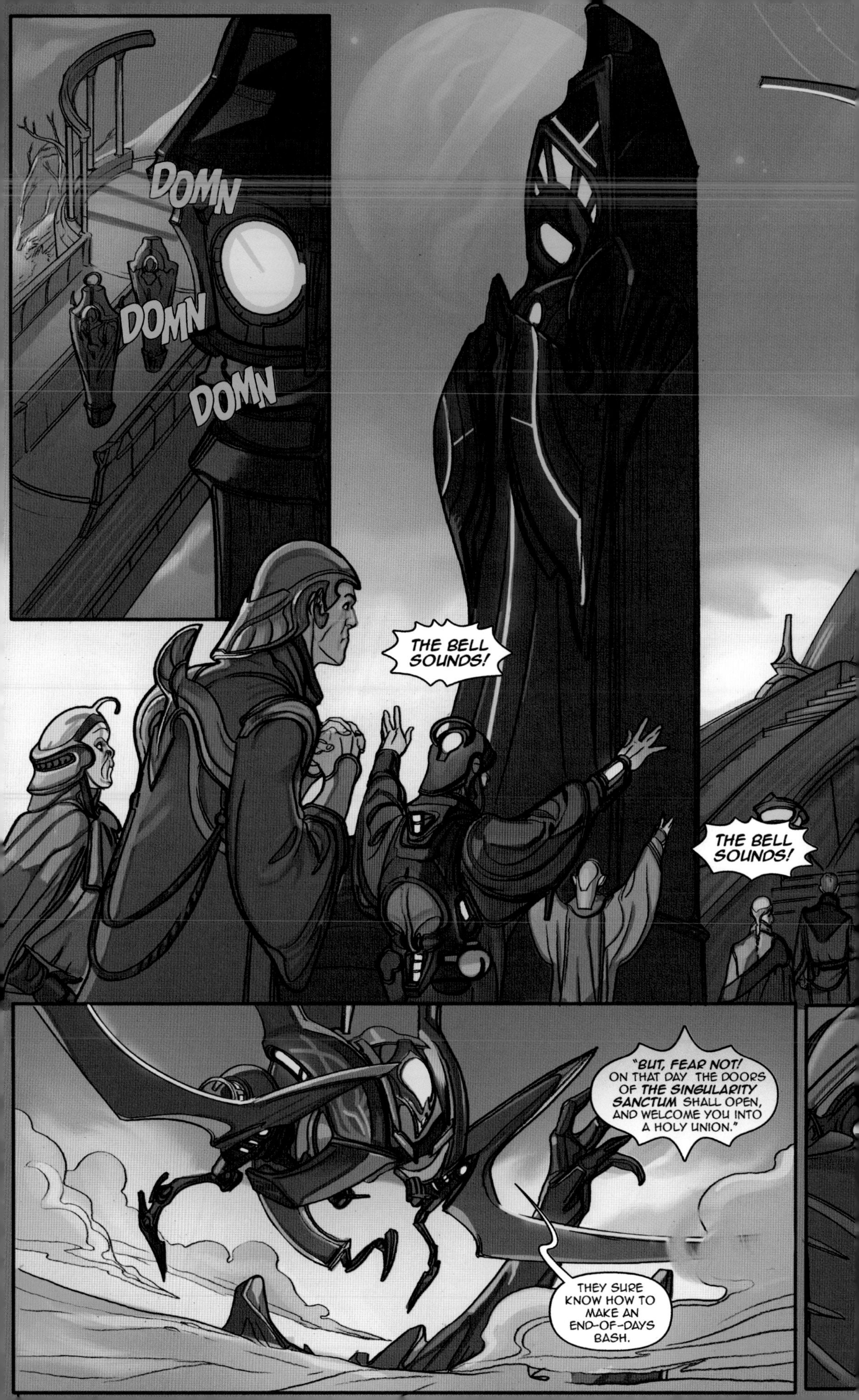
DOMN
DOMN
DOMN
THE BELL SOUNDS!
THE BELL SOUNDS!
"BUT, FEAR NOT! ON THAT DAY THE DOORS OF THE SINGULARITY SANCTUM SHALL OPEN, AND WELCOME YOU INTO A HOLY UNION."
THEY SURE KNOW HOW TO MAKE AN END-OF-DAYS BASH.

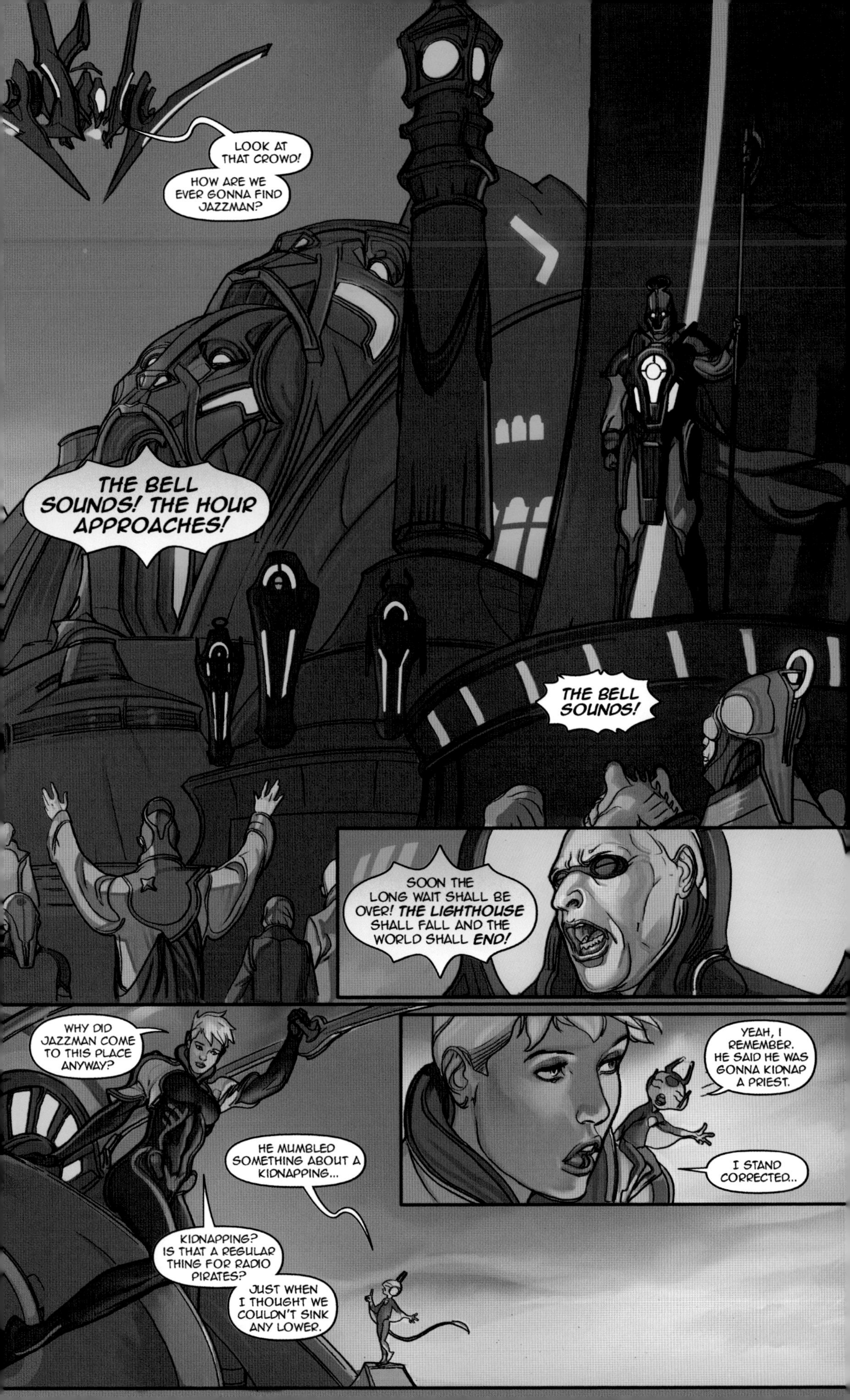
LOOK AT THAT CROWD!
HOW ARE WE EVER GONNA FIND JAZZMAN?
THE BELL SOUNDS! THE HOUR APPROACHES!
THE BELL SOUNDS!
SOON THE LONG WAIT SHALL BE OVER! THE LIGHTHOUSE SHALL FALL AND THE WORLD SHALL END!
WHY DID JAZZMAN COME TO THIS PLACE ANYWAY?
HE MUMBLED SOMETHING ABOUT A KIDNAPPING...
KIDNAPPING? IS THAT A REGULAR THING FOR RADIO PIRATES?
JUST WHEN I THOUGHT WE COULDN'T SINK ANY LOWER.
YEAH, I REMEMBER. HE SAID HE WAS GONNA KIDNAP A PRIEST.
I STAND CORRECTED...

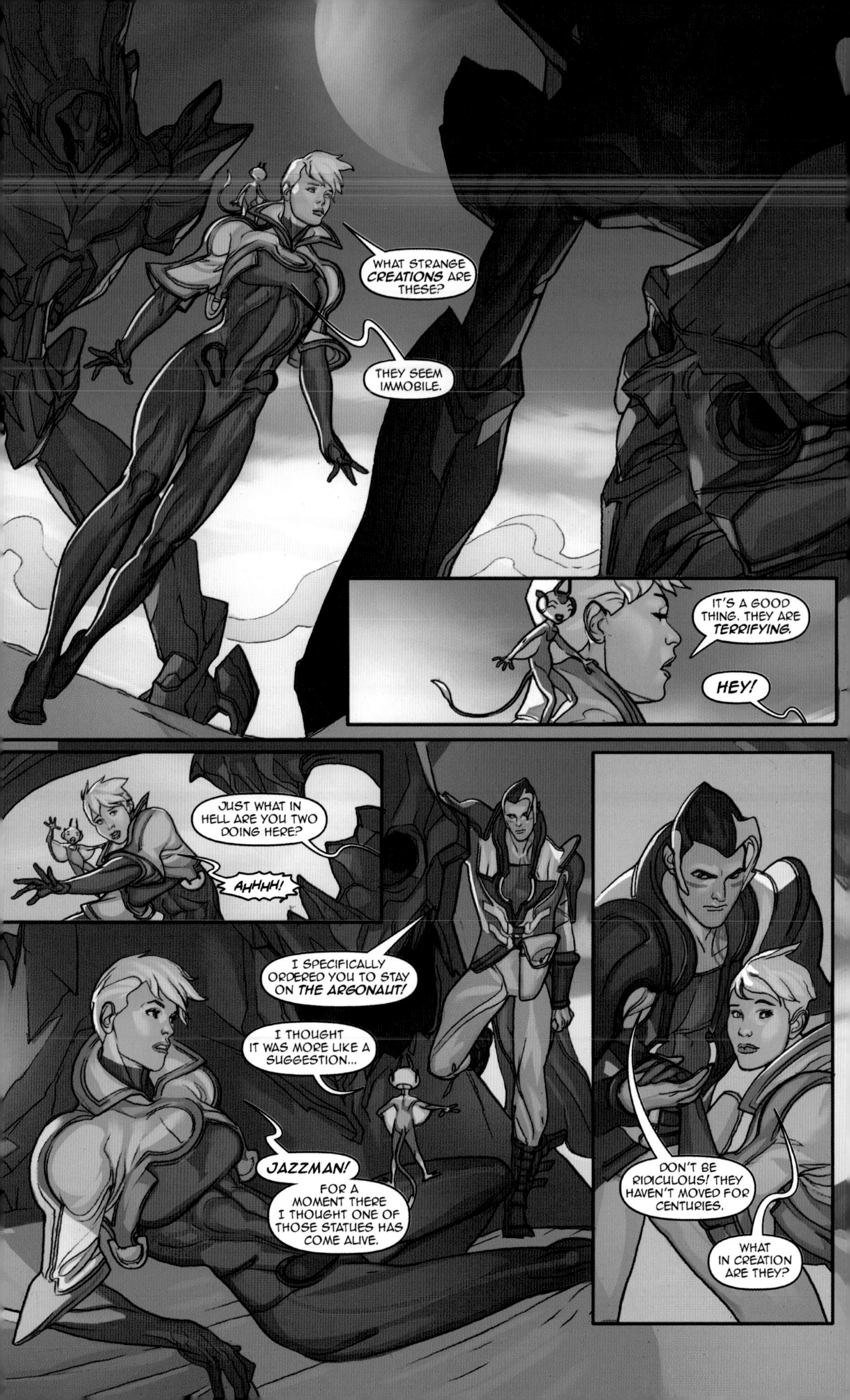
WHAT STRANGE CREATIONS ARE THESE?
THEY SEEM IMMOBILE.
IT'S A GOOD THING. THEY ARE TERRIFYING.
HEY!
JUST WHAT IN HELL ARE YOU TWO DOING HERE?
AHHHH!
I SPECIFICALLY ORDERED YOU TO STAY ON THE ARGONAUT!
I THOUGHT IT WAS MORE LIKE A SUGGESTION...
JAZZMAN!
FOR A MOMENT THERE I THOUGHT ONE OF THOSE STATUES HAS COME ALIVE.
DON'T BE RIDICULOUS! THEY HAVEN'T MOVED FOR CENTURIES.
WHAT IN CREATION ARE THEY?

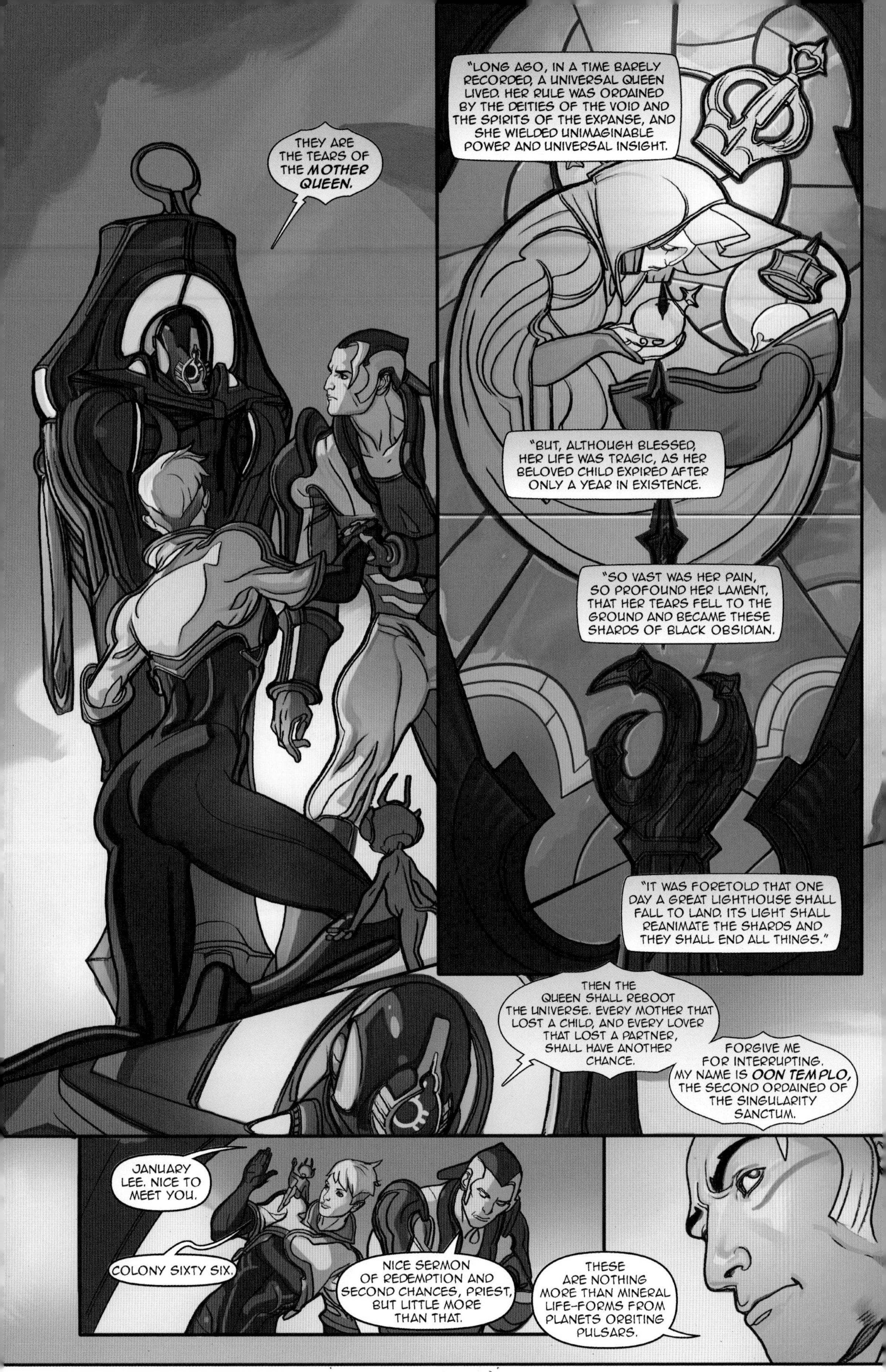
THEY ARE THE TEARS OF THE *MOTHER QUEEN.*
"LONG AGO, IN A TIME BARELY RECORDED, A UNIVERSAL QUEEN LIVED. HER RULE WAS ORDAINED BY THE DEITIES OF THE VOID AND THE SPIRITS OF THE EXPANSE, AND SHE WIELDED UNIMAGINABLE POWER AND UNIVERSAL INSIGHT.
"BUT, ALTHOUGH BLESSED, HER LIFE WAS TRAGIC, AS HER BELOVED CHILD EXPIRED AFTER ONLY A YEAR IN EXISTENCE.
"SO VAST WAS HER PAIN, SO PROFOUND HER LAMENT, THAT HER TEARS FELL TO THE GROUND AND BECAME THESE SHARDS OF BLACK OBSIDIAN.
"IT WAS FORETOLD THAT ONE DAY A GREAT LIGHTHOUSE SHALL FALL TO LAND. ITS LIGHT SHALL REANIMATE THE SHARDS AND THEY SHALL END ALL THINGS."
THEN THE QUEEN SHALL REBOOT THE UNIVERSE. EVERY MOTHER THAT LOST A CHILD, AND EVERY LOVER THAT LOST A PARTNER, SHALL HAVE ANOTHER CHANCE.
FORGIVE ME FOR INTERRUPTING. MY NAME IS *OON TEMPLO,* THE SECOND ORDAINED OF THE SINGULARITY SANCTUM.
JANUARY LEE. NICE TO MEET YOU.
COLONY SIXTY SIX.
NICE SERMON OF REDEMPTION AND SECOND CHANCES, PRIEST, BUT LITTLE MORE THAN THAT.
THESE ARE NOTHING MORE THAN MINERAL LIFE-FORMS FROM PLANETS ORBITING PULSARS.

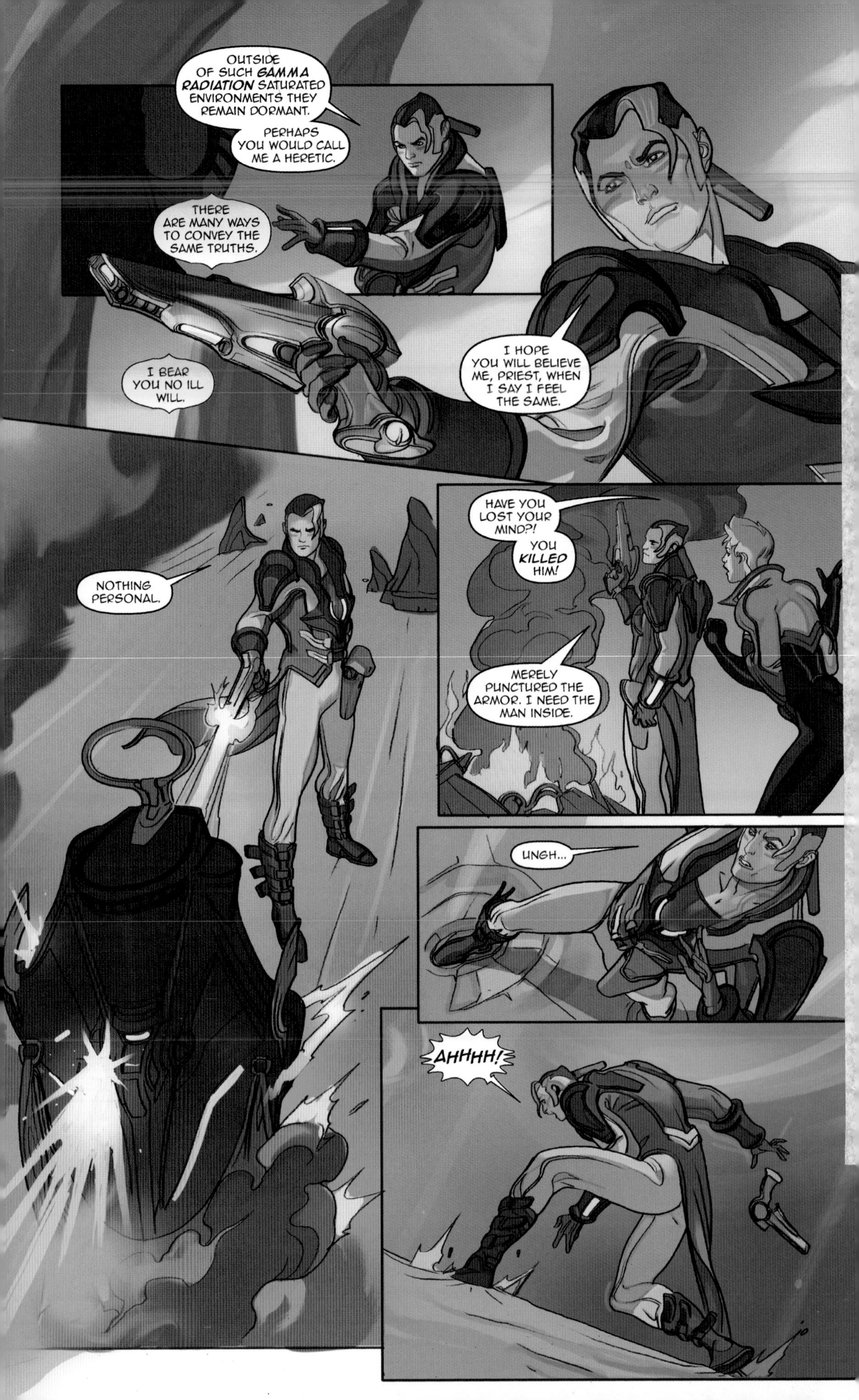
OUTSIDE OF SUCH GAMMA RADIATION SATURATED ENVIRONMENTS THEY REMAIN DORMANT.
PERHAPS YOU WOULD CALL ME A HERETIC.
THERE ARE MANY WAYS TO CONVEY THE SAME TRUTHS.
I BEAR YOU NO ILL WILL.
I HOPE YOU WILL BELIEVE ME, PRIEST, WHEN I SAY I FEEL THE SAME.
NOTHING PERSONAL.
HAVE YOU LOST YOUR MIND?!
YOU KILLED HIM!
MERELY PUNCTURED THE ARMOR. I NEED THE MAN INSIDE.
UNGH...
AHHHH!

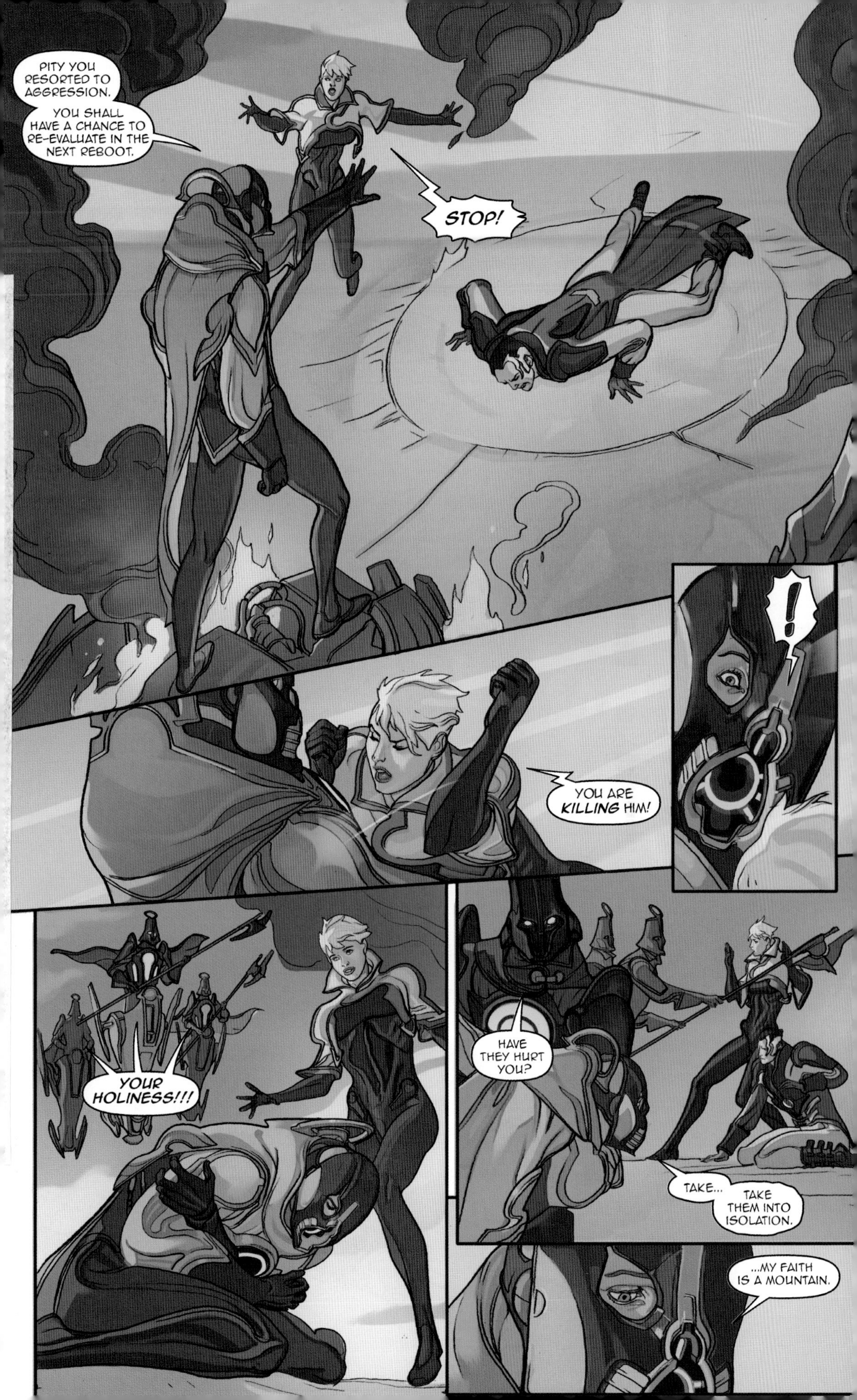

PITY YOU RESORTED TO AGGRESSION.
YOU SHALL HAVE A CHANCE TO RE-EVALUATE IN THE NEXT REBOOT.
STOP!
!
YOU ARE KILLING HIM!
YOUR HOLINESS!!!
HAVE THEY HURT YOU?
TAKE...
TAKE THEM INTO ISOLATION.
...MY FAITH IS A MOUNTAIN.

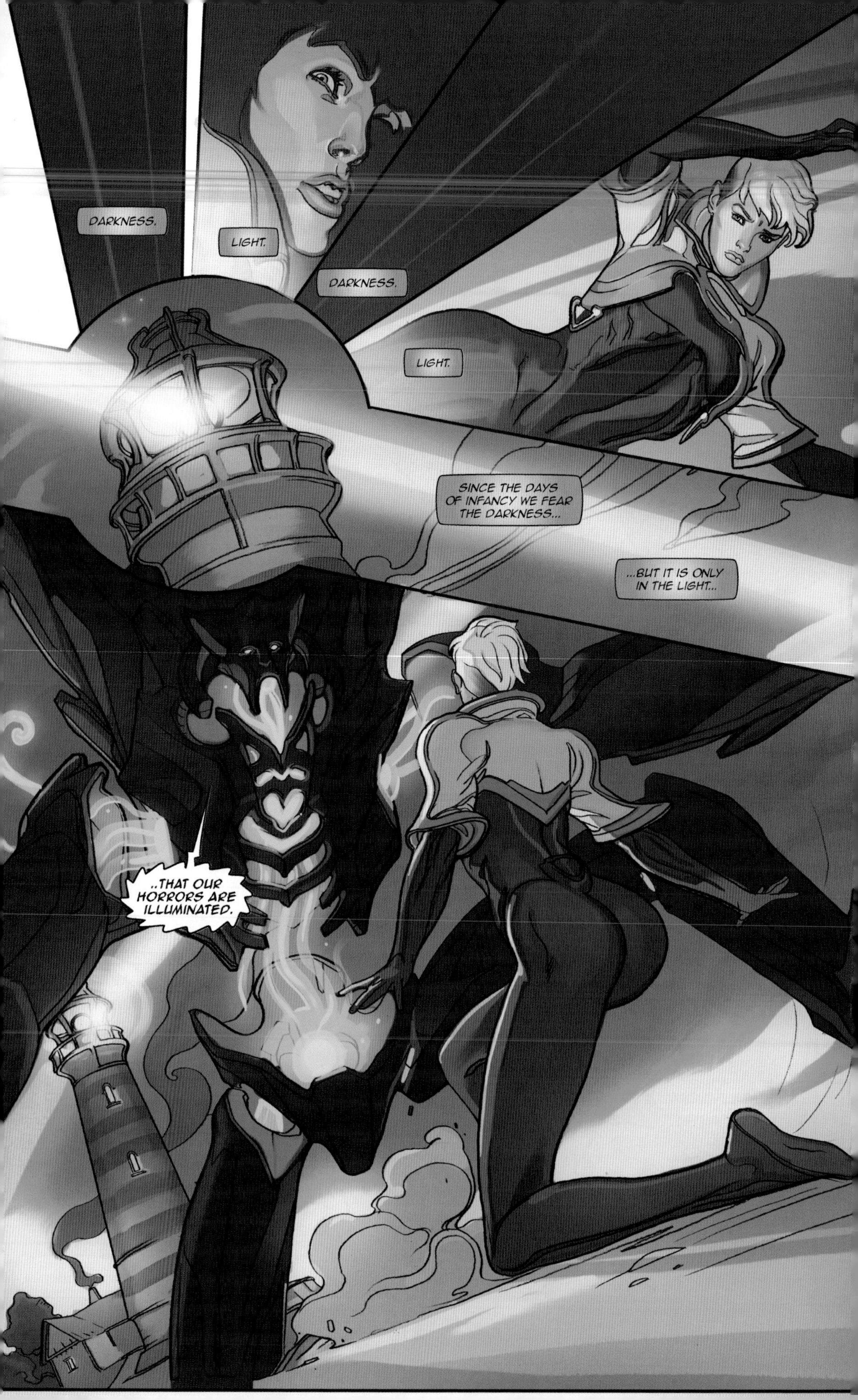
DARKNESS.
LIGHT.
DARKNESS.
LIGHT.
SINCE THE DAYS OF INFANCY WE FEAR THE DARKNESS...
...BUT IT IS ONLY IN THE LIGHT...
..THAT OUR HORRORS ARE ILLUMINATED.

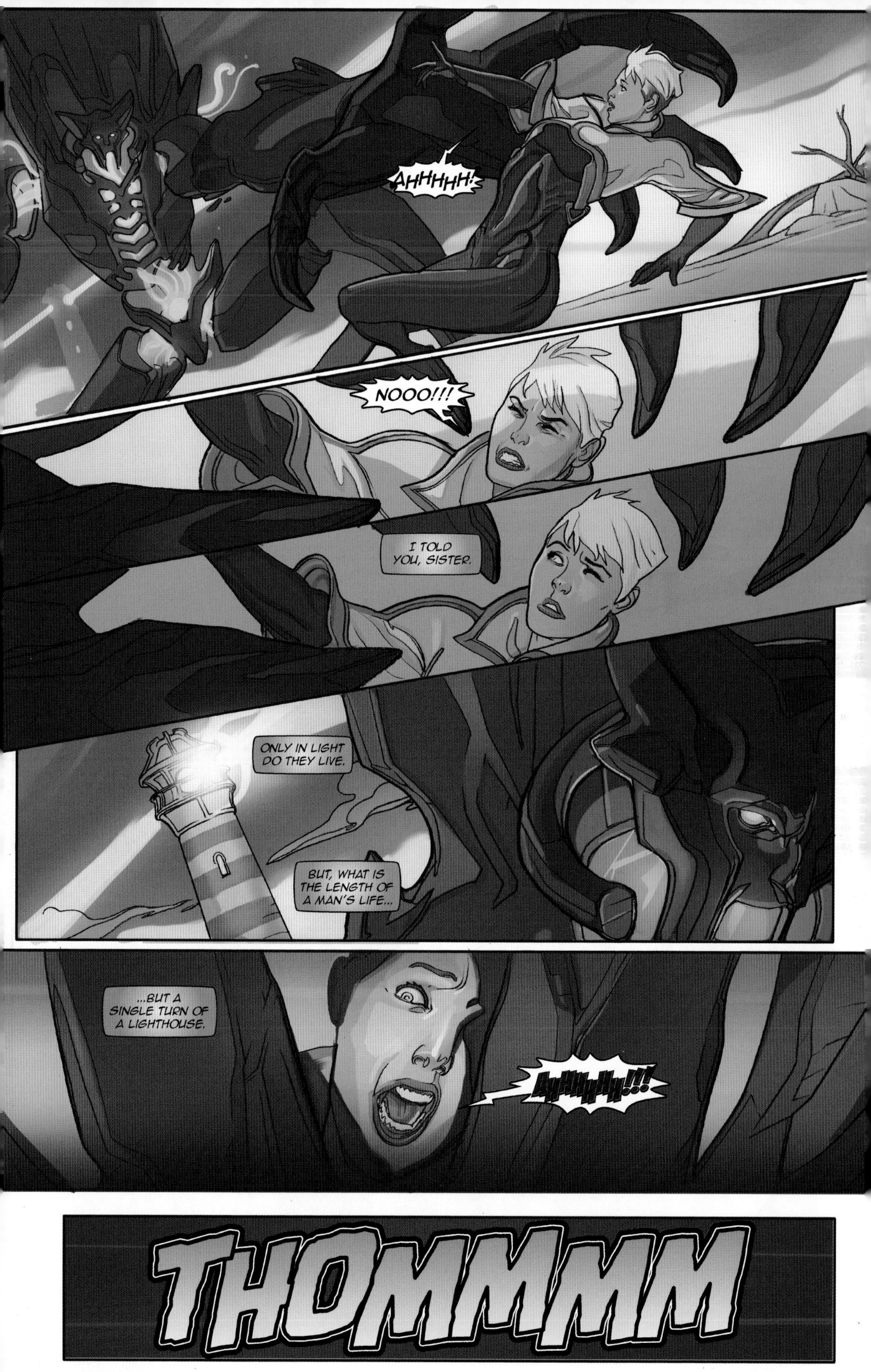
AHHHHH!
NOOO!!!
I TOLD YOU, SISTER.
ONLY IN LIGHT DO THEY LIVE.
BUT, WHAT IS THE LENGTH OF A MAN'S LIFE...
...BUT A SINGLE TURN OF A LIGHTHOUSE.
THOMMMM

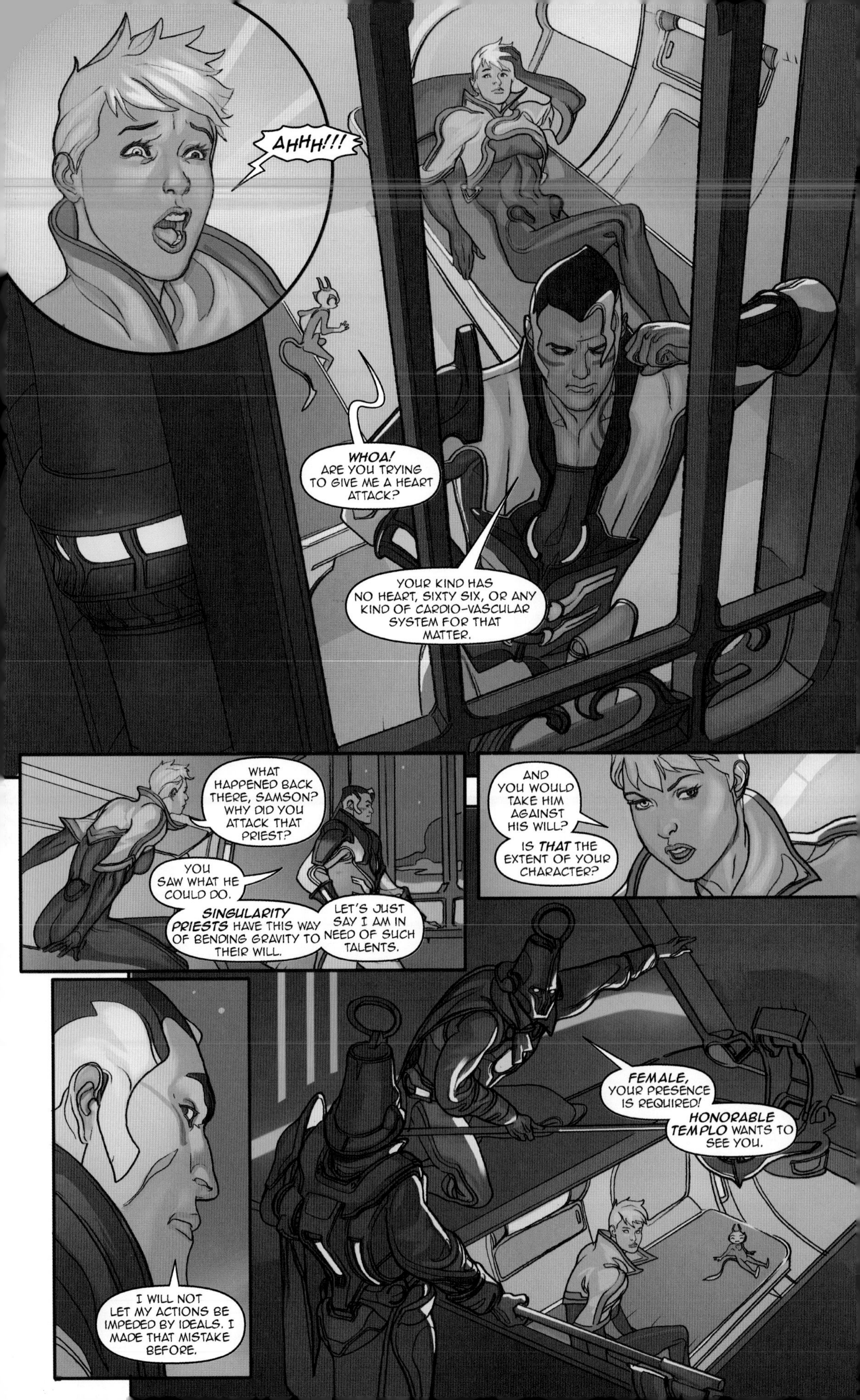
AHHH!!!
WHOA! ARE YOU TRYING TO GIVE ME A HEART ATTACK?
YOUR KIND HAS NO HEART, SIXTY SIX, OR ANY KIND OF CARDIO-VASCULAR SYSTEM FOR THAT MATTER.
WHAT HAPPENED BACK THERE, SAMSON? WHY DID YOU ATTACK THAT PRIEST?
YOU SAW WHAT HE COULD DO.
SINGULARITY PRIESTS HAVE THIS WAY OF BENDING GRAVITY TO THEIR WILL.
LET'S JUST SAY I AM IN NEED OF SUCH TALENTS.
AND YOU WOULD TAKE HIM AGAINST HIS WILL?
IS THAT THE EXTENT OF YOUR CHARACTER?
I WILL NOT LET MY ACTIONS BE IMPEDED BY IDEALS. I MADE THAT MISTAKE BEFORE.
FEMALE, YOUR PRESENCE IS REQUIRED!
HONORABLE TEMPLO WANTS TO SEE YOU.

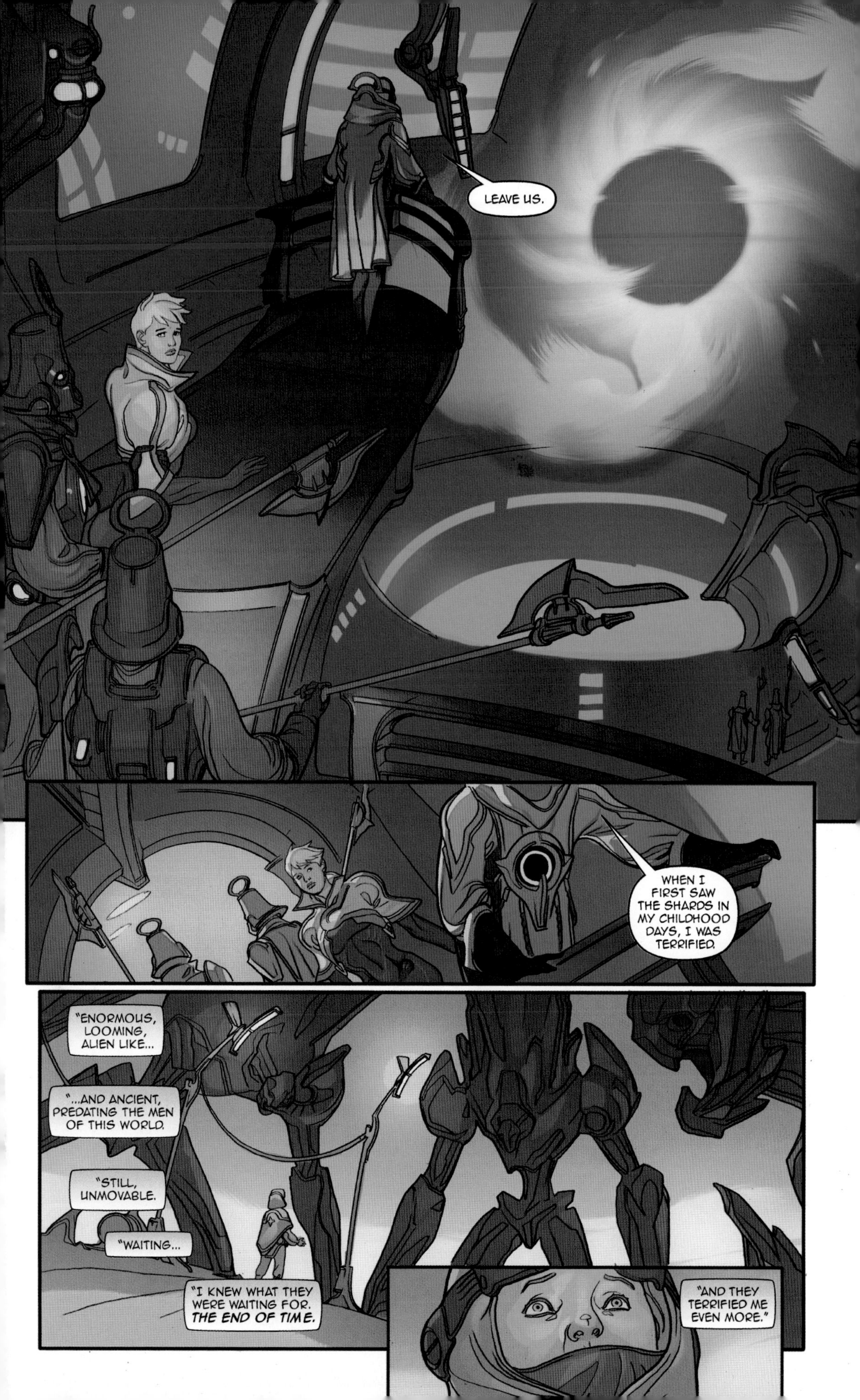
LEAVE US.
WHEN I FIRST SAW THE SHARDS IN MY CHILDHOOD DAYS, I WAS TERRIFIED.
"ENORMOUS, LOOMING, ALIEN LIKE...
"...AND ANCIENT, PREDATING THE MEN OF THIS WORLD.
"STILL, UNMOVABLE.
"WAITING...
"I KNEW WHAT THEY WERE WAITING FOR. *THE END OF TIME*.
"AND THEY TERRIFIED ME EVEN MORE."

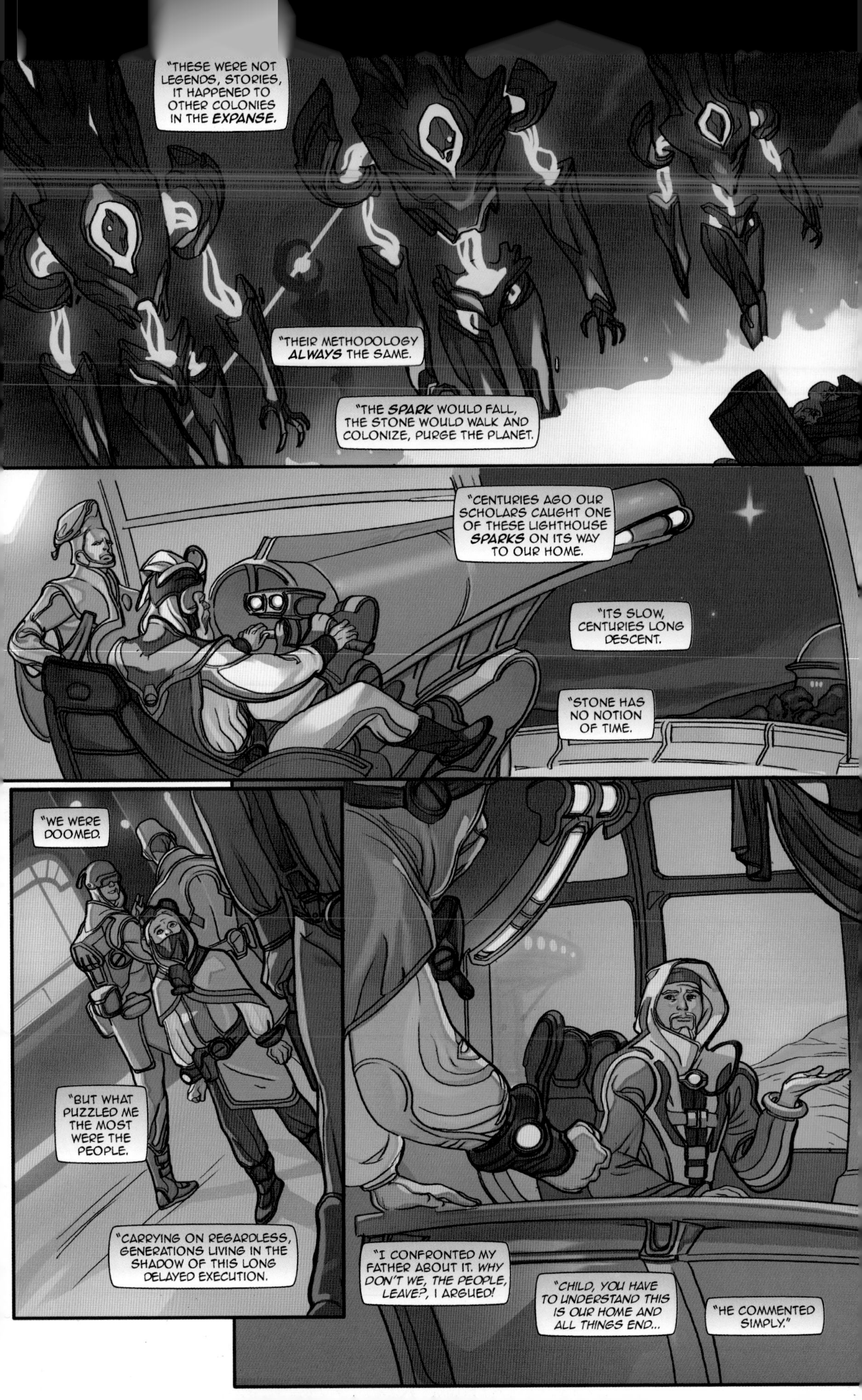
"THESE WERE NOT LEGENDS, STORIES, IT HAPPENED TO OTHER COLONIES IN THE EXPANSE.
"THEIR METHODOLOGY ALWAYS THE SAME.
"THE SPARK WOULD FALL, THE STONE WOULD WALK AND COLONIZE, PURGE THE PLANET.
"CENTURIES AGO OUR SCHOLARS CAUGHT ONE OF THESE LIGHTHOUSE SPARKS ON ITS WAY TO OUR HOME.
"ITS SLOW, CENTURIES LONG DESCENT.
"STONE HAS NO NOTION OF TIME.
"WE WERE DOOMED.
"BUT WHAT PUZZLED ME THE MOST WERE THE PEOPLE.
"CARRYING ON REGARDLESS, GENERATIONS LIVING IN THE SHADOW OF THIS LONG DELAYED EXECUTION.
"I CONFRONTED MY FATHER ABOUT IT. WHY DON'T WE, THE PEOPLE, LEAVE?, I ARGUED!
"CHILD, YOU HAVE TO UNDERSTAND THIS IS OUR HOME AND ALL THINGS END...
"HE COMMENTED SIMPLY."

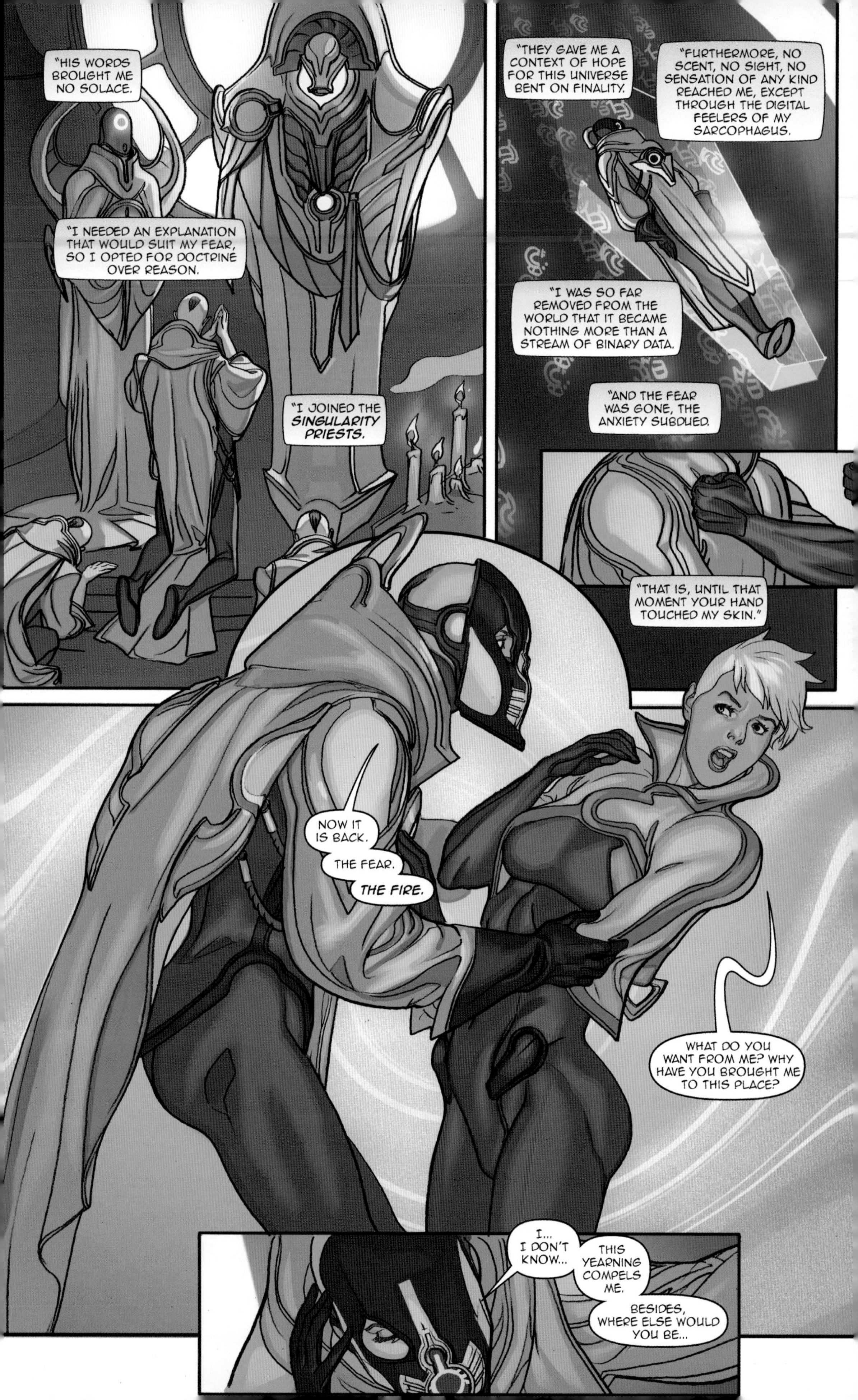
"HIS WORDS BROUGHT ME NO SOLACE.
"I NEEDED AN EXPLANATION THAT WOULD SUIT MY FEAR, SO I OPTED FOR DOCTRINE OVER REASON.
"I JOINED THE *SINGULARITY PRIESTS.*
"THEY GAVE ME A CONTEXT OF HOPE FOR THIS UNIVERSE BENT ON FINALITY.
"FURTHERMORE, NO SCENT, NO SIGHT, NO SENSATION OF ANY KIND REACHED ME, EXCEPT THROUGH THE DIGITAL FEELERS OF MY SARCOPHAGUS.
"I WAS SO FAR REMOVED FROM THE WORLD THAT IT BECAME NOTHING MORE THAN A STREAM OF BINARY DATA.
"AND THE FEAR WAS GONE, THE ANXIETY SUBDUED.
"THAT IS, UNTIL THAT MOMENT YOUR HAND TOUCHED MY SKIN."
NOW IT IS BACK.
THE FEAR.
THE FIRE.
WHAT DO YOU WANT FROM ME? WHY HAVE YOU BROUGHT ME TO THIS PLACE?
I... I DON'T KNOW...
THIS YEARNING COMPELS ME.
BESIDES, WHERE ELSE WOULD YOU BE...

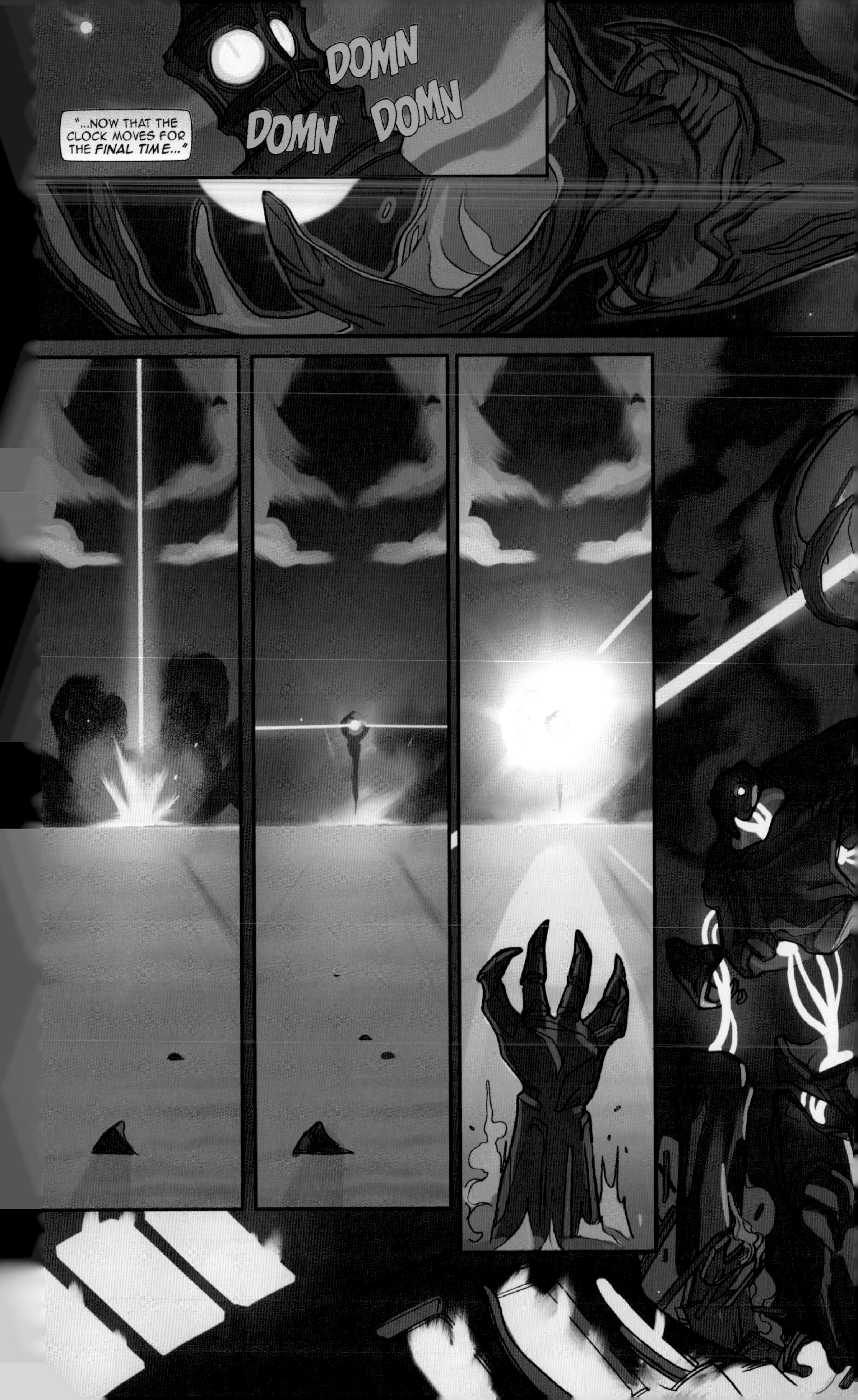
"...NOW THAT THE CLOCK MOVES FOR THE FINAL TIME..."
DOMN
DOMN
DOMN

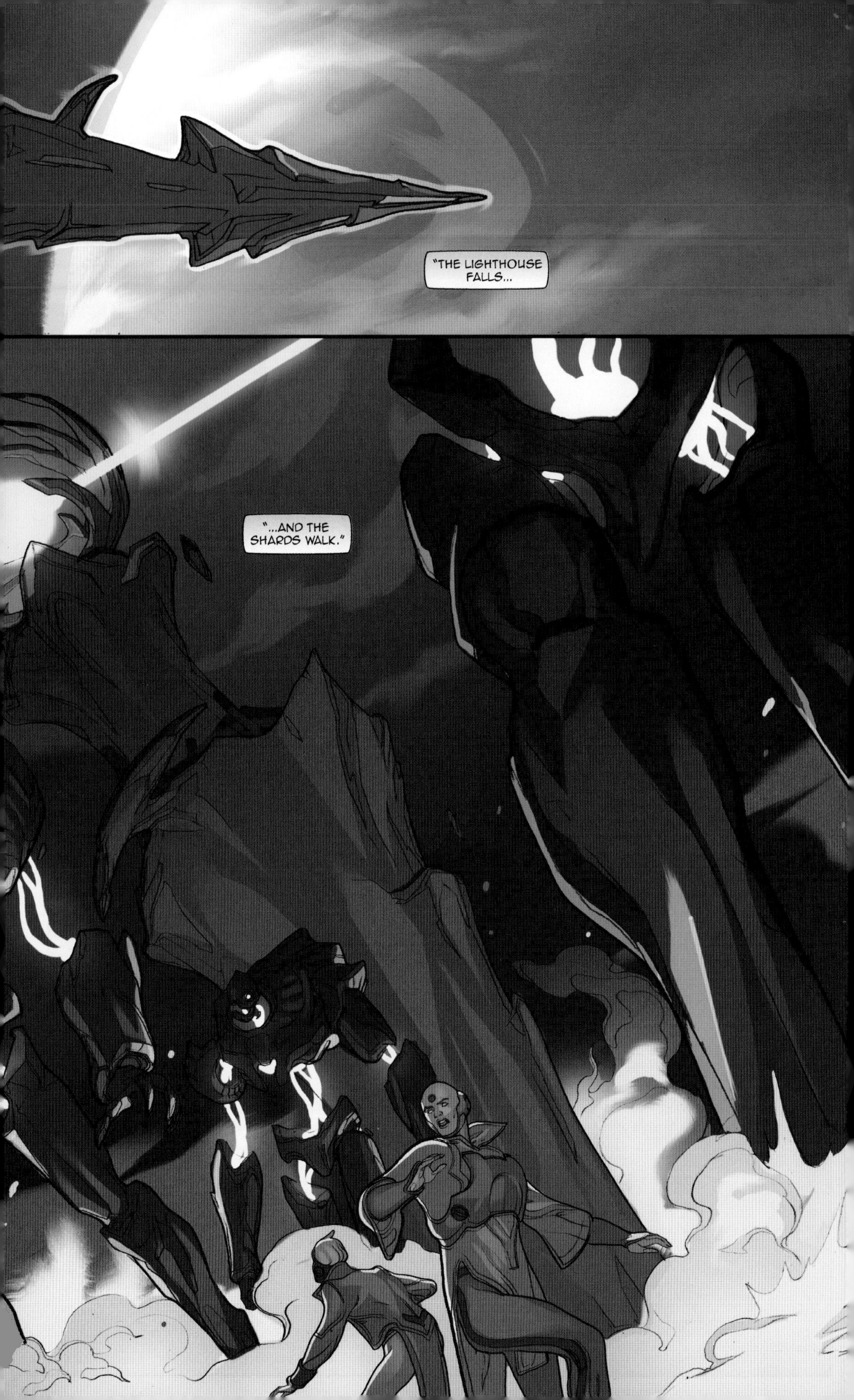
"THE LIGHTHOUSE FALLS...
"...AND THE SHARDS WALK."

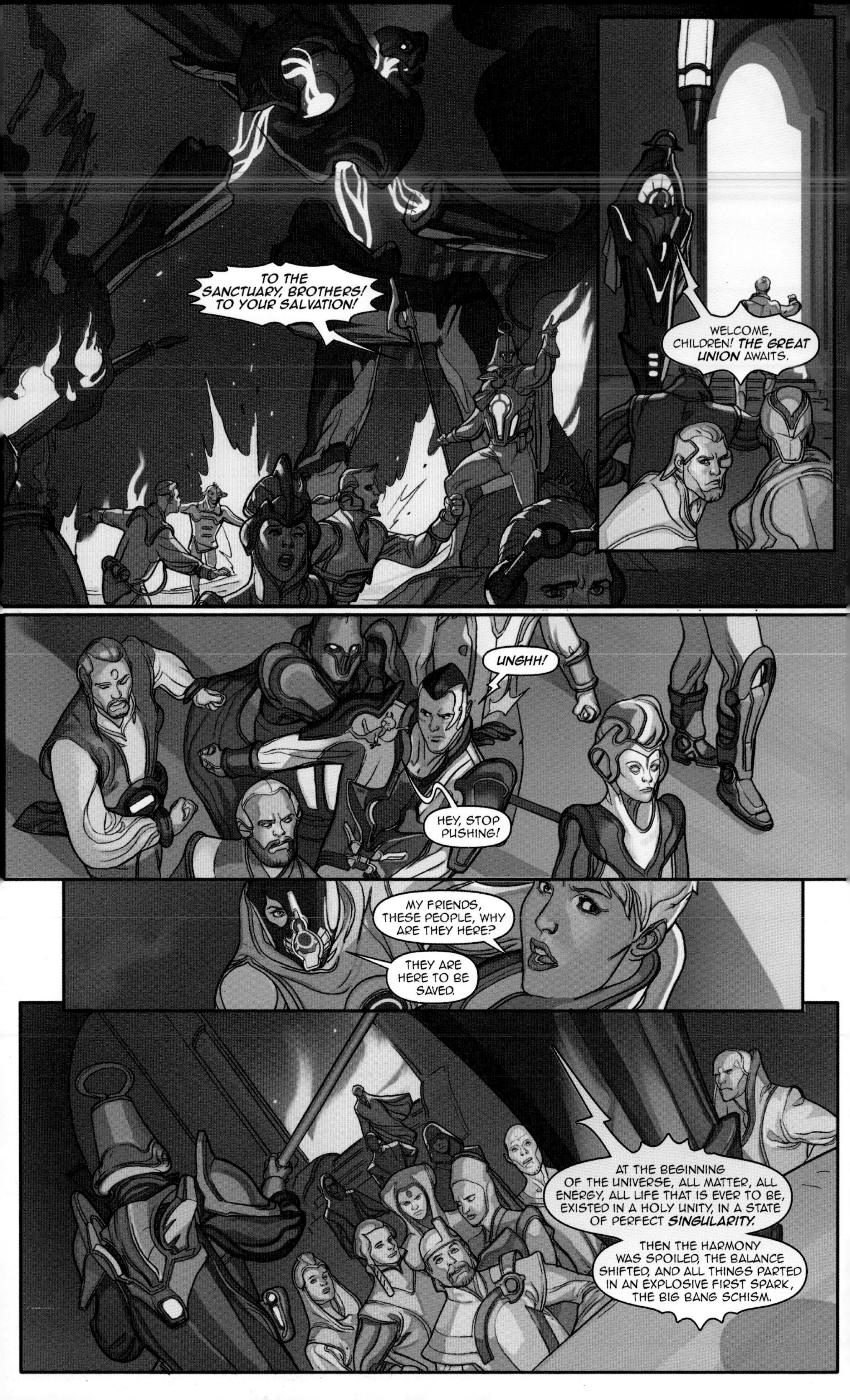
TO THE SANCTUARY, BROTHERS! TO YOUR SALVATION!
WELCOME, CHILDREN! THE GREAT UNION AWAITS.
UNGHH!
HEY, STOP PUSHING!
MY FRIENDS, THESE PEOPLE, WHY ARE THEY HERE?
THEY ARE HERE TO BE SAVED.
AT THE BEGINNING OF THE UNIVERSE, ALL MATTER, ALL ENERGY, ALL LIFE THAT IS EVER TO BE, EXISTED IN A HOLY UNITY, IN A STATE OF PERFECT SINGULARITY.
THEN THE HARMONY WAS SPOILED, THE BALANCE SHIFTED, AND ALL THINGS PARTED IN AN EXPLOSIVE FIRST SPARK, THE BIG BANG SCHISM.

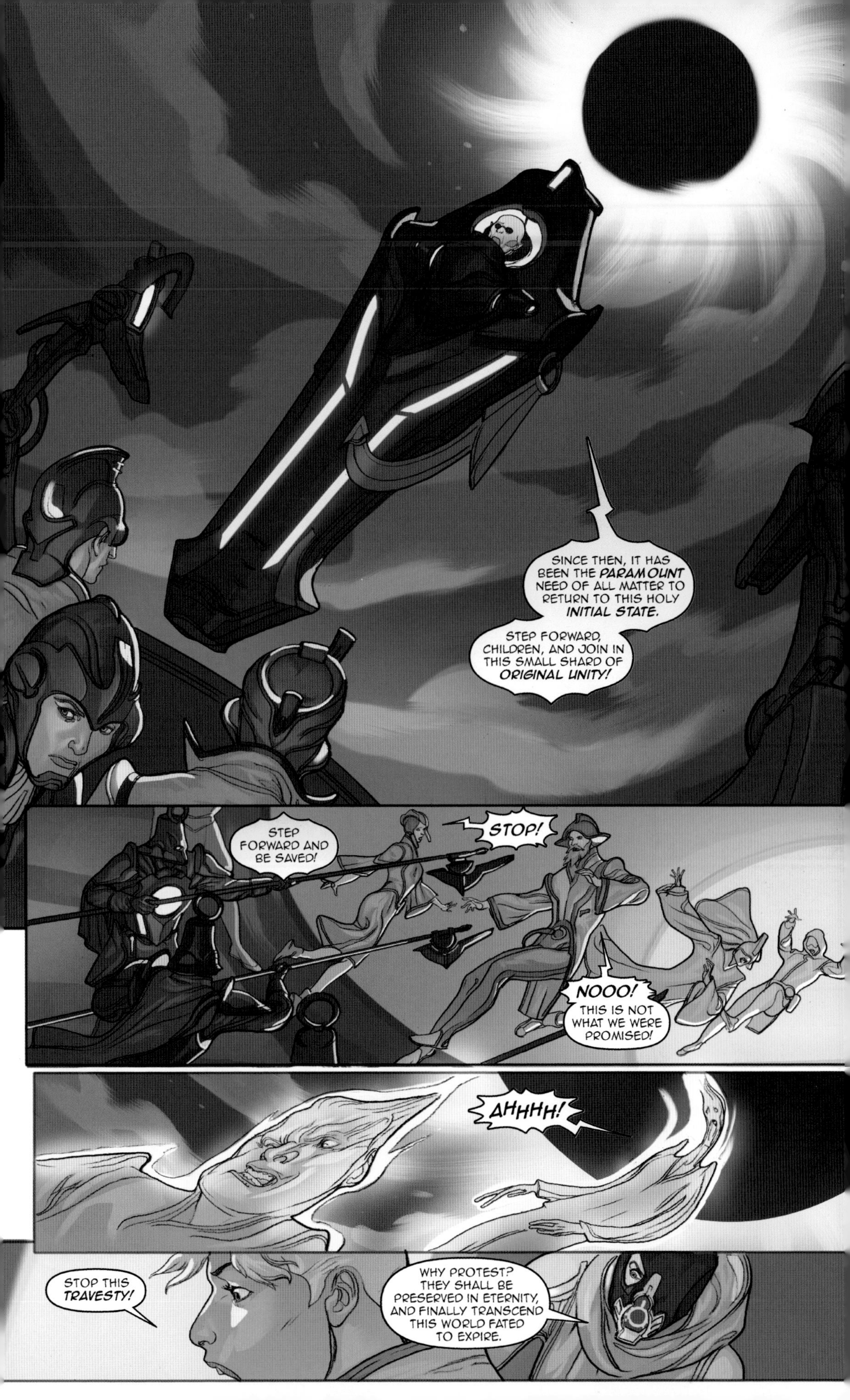
SINCE THEN, IT HAS BEEN THE PARAMOUNT NEED OF ALL MATTER TO RETURN TO THIS HOLY INITIAL STATE.
STEP FORWARD, CHILDREN, AND JOIN IN THIS SMALL SHARD OF ORIGINAL UNITY!
STEP FORWARD AND BE SAVED!
STOP!
NOOO!
THIS IS NOT WHAT WE WERE PROMISED!
AHHHH!
STOP THIS TRAVESTY!
WHY PROTEST? THEY SHALL BE PRESERVED IN ETERNITY, AND FINALLY TRANSCEND THIS WORLD FATED TO EXPIRE.

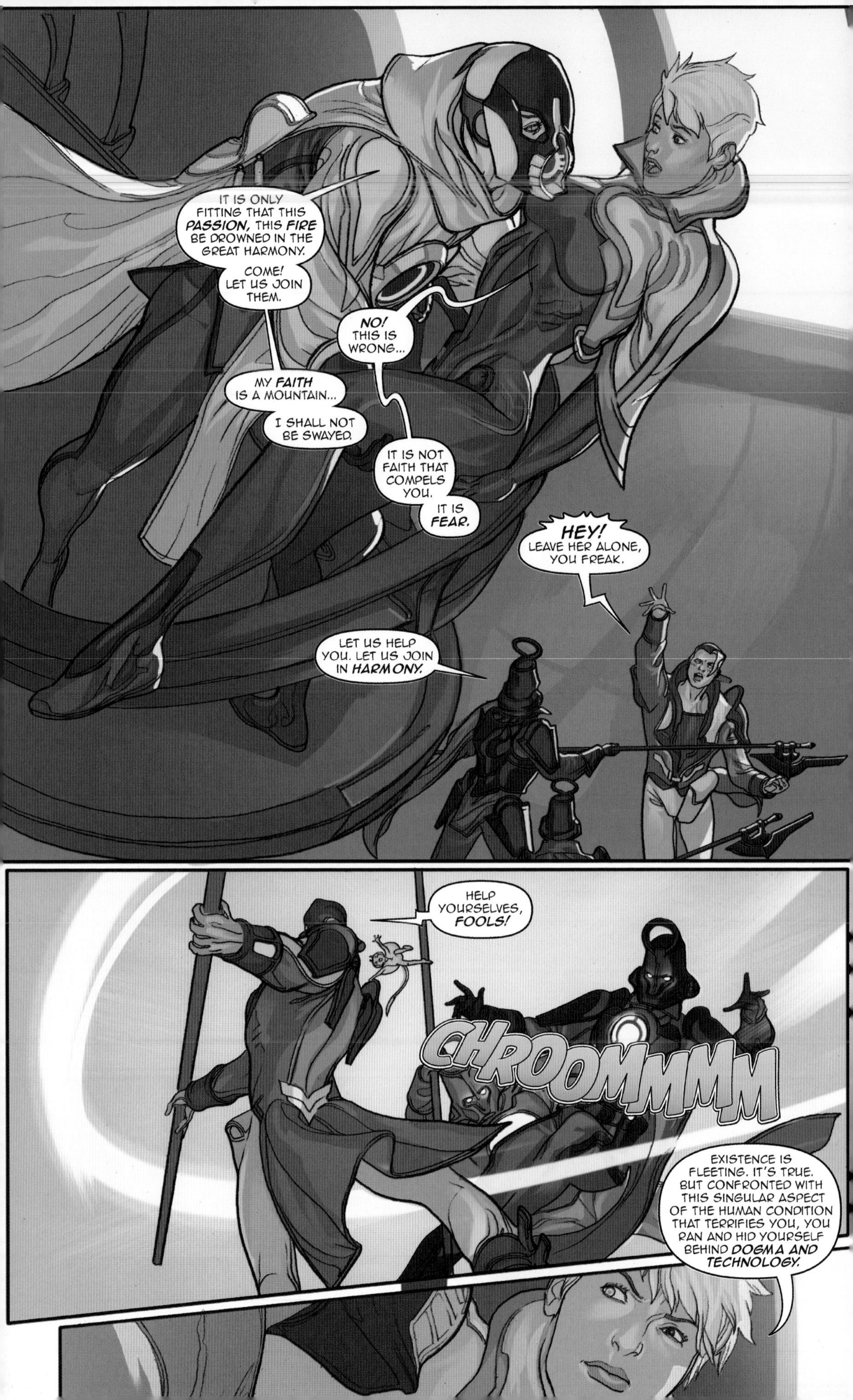

IT IS ONLY FITTING THAT THIS PASSION, THIS FIRE BE DROWNED IN THE GREAT HARMONY.
COME! LET US JOIN THEM.
NO! THIS IS WRONG...
MY FAITH IS A MOUNTAIN...
I SHALL NOT BE SWAYED.
IT IS NOT FAITH THAT COMPELS YOU.
IT IS FEAR.
HEY! LEAVE HER ALONE, YOU FREAK.
LET US HELP YOU. LET US JOIN IN HARMONY.
HELP YOURSELVES, FOOLS!
CHROOMMMMM
EXISTENCE IS FLEETING. IT'S TRUE. BUT CONFRONTED WITH THIS SINGULAR ASPECT OF THE HUMAN CONDITION THAT TERRIFIES YOU, YOU RAN AND HID YOURSELF BEHIND DOGMA AND TECHNOLOGY.

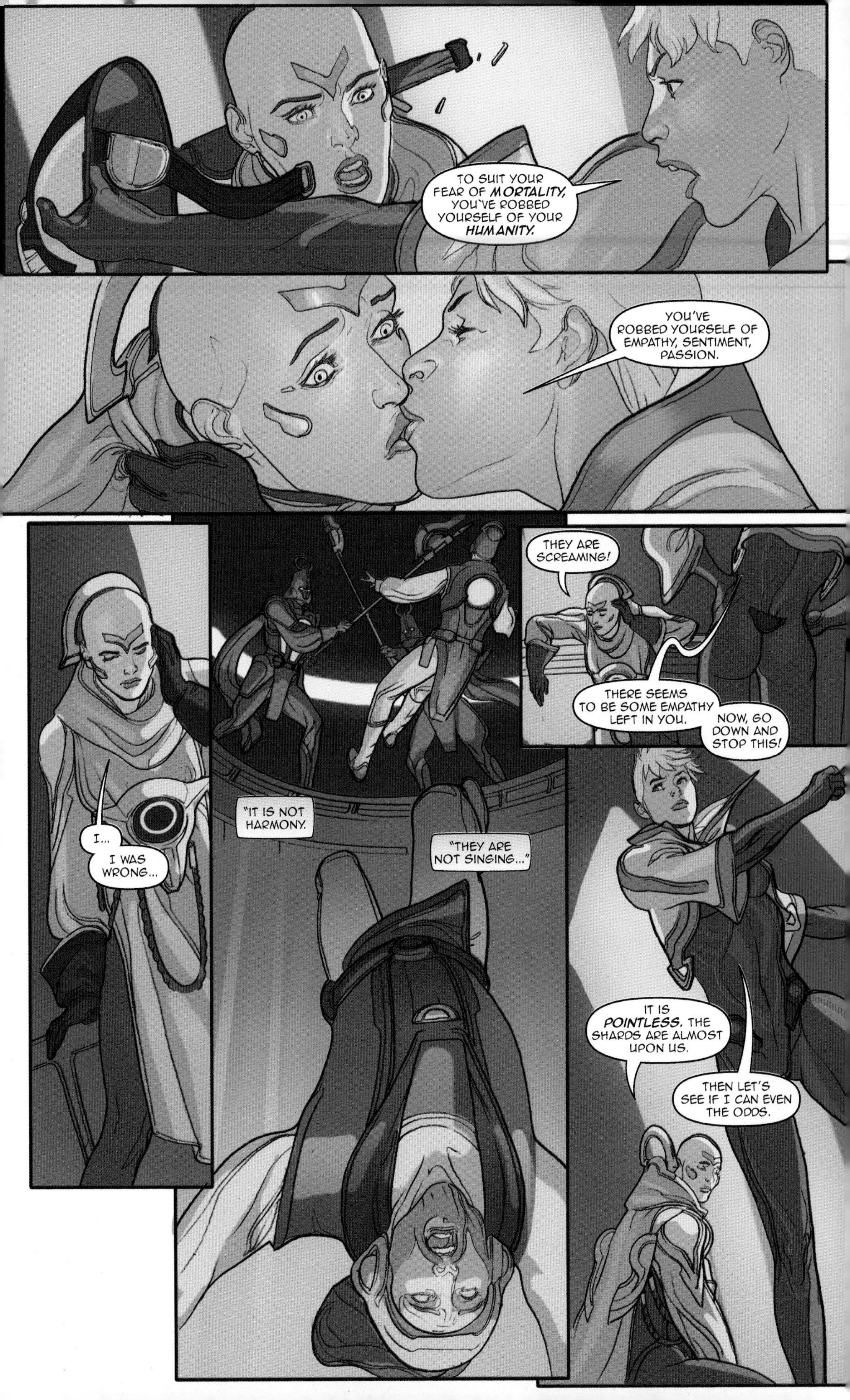
TO SUIT YOUR FEAR OF MORTALITY, YOU'VE ROBBED YOURSELF OF YOUR HUMANITY.
YOU'VE ROBBED YOURSELF OF EMPATHY, SENTIMENT, PASSION.
I... I WAS WRONG...
"IT IS NOT HARMONY.
"THEY ARE NOT SINGING..."
THEY ARE SCREAMING!
THERE SEEMS TO BE SOME EMPATHY LEFT IN YOU.
NOW, GO DOWN AND STOP THIS!
IT IS POINTLESS. THE SHARDS ARE ALMOST UPON US.
THEN LET'S SEE IF I CAN EVEN THE ODDS.

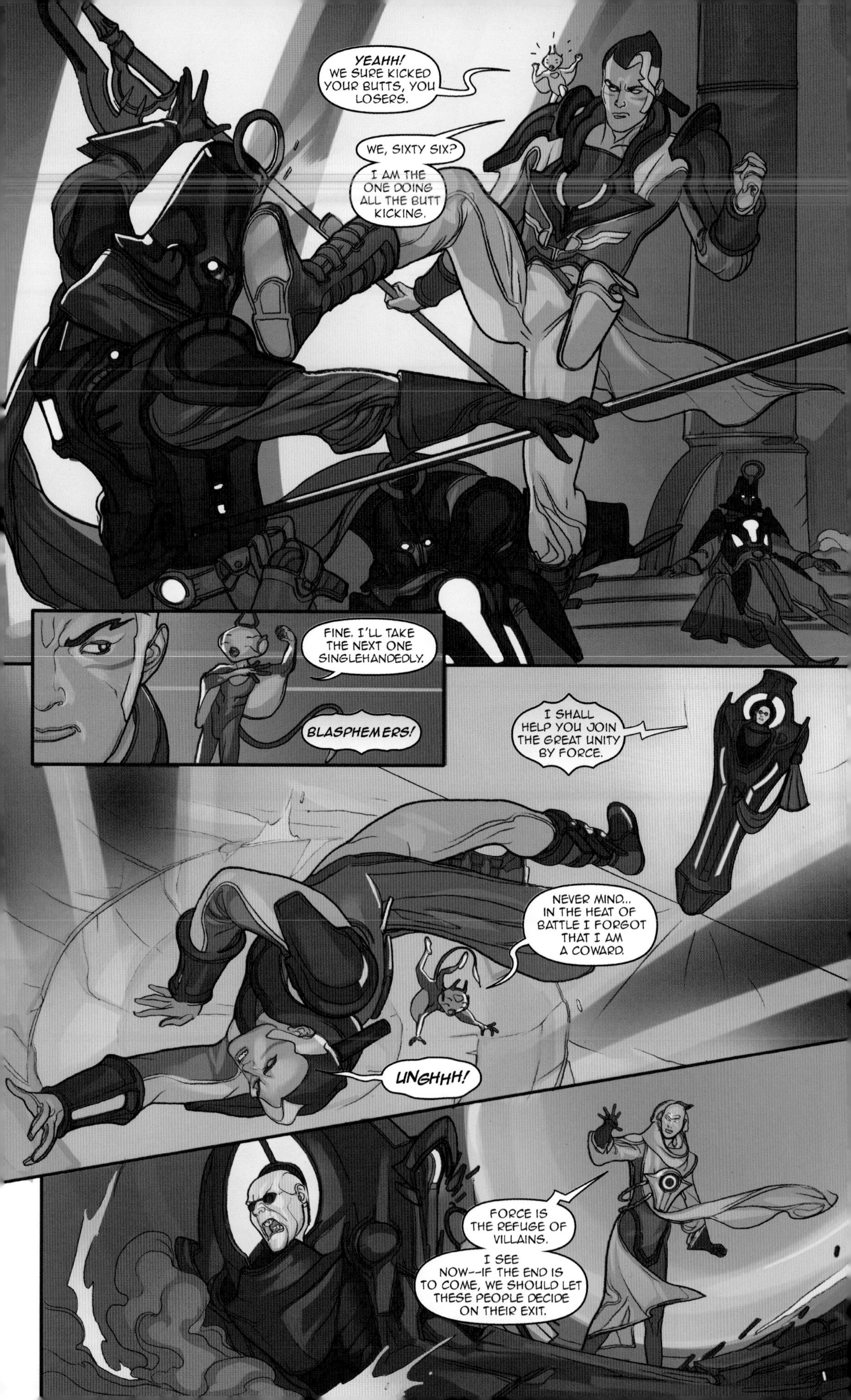

YEAHH! WE SURE KICKED YOUR BUTTS, YOU LOSERS.
WE, SIXTY SIX?
I AM THE ONE DOING ALL THE BUTT KICKING.
FINE. I'LL TAKE THE NEXT ONE SINGLEHANDEDLY.
BLASPHEMERS!
I SHALL HELP YOU JOIN THE GREAT UNITY BY FORCE.
NEVER MIND... IN THE HEAT OF BATTLE I FORGOT THAT I AM A COWARD.
UNGHHH!
FORCE IS THE REFUGE OF VILLAINS.
I SEE NOW--IF THE END IS TO COME, WE SHOULD LET THESE PEOPLE DECIDE ON THEIR EXIT.

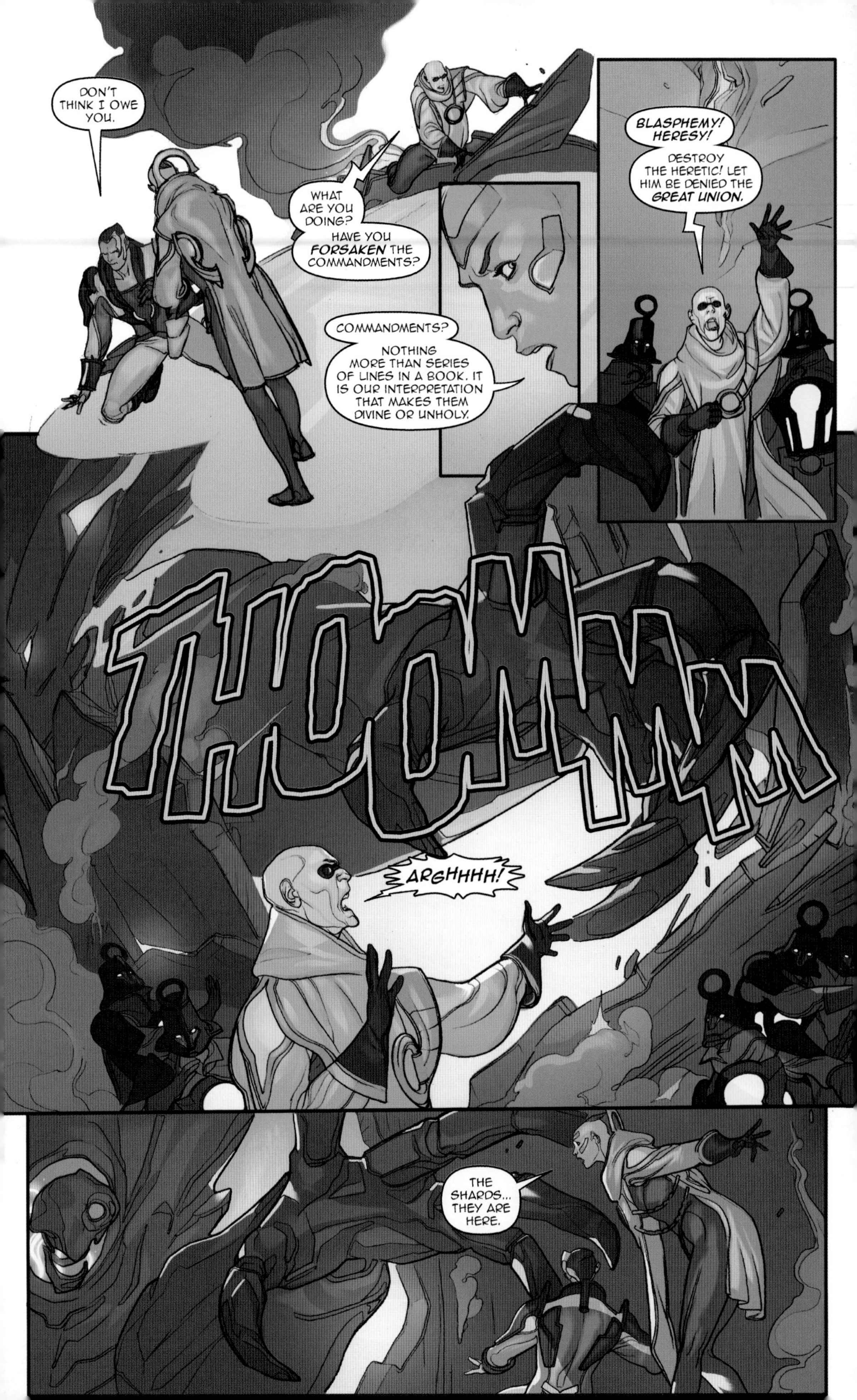
DON'T THINK I OWE YOU.
WHAT ARE YOU DOING?
HAVE YOU *FORSAKEN* THE COMMANDMENTS?
COMMANDMENTS?
NOTHING MORE THAN SERIES OF LINES IN A BOOK. IT IS OUR INTERPRETATION THAT MAKES THEM DIVINE OR UNHOLY.
BLASPHEMY! HERESY!
DESTROY THE HERETIC! LET HIM BE DENIED THE *GREAT UNION.*
THOOMMMM
ARGHHHH!
THE SHARDS... THEY ARE HERE.

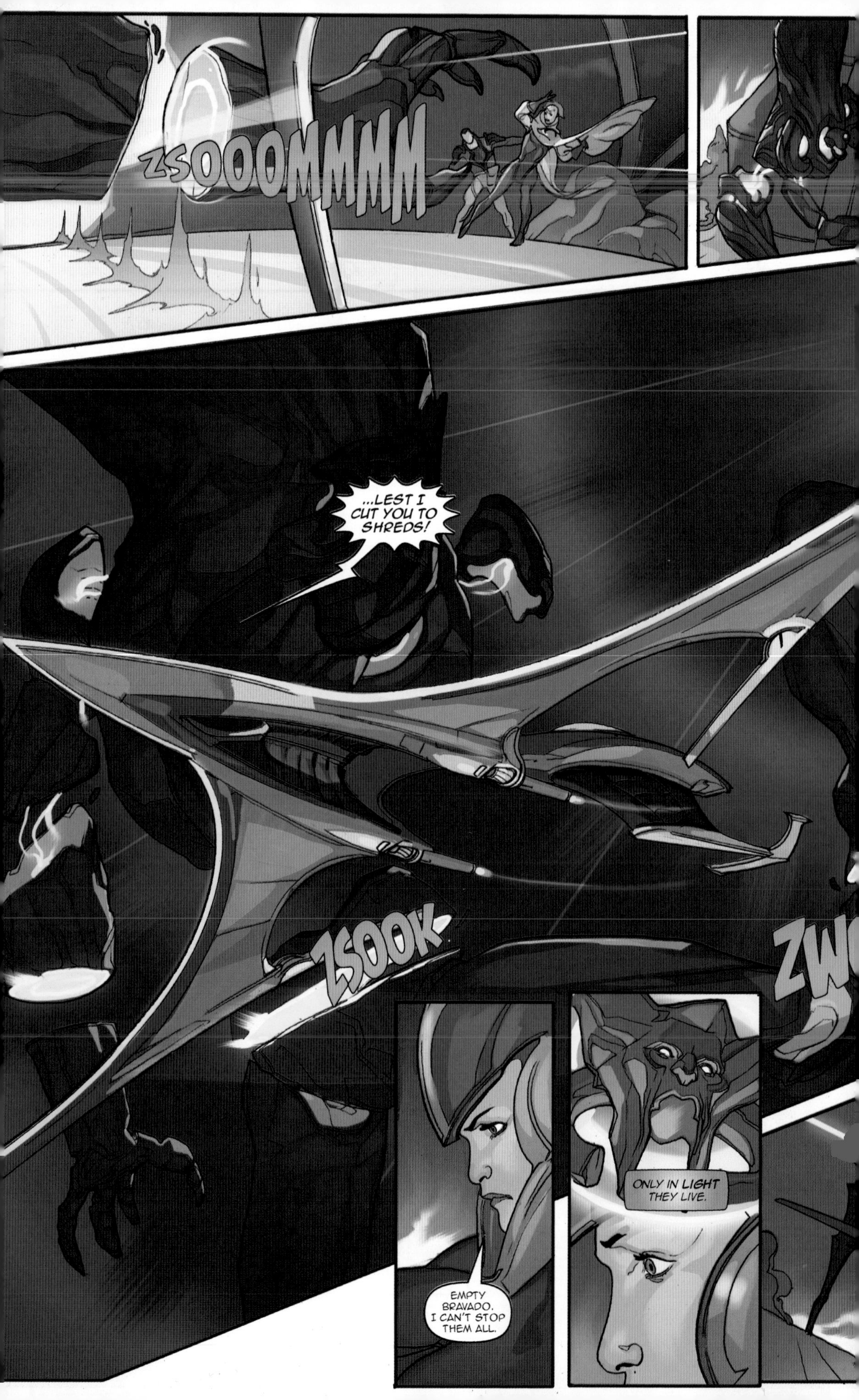
ZSOOOMMMM
...LEST I CUT YOU TO SHREDS!
ZSOOK
ZW
EMPTY BRAVADO. I CAN'T STOP THEM ALL.
ONLY IN LIGHT THEY LIVE.

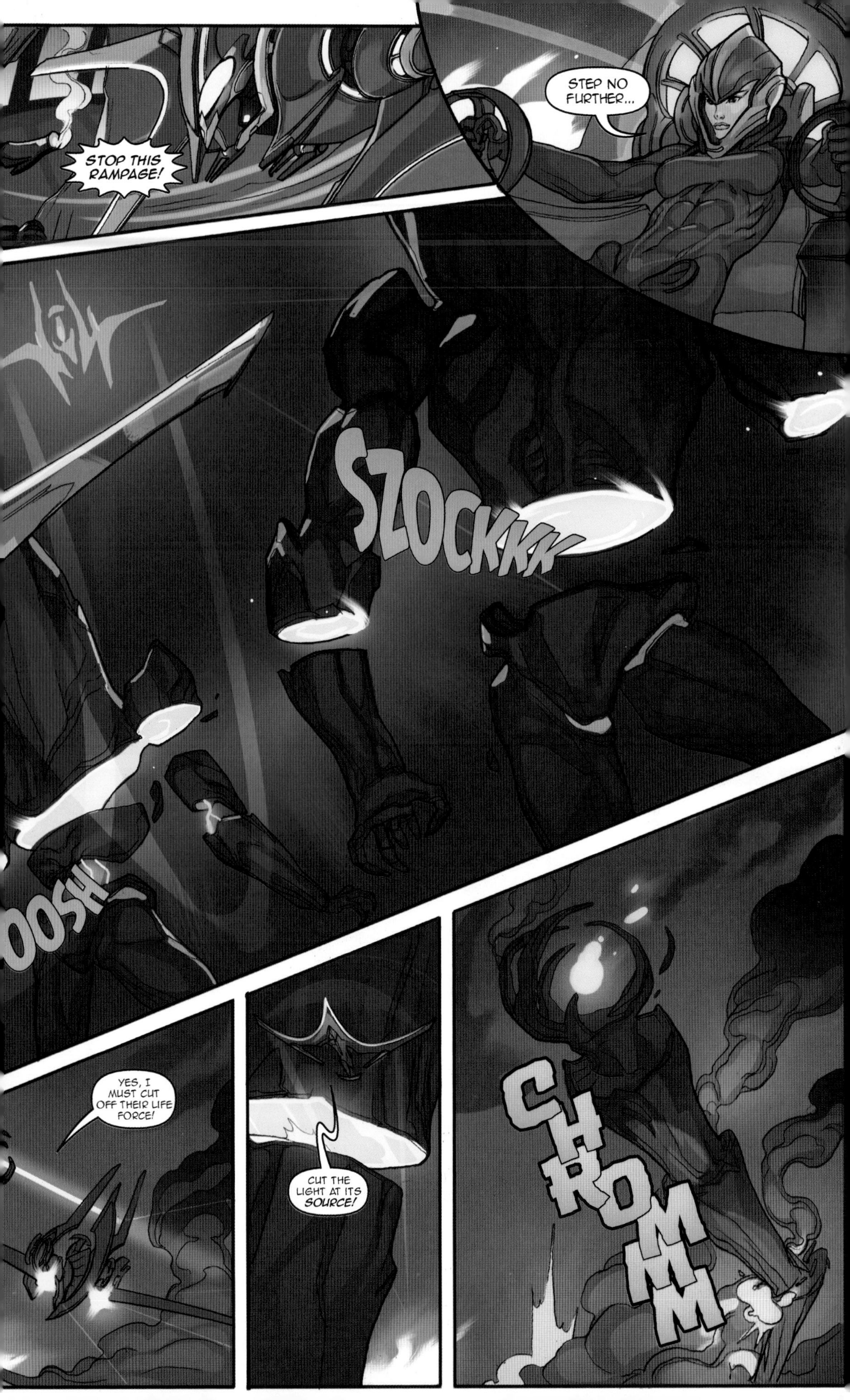
STOP THIS RAMPAGE!
STEP NO FURTHER...
SZOCKKK
OOSH
YES, I MUST CUT OFF THEIR LIFE FORCE!
CUT THE LIGHT AT ITS SOURCE!
CHROMMM

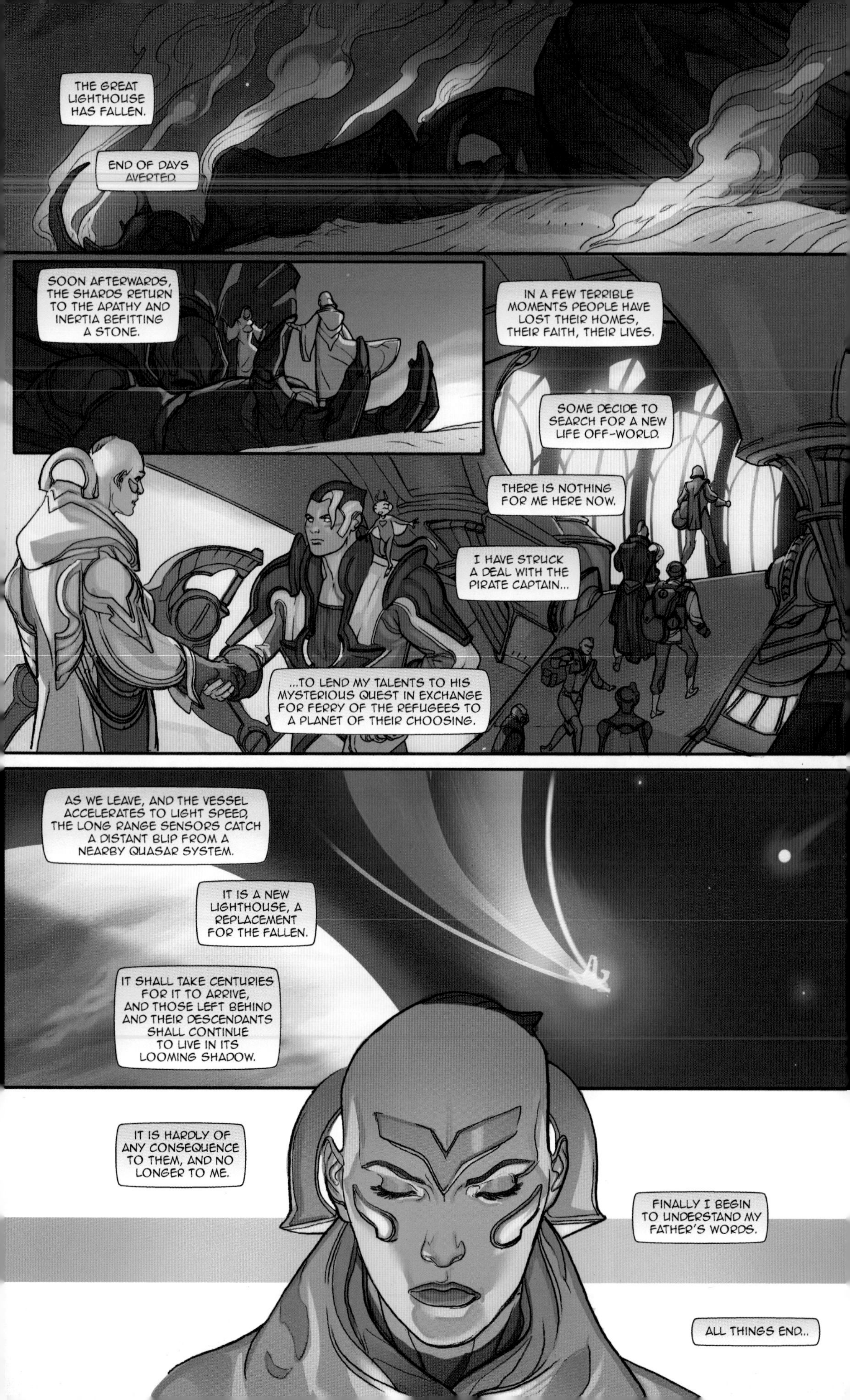
THE GREAT LIGHTHOUSE HAS FALLEN.
END OF DAYS AVERTED.
SOON AFTERWARDS, THE SHARDS RETURN TO THE APATHY AND INERTIA BEFITTING A STONE.
IN A FEW TERRIBLE MOMENTS PEOPLE HAVE LOST THEIR HOMES, THEIR FAITH, THEIR LIVES.
SOME DECIDE TO SEARCH FOR A NEW LIFE OFF-WORLD.
THERE IS NOTHING FOR ME HERE NOW.
I HAVE STRUCK A DEAL WITH THE PIRATE CAPTAIN...
...TO LEND MY TALENTS TO HIS MYSTERIOUS QUEST IN EXCHANGE FOR FERRY OF THE REFUGEES TO A PLANET OF THEIR CHOOSING.
AS WE LEAVE, AND THE VESSEL ACCELERATES TO LIGHT SPEED, THE LONG RANGE SENSORS CATCH A DISTANT BLIP FROM A NEARBY QUASAR SYSTEM.
IT IS A NEW LIGHTHOUSE, A REPLACEMENT FOR THE FALLEN.
IT SHALL TAKE CENTURIES FOR IT TO ARRIVE, AND THOSE LEFT BEHIND AND THEIR DESCENDANTS SHALL CONTINUE TO LIVE IN ITS LOOMING SHADOW.
IT IS HARDLY OF ANY CONSEQUENCE TO THEM, AND NO LONGER TO ME.
FINALLY I BEGIN TO UNDERSTAND MY FATHER'S WORDS.
ALL THINGS END...

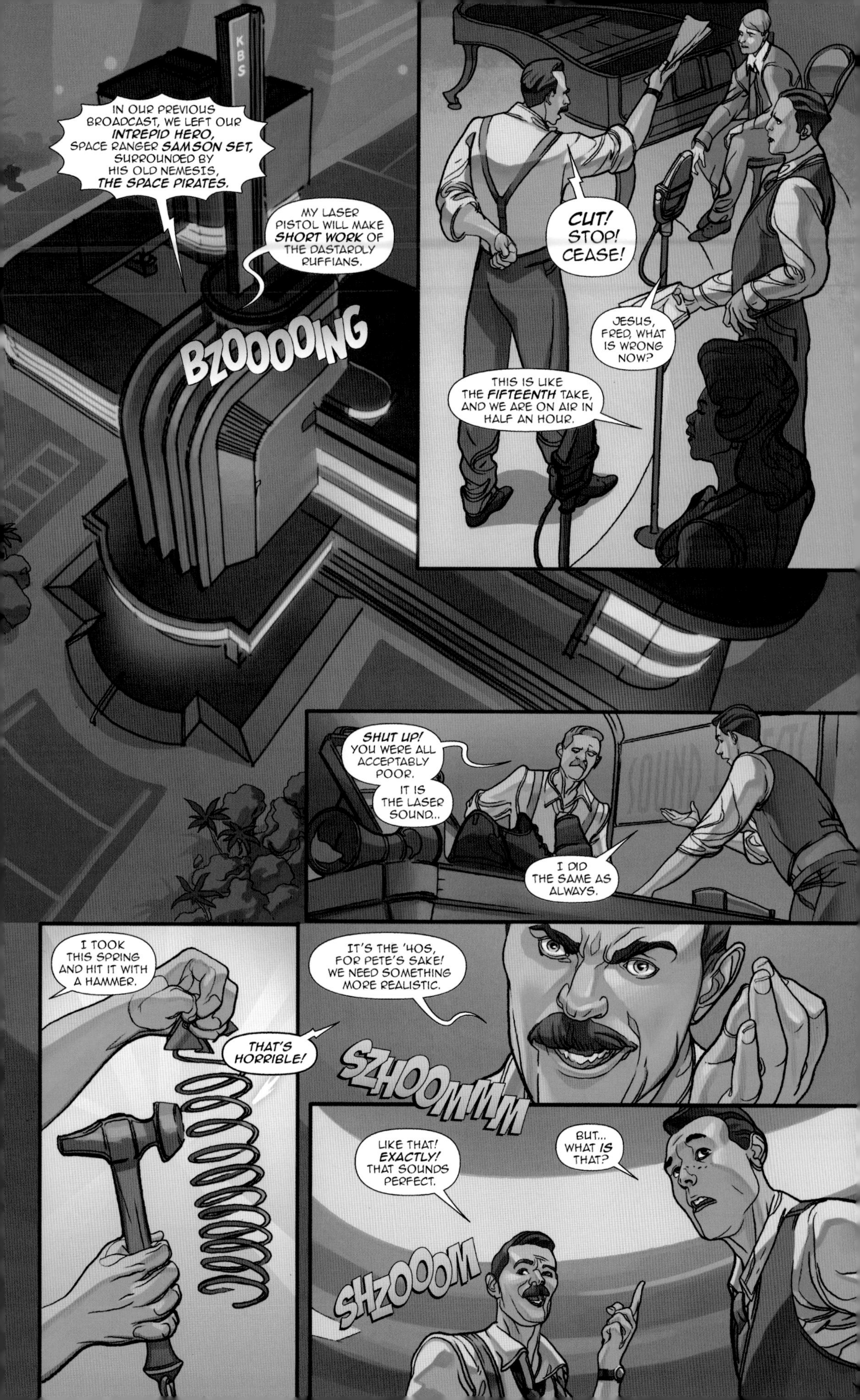
KBS
IN OUR PREVIOUS BROADCAST, WE LEFT OUR **INTREPID HERO,** SPACE RANGER **SAMSON SET,** SURROUNDED BY HIS OLD NEMESIS, **THE SPACE PIRATES.**
MY LASER PISTOL WILL MAKE **SHORT WORK** OF THE DASTARDLY RUFFIANS.
BZOOOOOING
CUT! STOP! CEASE!
JESUS, FRED, WHAT IS WRONG NOW?
THIS IS LIKE THE **FIFTEENTH** TAKE, AND WE ARE ON AIR IN HALF AN HOUR.
SHUT UP! YOU WERE ALL ACCEPTABLY POOR.
IT IS THE LASER SOUND..
I DID THE SAME AS ALWAYS.
I TOOK THIS SPRING AND HIT IT WITH A HAMMER.
THAT'S HORRIBLE!
IT'S THE '40S, FOR PETE'S SAKE! WE NEED SOMETHING MORE REALISTIC.
SZHOOMMMM
LIKE THAT! **EXACTLY!** THAT SOUNDS PERFECT.
BUT... WHAT *IS* THAT?
SHZOOOM

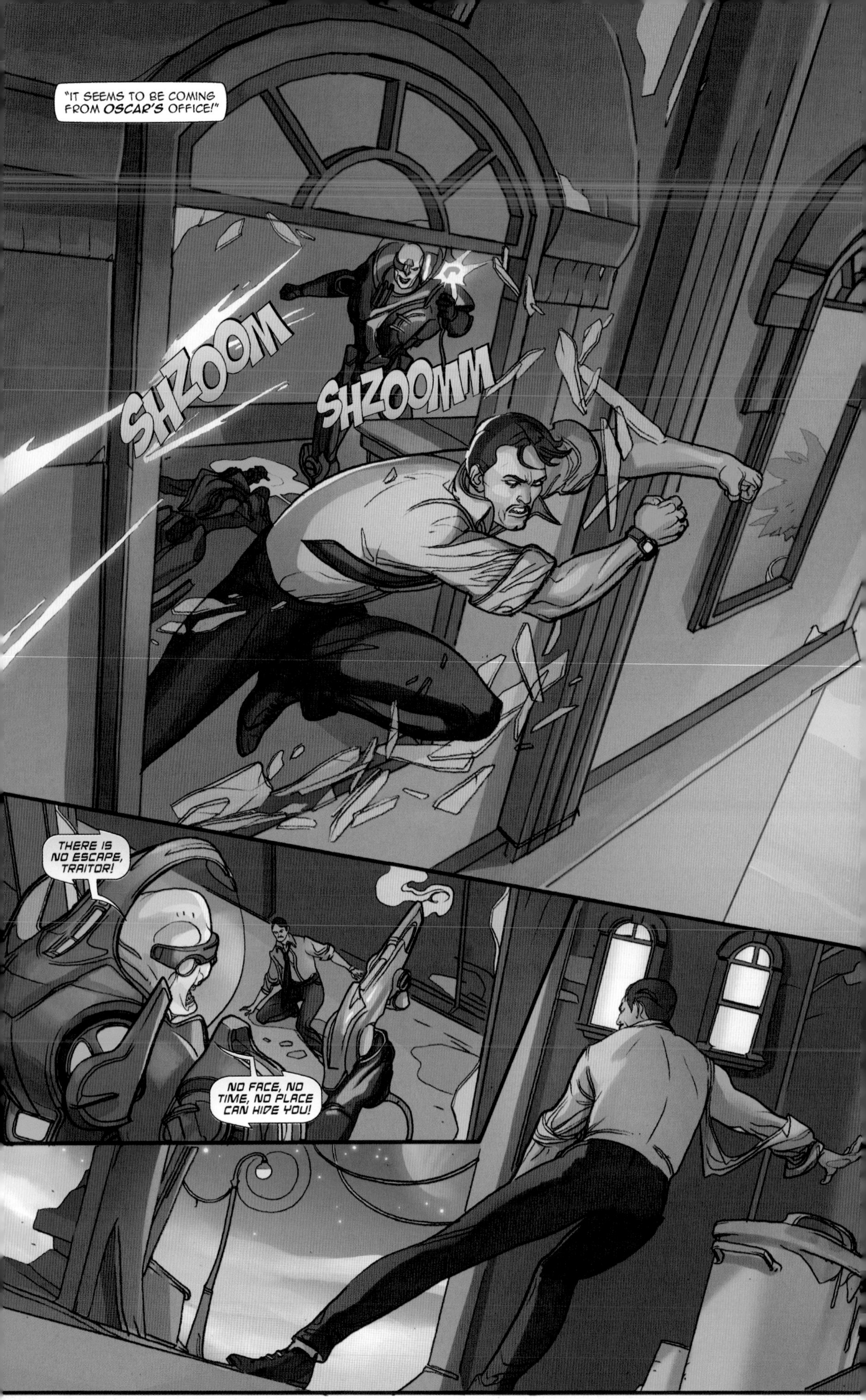
"IT SEEMS TO BE COMING FROM OSCAR'S OFFICE!"
SHZOOM
SHZOOMM
THERE IS NO ESCAPE, TRAITOR!
NO FACE, NO TIME, NO PLACE CAN HIDE YOU!

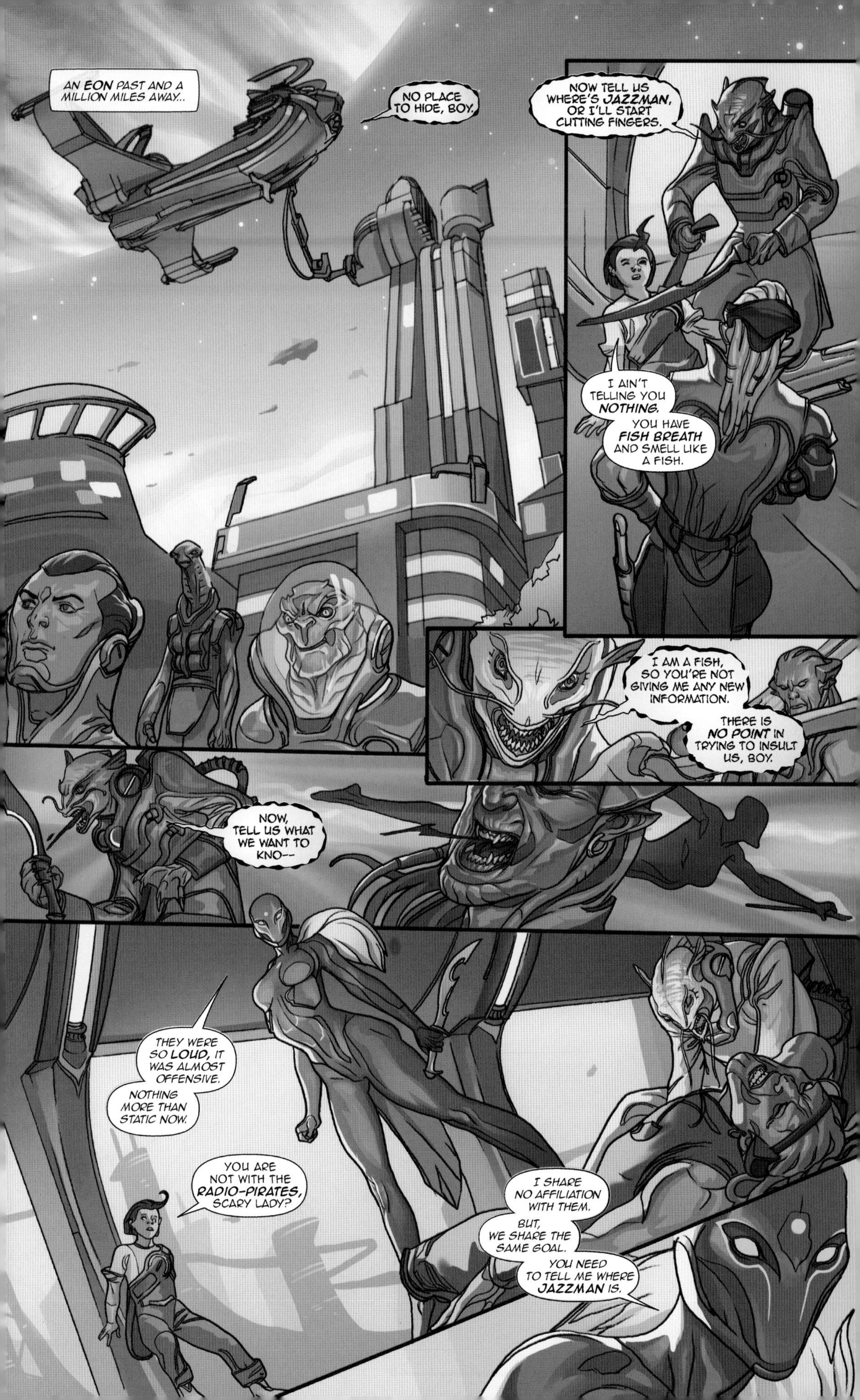
AN EON PAST AND A MILLION MILES AWAY...
NO PLACE TO HIDE, BOY.
NOW TELL US WHERE'S JAZZMAN, OR I'LL START CUTTING FINGERS.
I AIN'T TELLING YOU NOTHING.
YOU HAVE FISH BREATH AND SMELL LIKE A FISH.
I AM A FISH, SO YOU'RE NOT GIVING ME ANY NEW INFORMATION.
THERE IS NO POINT IN TRYING TO INSULT US, BOY.
NOW, TELL US WHAT WE WANT TO KNO--
THEY WERE SO LOUD, IT WAS ALMOST OFFENSIVE.
NOTHING MORE THAN STATIC NOW.
YOU ARE NOT WITH THE RADIO-PIRATES, SCARY LADY?
I SHARE NO AFFILIATION WITH THEM.
BUT, WE SHARE THE SAME GOAL.
YOU NEED TO TELL ME WHERE JAZZMAN IS.

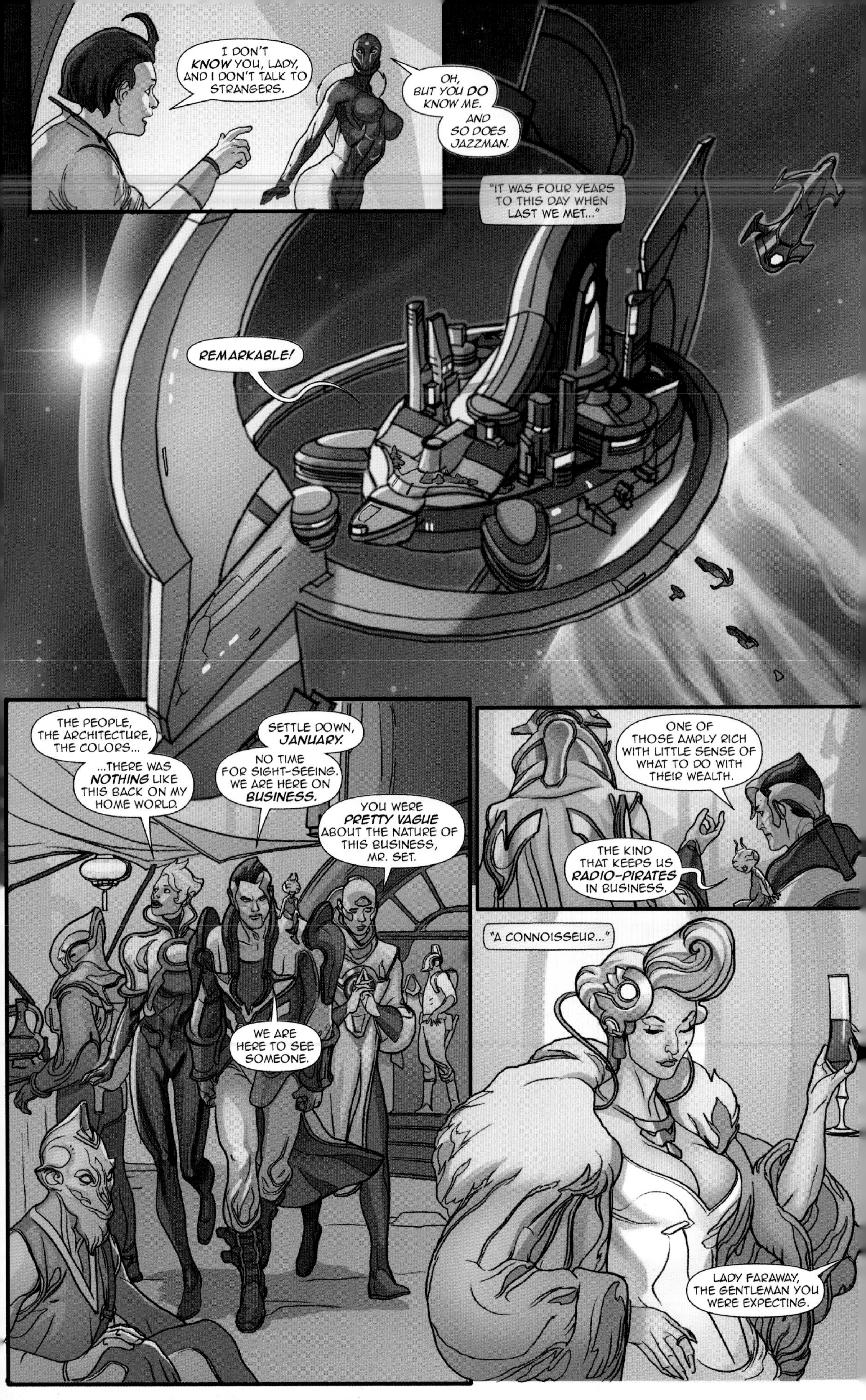

I DON'T KNOW YOU, LADY, AND I DON'T TALK TO STRANGERS.
OH, BUT YOU DO KNOW ME.
AND SO DOES JAZZMAN.
"IT WAS FOUR YEARS TO THIS DAY WHEN LAST WE MET..."
REMARKABLE!
THE PEOPLE, THE ARCHITECTURE, THE COLORS...
...THERE WAS NOTHING LIKE THIS BACK ON MY HOME WORLD.
SETTLE DOWN, JANUARY.
NO TIME FOR SIGHT-SEEING. WE ARE HERE ON BUSINESS.
YOU WERE PRETTY VAGUE ABOUT THE NATURE OF THIS BUSINESS, MR. SET.
WE ARE HERE TO SEE SOMEONE.
ONE OF THOSE AMPLY RICH WITH LITTLE SENSE OF WHAT TO DO WITH THEIR WEALTH.
THE KIND THAT KEEPS US RADIO-PIRATES IN BUSINESS.
"A CONNOISSEUR..."
LADY FARAWAY, THE GENTLEMAN YOU WERE EXPECTING.

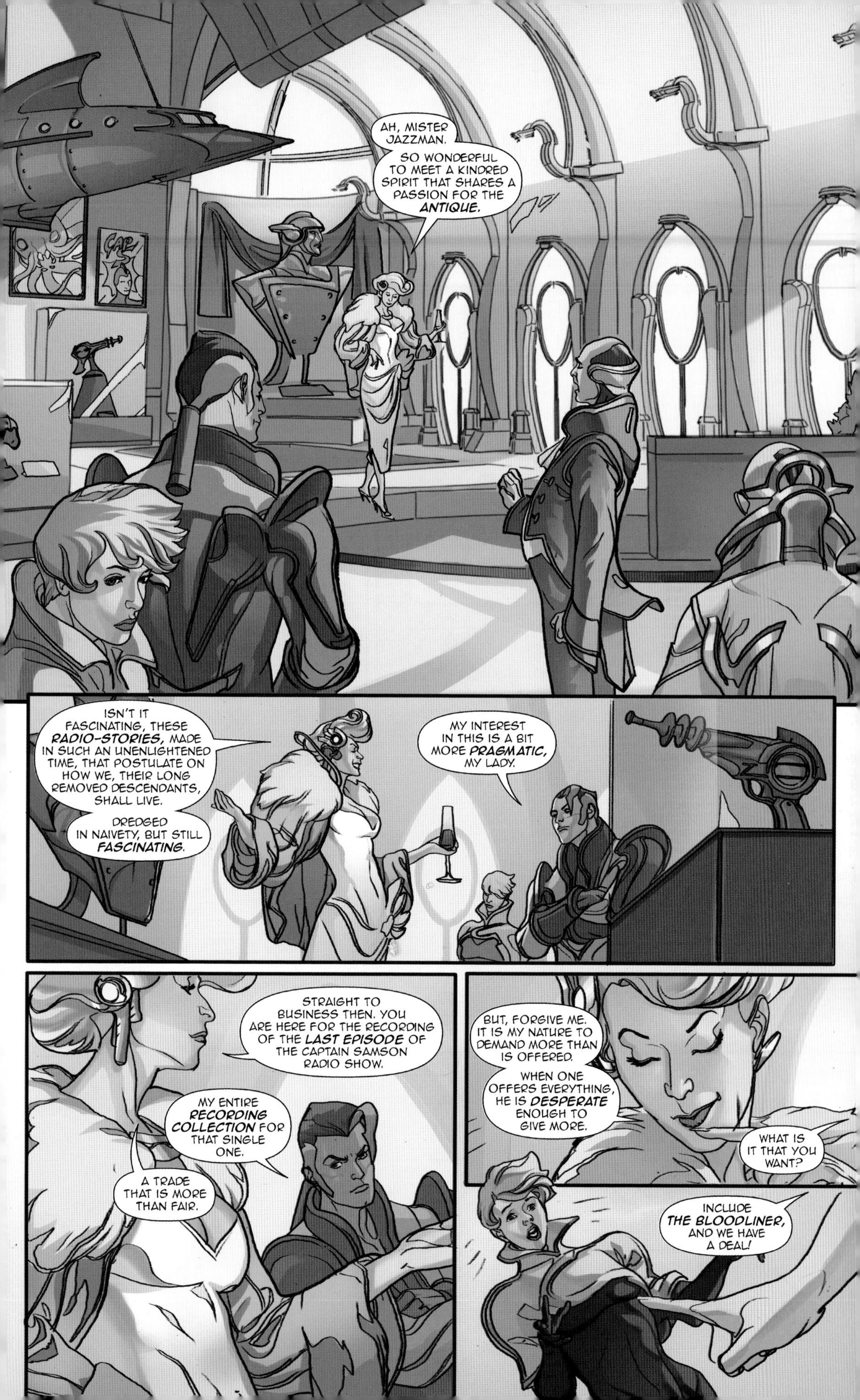
AH, MISTER JAZZMAN.
SO WONDERFUL TO MEET A KINDRED SPIRIT THAT SHARES A PASSION FOR THE ANTIQUE.
ISN'T IT FASCINATING, THESE RADIO-STORIES, MADE IN SUCH AN UNENLIGHTENED TIME, THAT POSTULATE ON HOW WE, THEIR LONG REMOVED DESCENDANTS, SHALL LIVE.
DREDGED IN NAIVETY, BUT STILL FASCINATING.
MY INTEREST IN THIS IS A BIT MORE PRAGMATIC, MY LADY.
STRAIGHT TO BUSINESS THEN. YOU ARE HERE FOR THE RECORDING OF THE LAST EPISODE OF THE CAPTAIN SAMSON RADIO SHOW.
MY ENTIRE RECORDING COLLECTION FOR THAT SINGLE ONE.
A TRADE THAT IS MORE THAN FAIR.
BUT, FORGIVE ME. IT IS MY NATURE TO DEMAND MORE THAN IS OFFERED.
WHEN ONE OFFERS EVERYTHING, HE IS DESPERATE ENOUGH TO GIVE MORE.
WHAT IS IT THAT YOU WANT?
INCLUDE THE BLOODLINER, AND WE HAVE A DEAL!

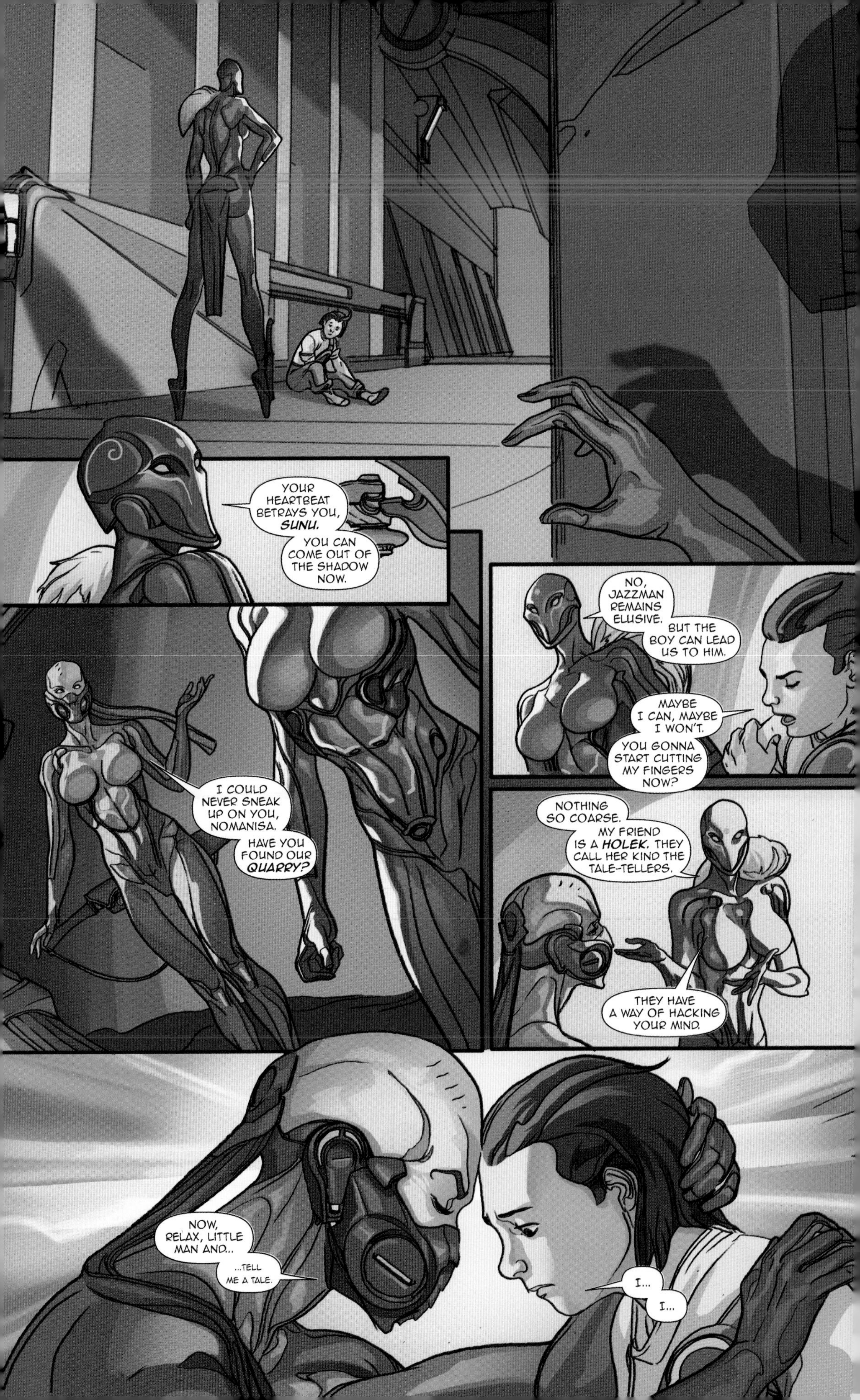
YOUR HEARTBEAT BETRAYS YOU, SUNU.
YOU CAN COME OUT OF THE SHADOW NOW.
I COULD NEVER SNEAK UP ON YOU, NOMANISA.
HAVE YOU FOUND OUR QUARRY?
NO, JAZZMAN REMAINS ELUSIVE.
BUT THE BOY CAN LEAD US TO HIM.
MAYBE I CAN, MAYBE I WON'T.
YOU GONNA START CUTTING MY FINGERS NOW?
NOTHING SO COARSE.
MY FRIEND IS A HOLEK. THEY CALL HER KIND THE TALE-TELLERS.
THEY HAVE A WAY OF HACKING YOUR MIND.
NOW, RELAX, LITTLE MAN AND...
...TELL ME A TALE.
I...
I...

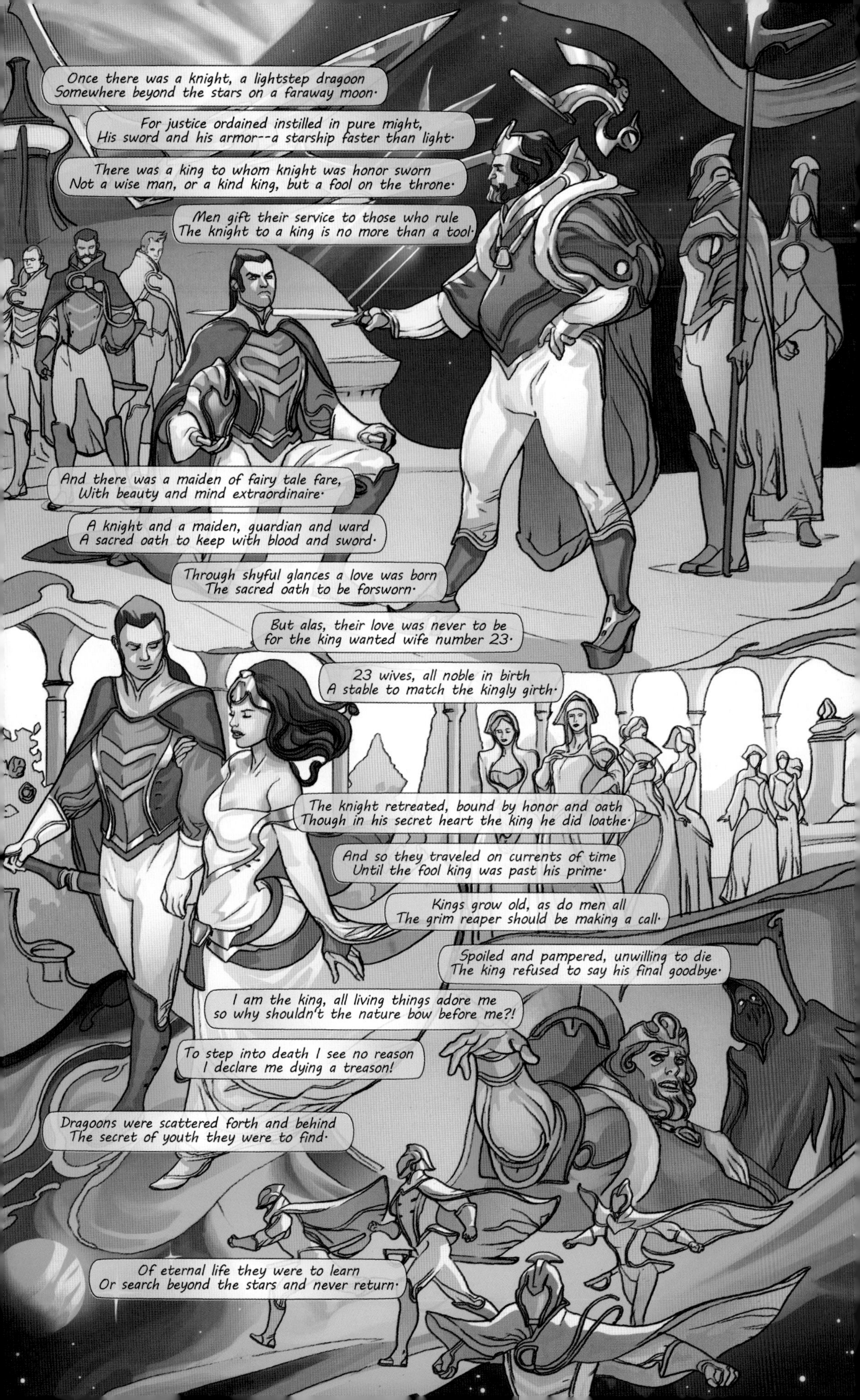
Once there was a knight, a lightstep dragoon Somewhere beyond the stars on a faraway moon.
For justice ordained instilled in pure might, His sword and his armor--a starship faster than light.
There was a king to whom knight was honor sworn Not a wise man, or a kind king, but a fool on the throne.
Men gift their service to those who rule The knight to a king is no more than a tool.
And there was a maiden of fairy tale fare, With beauty and mind extraordinaire.
A knight and a maiden, guardian and ward A sacred oath to keep with blood and sword.
Through shyful glances a love was born The sacred oath to be forsworn.
But alas, their love was never to be for the king wanted wife number 23.
23 wives, all noble in birth A stable to match the kingly girth.
The knight retreated, bound by honor and oath Though in his secret heart the king he did loathe.
And so they traveled on currents of time Until the fool king was past his prime.
Kings grow old, as do men all The grim reaper should be making a call.
Spoiled and pampered, unwilling to die The king refused to say his final goodbye.
I am the king, all living things adore me so why shouldn't the nature bow before me?!
To step into death I see no reason I declare me dying a treason!
Dragoons were scattered forth and behind The secret of youth they were to find.
Of eternal life they were to learn Or search beyond the stars and never return.

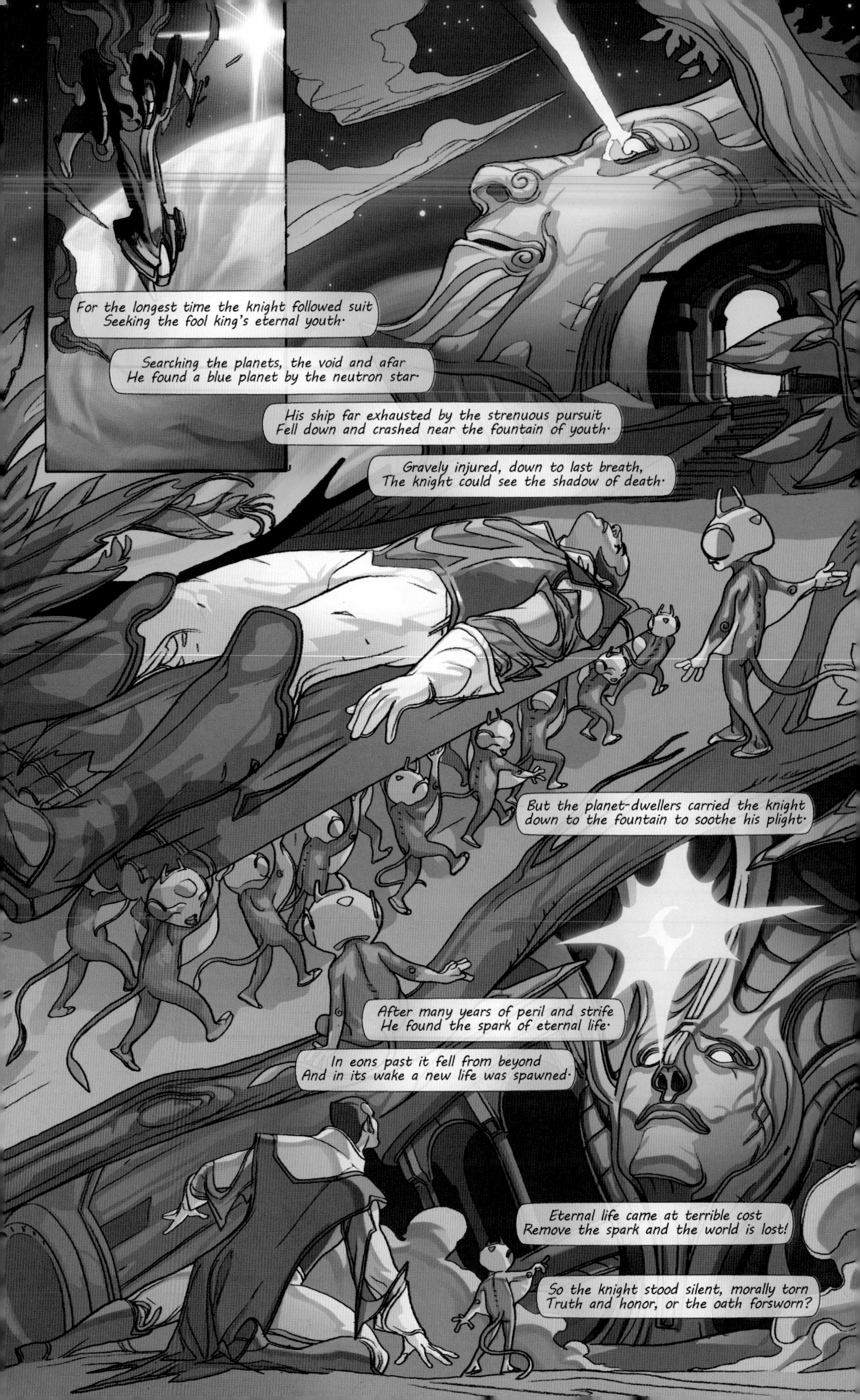

For the longest time the knight followed suit
Seeking the fool king's eternal youth.
Searching the planets, the void and afar
He found a blue planet by the neutron star.
His ship far exhausted by the strenuous pursuit
Fell down and crashed near the fountain of youth.
Gravely injured, down to last breath,
The knight could see the shadow of death.
But the planet-dwellers carried the knight
down to the fountain to soothe his plight.
After many years of peril and strife
He found the spark of eternal life.
In eons past it fell from beyond
And in its wake a new life was spawned.
Eternal life came at terrible cost
Remove the spark and the world is lost!
So the knight stood silent, morally torn
Truth and honor, or the oath forsworn?

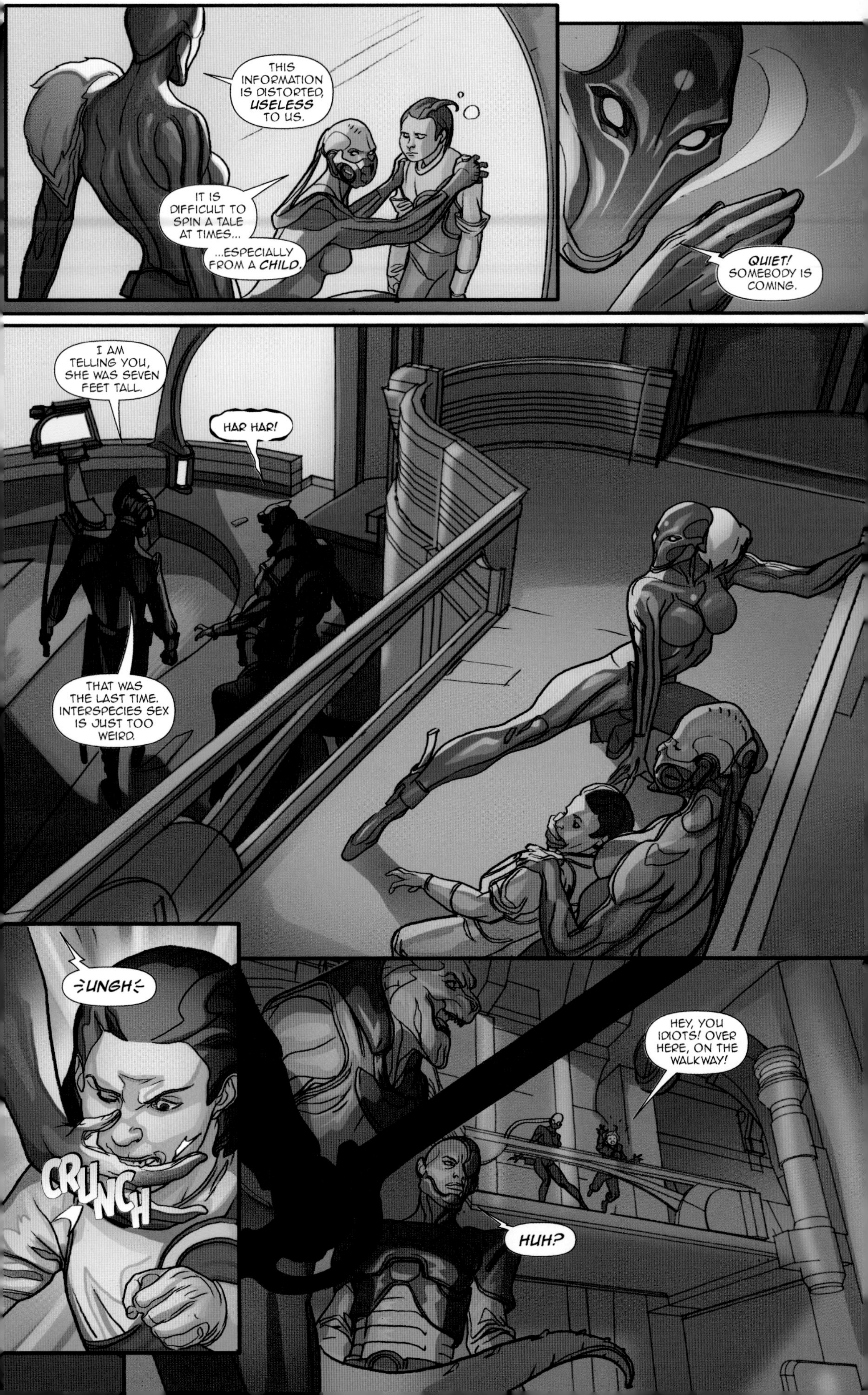
THIS INFORMATION IS DISTORTED, USELESS TO US.
IT IS DIFFICULT TO SPIN A TALE AT TIMES...
...ESPECIALLY FROM A CHILD.
QUIET! SOMEBODY IS COMING.
I AM TELLING YOU, SHE WAS SEVEN FEET TALL.
HAR HAR!
THAT WAS THE LAST TIME. INTERSPECIES SEX IS JUST TOO WEIRD.
UNGH
CRUNCH
HEY, YOU IDIOTS! OVER HERE, ON THE WALKWAY!
HUH?

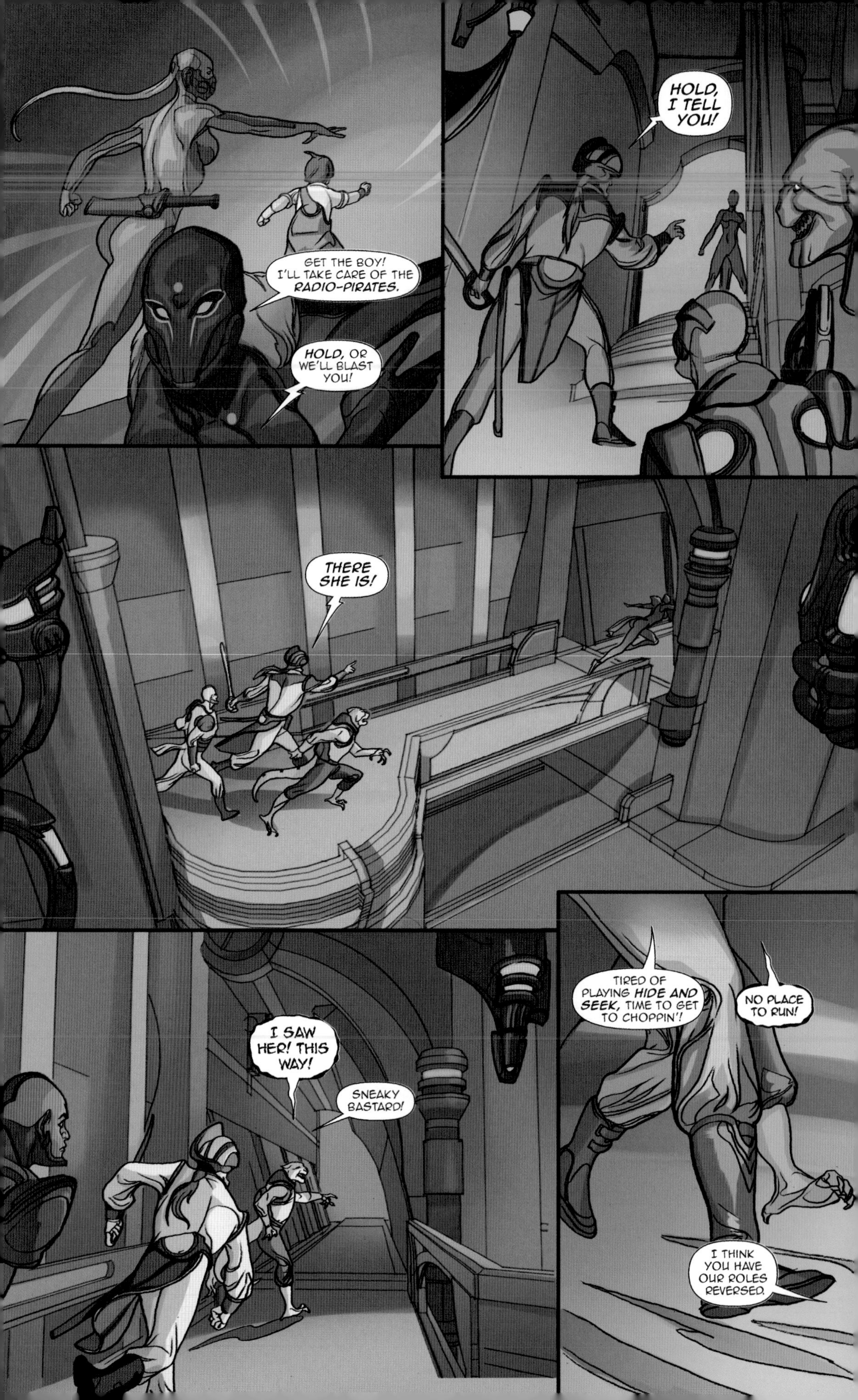
GET THE BOY! I'LL TAKE CARE OF THE RADIO-PIRATES.
HOLD, OR WE'LL BLAST YOU!
HOLD, I TELL YOU!
THERE SHE IS!
I SAW HER! THIS WAY!
SNEAKY BASTARD!
TIRED OF PLAYING HIDE AND SEEK, TIME TO GET TO CHOPPIN'!
NO PLACE TO RUN!
I THINK YOU HAVE OUR ROLES REVERSED.

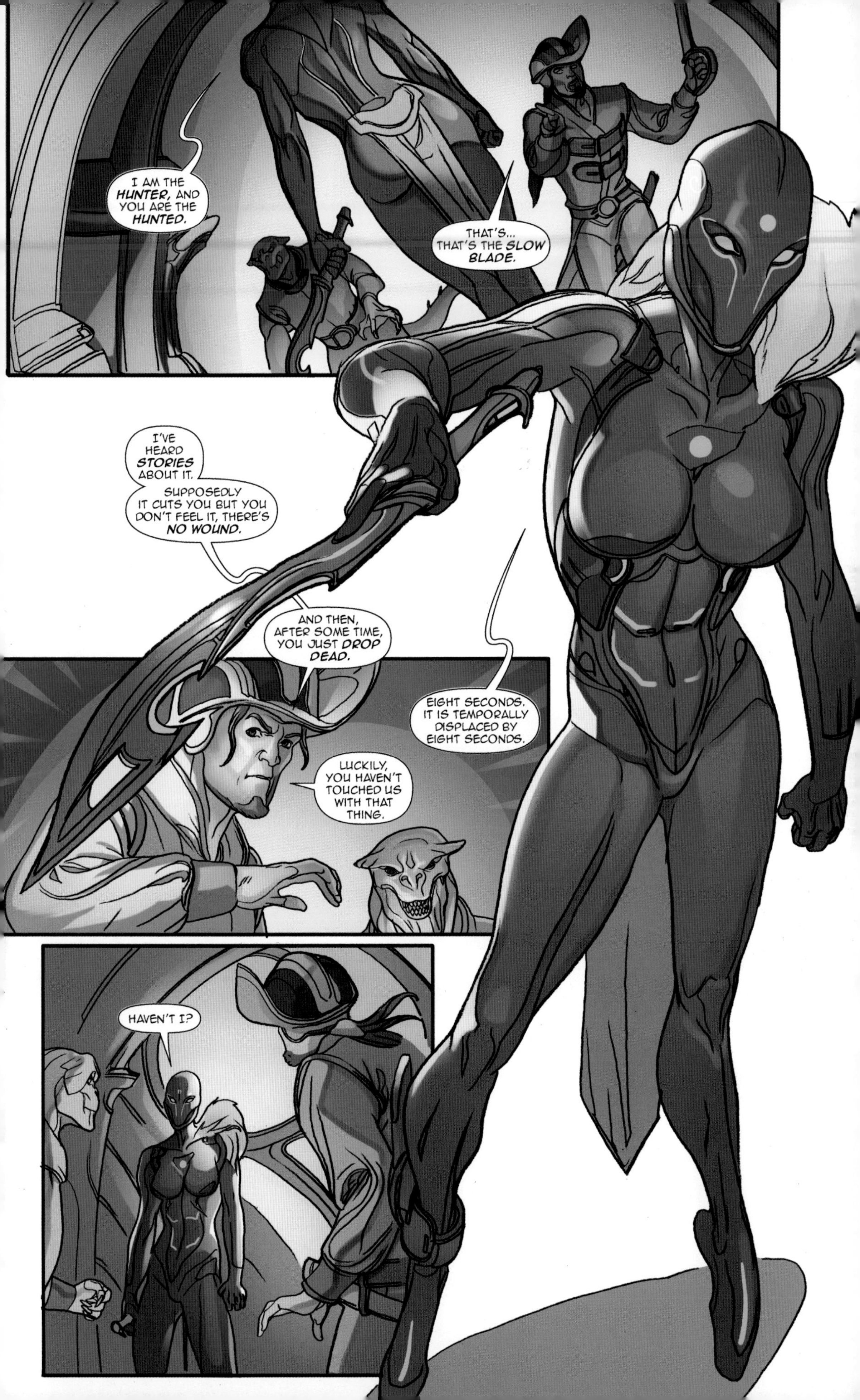
I AM THE HUNTER, AND YOU ARE THE HUNTED.
THAT'S... THAT'S THE SLOW BLADE.
I'VE HEARD STORIES ABOUT IT.
SUPPOSEDLY IT CUTS YOU BUT YOU DON'T FEEL IT, THERE'S NO WOUND.
AND THEN, AFTER SOME TIME, YOU JUST DROP DEAD.
EIGHT SECONDS. IT IS TEMPORALLY DISPLACED BY EIGHT SECONDS.
LUCKILY, YOU HAVEN'T TOUCHED US WITH THAT THING.
HAVEN'T I?

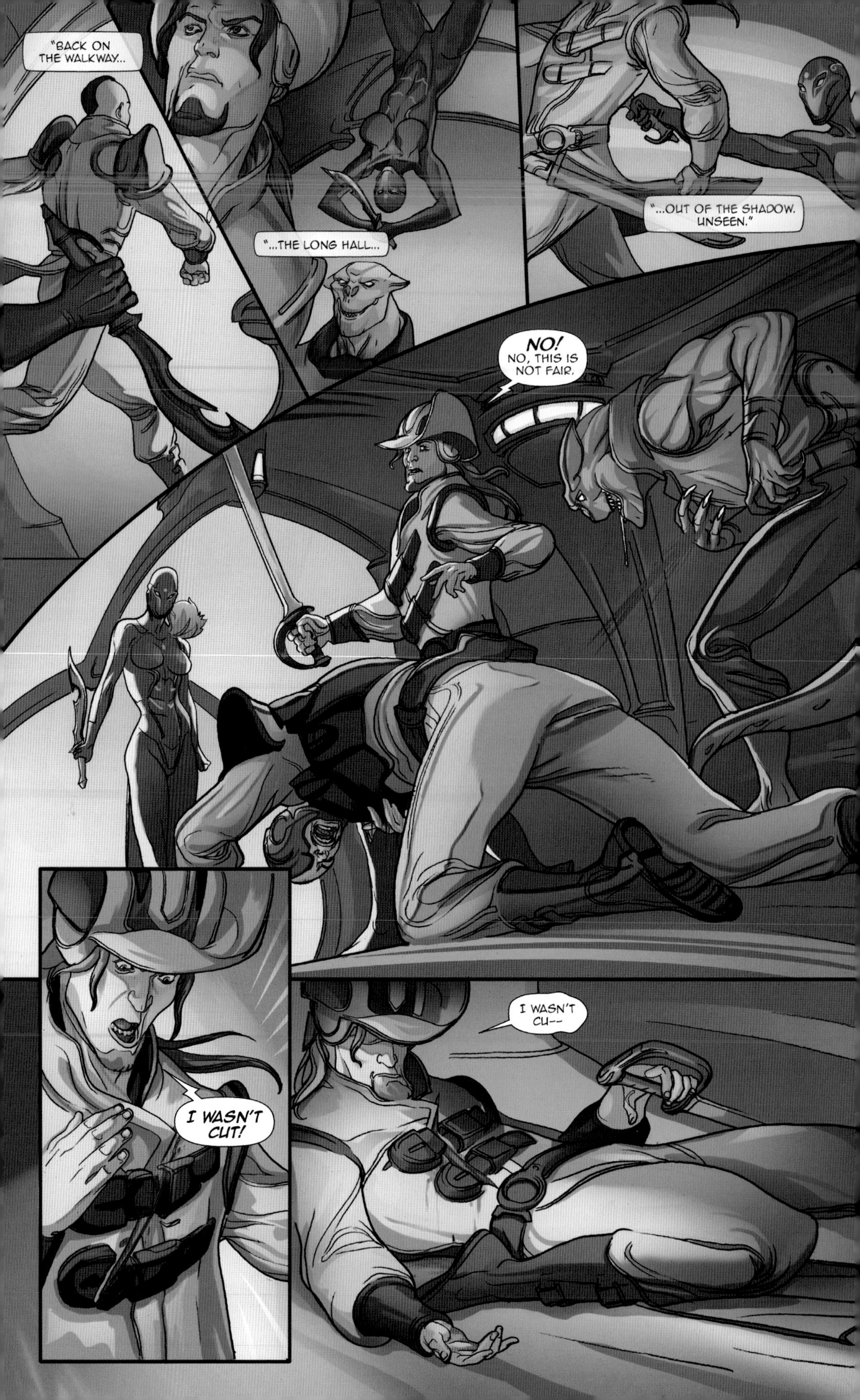
"BACK ON THE WALKWAY...
"...THE LONG HALL...
"...OUT OF THE SHADOW. UNSEEN."
NO! NO, THIS IS NOT FAIR.
I WASN'T CUT!
I WASN'T CU--

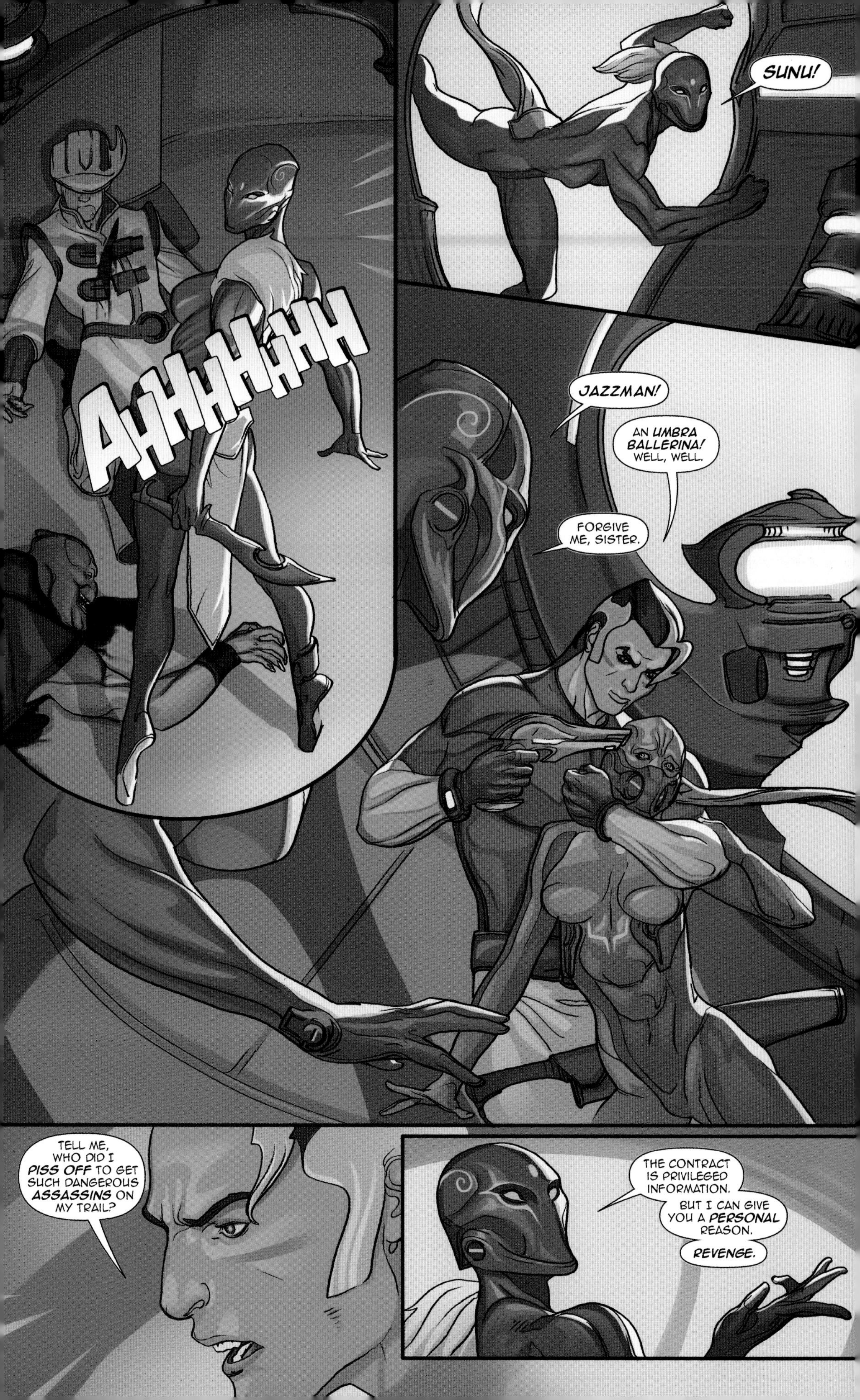
AHHHHHHH
SUNU!
JAZZMAN!
AN UMBRA BALLERINA! WELL, WELL.
FORGIVE ME, SISTER.
TELL ME, WHO DID I PISS OFF TO GET SUCH DANGEROUS ASSASSINS ON MY TRAIL?
THE CONTRACT IS PRIVILEGED INFORMATION.
BUT I CAN GIVE YOU A PERSONAL REASON.
REVENGE.

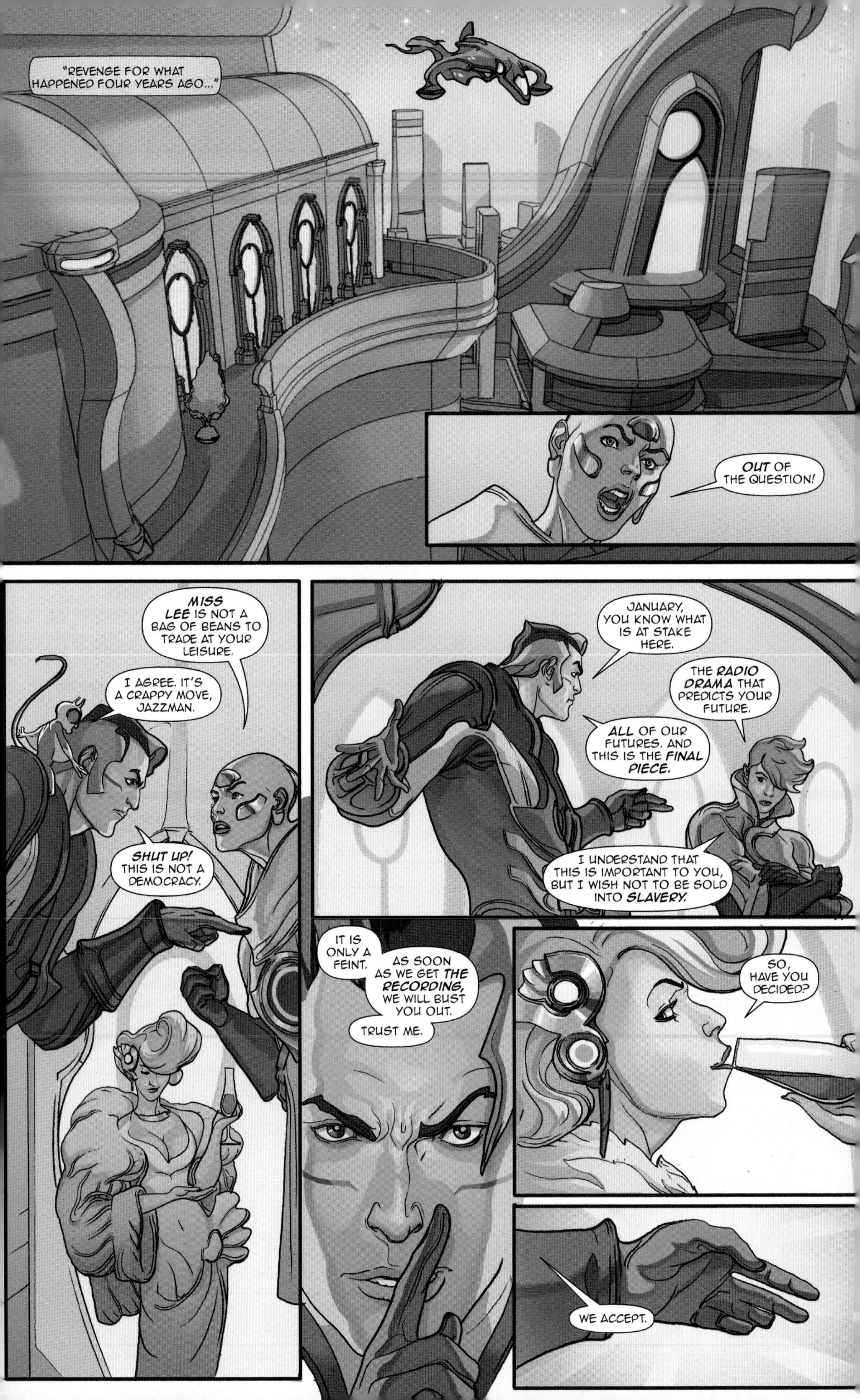
"REVENGE FOR WHAT HAPPENED FOUR YEARS AGO..."
OUT OF THE QUESTION!
MISS LEE IS NOT A BAG OF BEANS TO TRADE AT YOUR LEISURE.
I AGREE. IT'S A CRAPPY MOVE, JAZZMAN.
SHUT UP! THIS IS NOT A DEMOCRACY.
JANUARY, YOU KNOW WHAT IS AT STAKE HERE.
THE RADIO DRAMA THAT PREDICTS YOUR FUTURE.
ALL OF OUR FUTURES. AND THIS IS THE FINAL PIECE.
I UNDERSTAND THAT THIS IS IMPORTANT TO YOU, BUT I WISH NOT TO BE SOLD INTO SLAVERY.
IT IS ONLY A FEINT.
AS SOON AS WE GET THE RECORDING, WE WILL BUST YOU OUT.
TRUST ME.
SO, HAVE YOU DECIDED?
WE ACCEPT.

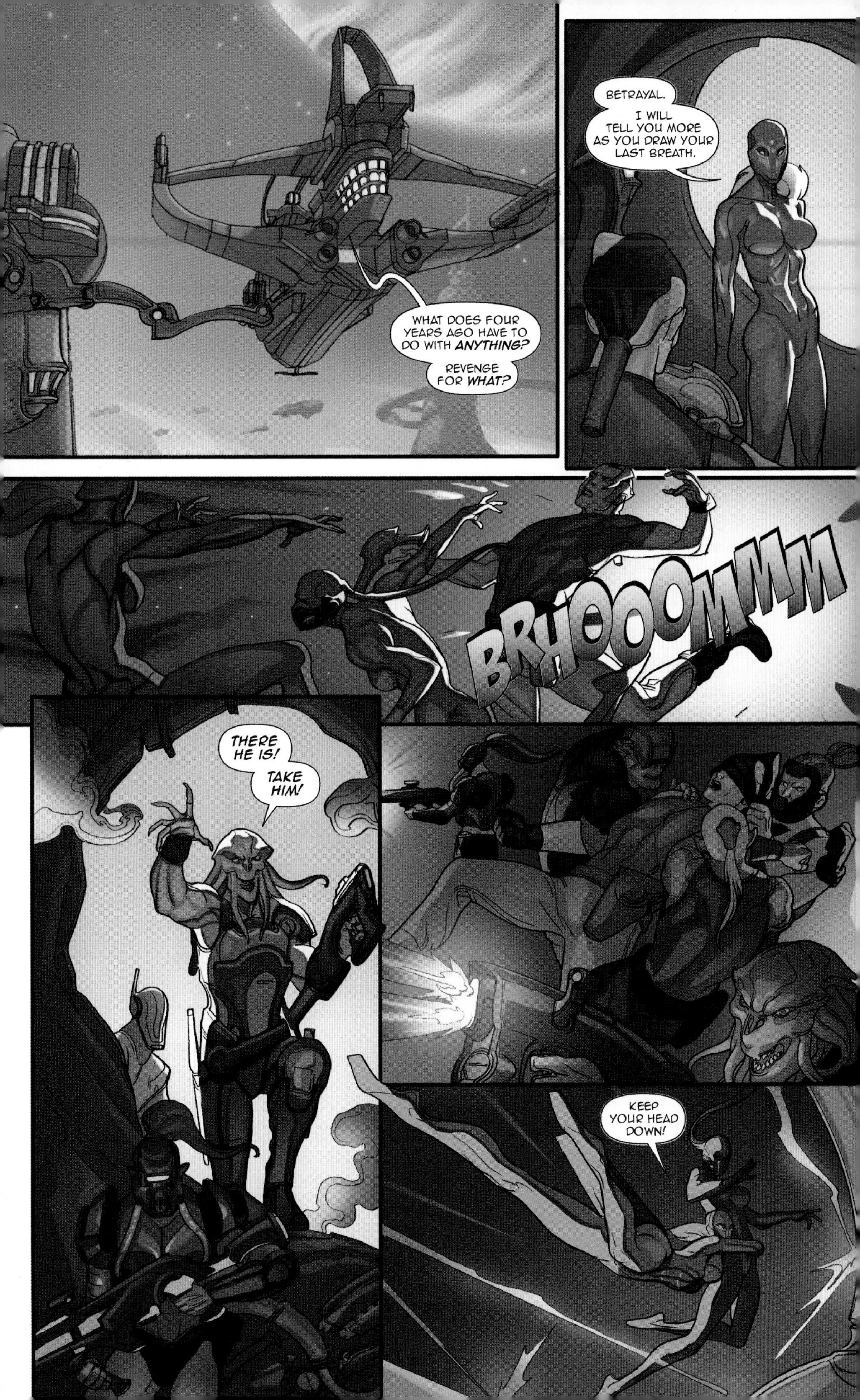
WHAT DOES FOUR YEARS AGO HAVE TO DO WITH ANYTHING?
REVENGE FOR WHAT?
BETRAYAL.
I WILL TELL YOU MORE AS YOU DRAW YOUR LAST BREATH.
BRHOOOMMM
THERE HE IS!
TAKE HIM!
KEEP YOUR HEAD DOWN!

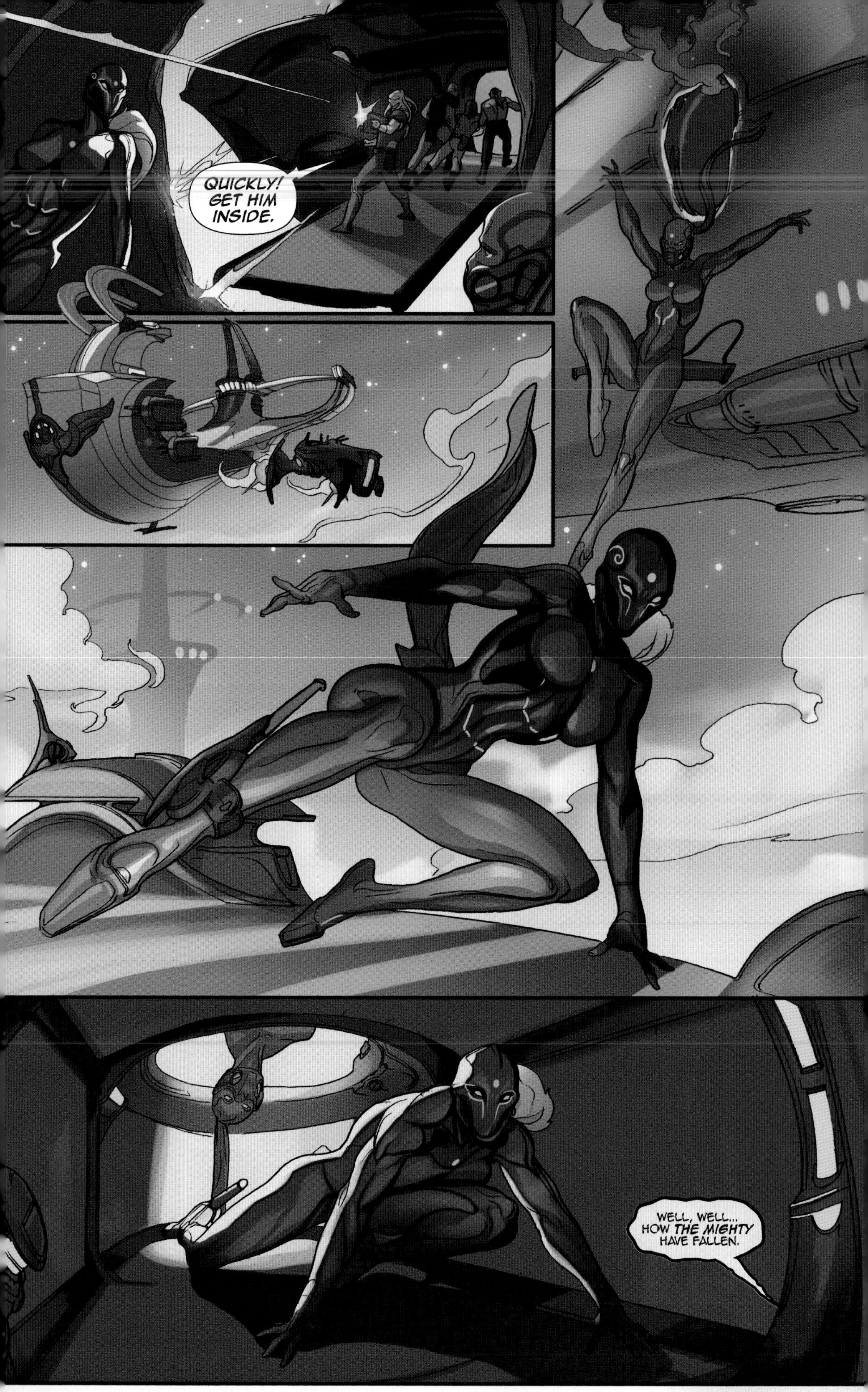
QUICKLY! GET HIM INSIDE.
WELL, WELL... HOW THE MIGHTY HAVE FALLEN.

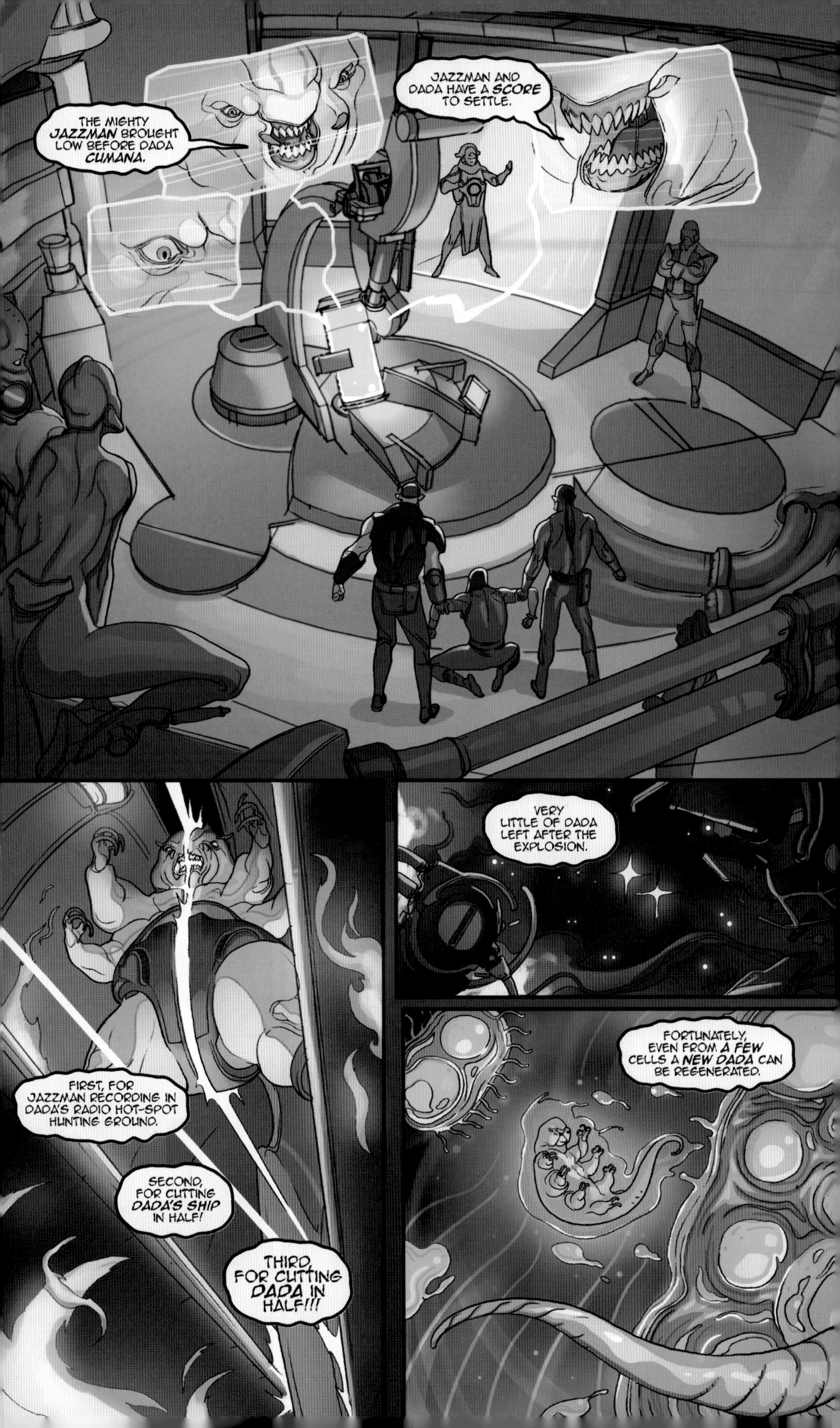
THE MIGHTY JAZZMAN BROUGHT LOW BEFORE DADA CUMANA.
JAZZMAN AND DADA HAVE A SCORE TO SETTLE.
FIRST, FOR JAZZMAN RECORDING IN DADA'S RADIO HOT-SPOT HUNTING GROUND.
SECOND, FOR CUTTING DADA'S SHIP IN HALF!
THIRD, FOR CUTTING DADA IN HALF!!!
VERY LITTLE OF DADA LEFT AFTER THE EXPLOSION.
FORTUNATELY, EVEN FROM A FEW CELLS A NEW DADA CAN BE REGENERATED.

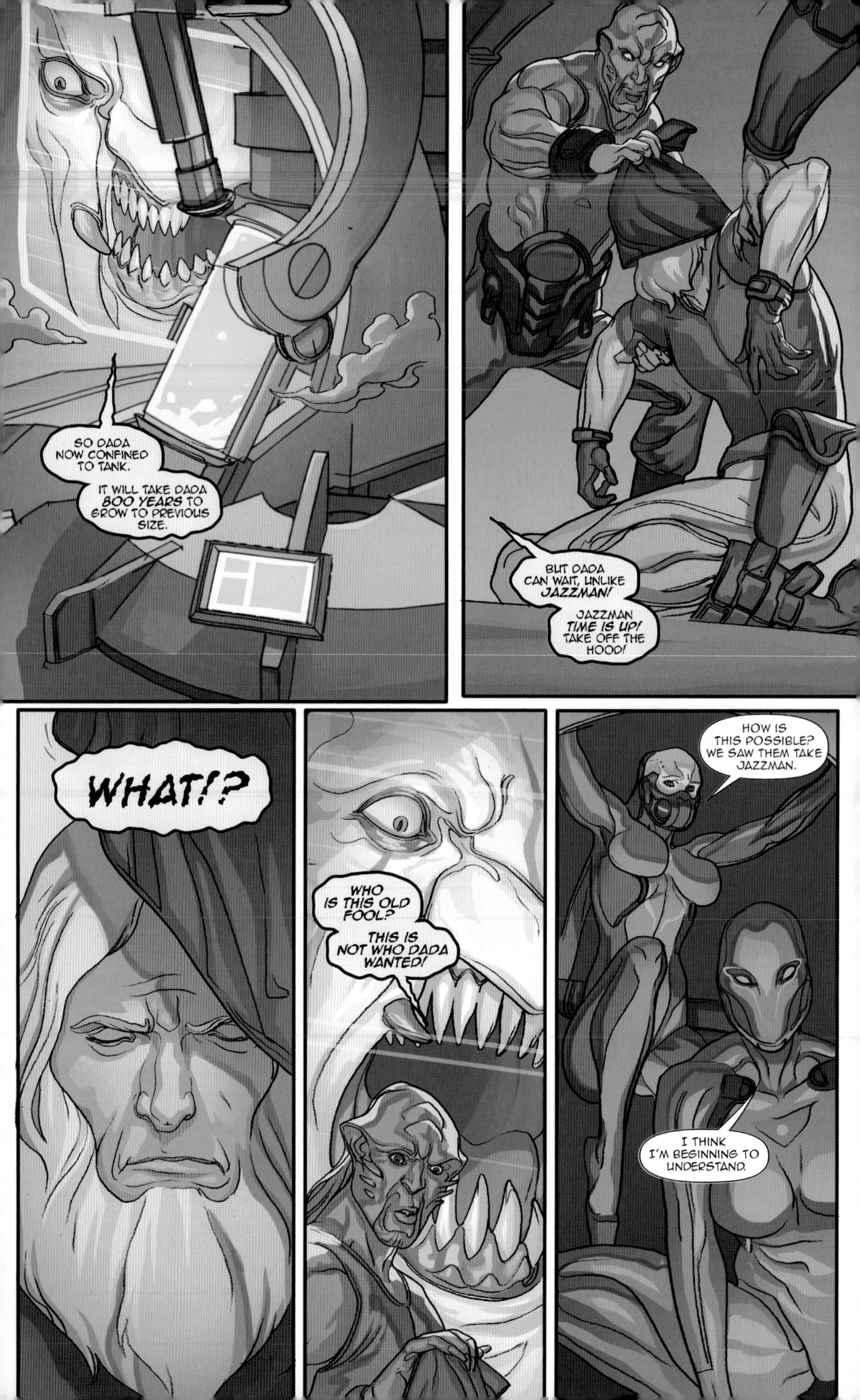
SO DADA NOW CONFINED TO TANK.
IT WILL TAKE DADA 800 YEARS TO GROW TO PREVIOUS SIZE.
BUT DADA CAN WAIT, UNLIKE JAZZMAN!
JAZZMAN TIME IS UP! TAKE OFF THE HOOD!
WHAT!?
WHO IS THIS OLD FOOL?
THIS IS NOT WHO DADA WANTED!
HOW IS THIS POSSIBLE? WE SAW THEM TAKE JAZZMAN.
I THINK I'M BEGINNING TO UNDERSTAND.

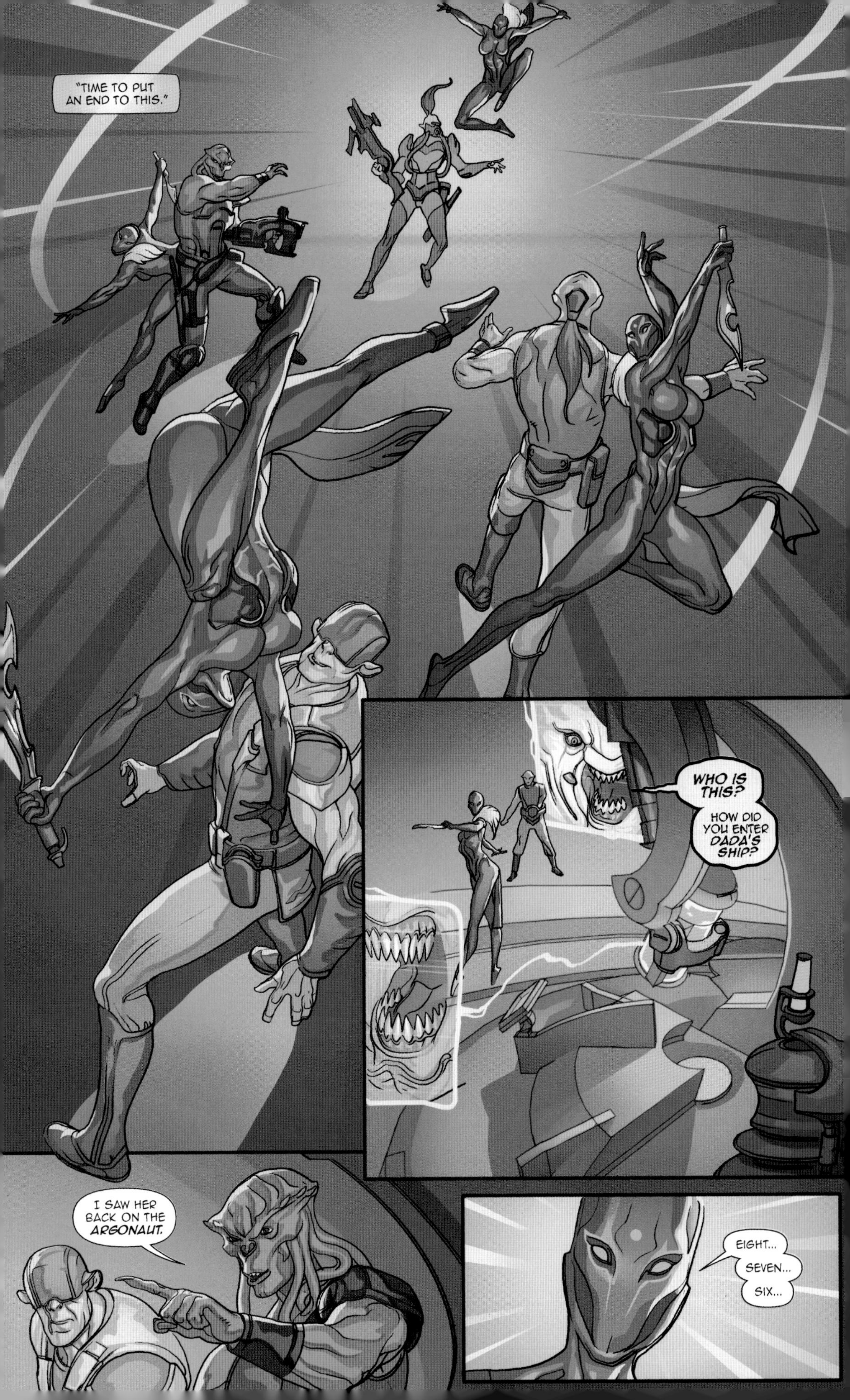
"TIME TO PUT AN END TO THIS."
WHO IS THIS?
HOW DID YOU ENTER DADA'S SHIP?
I SAW HER BACK ON THE ARGONAUT.
EIGHT...
SEVEN...
SIX...

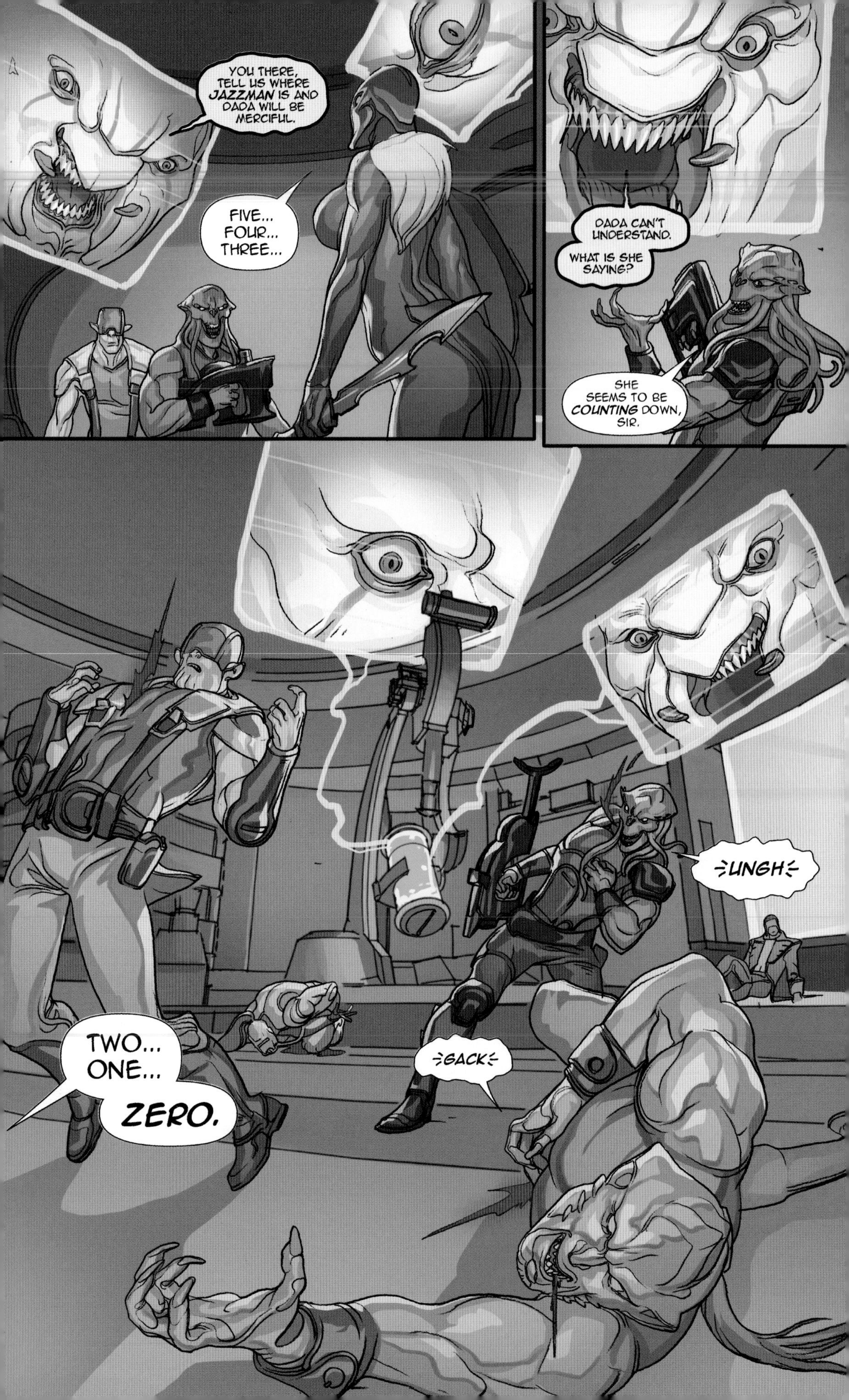
YOU THERE, TELL US WHERE JAZZMAN IS AND DADA WILL BE MERCIFUL.
FIVE... FOUR... THREE...
DADA CAN'T UNDERSTAND.
WHAT IS SHE SAYING?
SHE SEEMS TO BE COUNTING DOWN, SIR.
UNGH
TWO... ONE... ZERO.
GACK

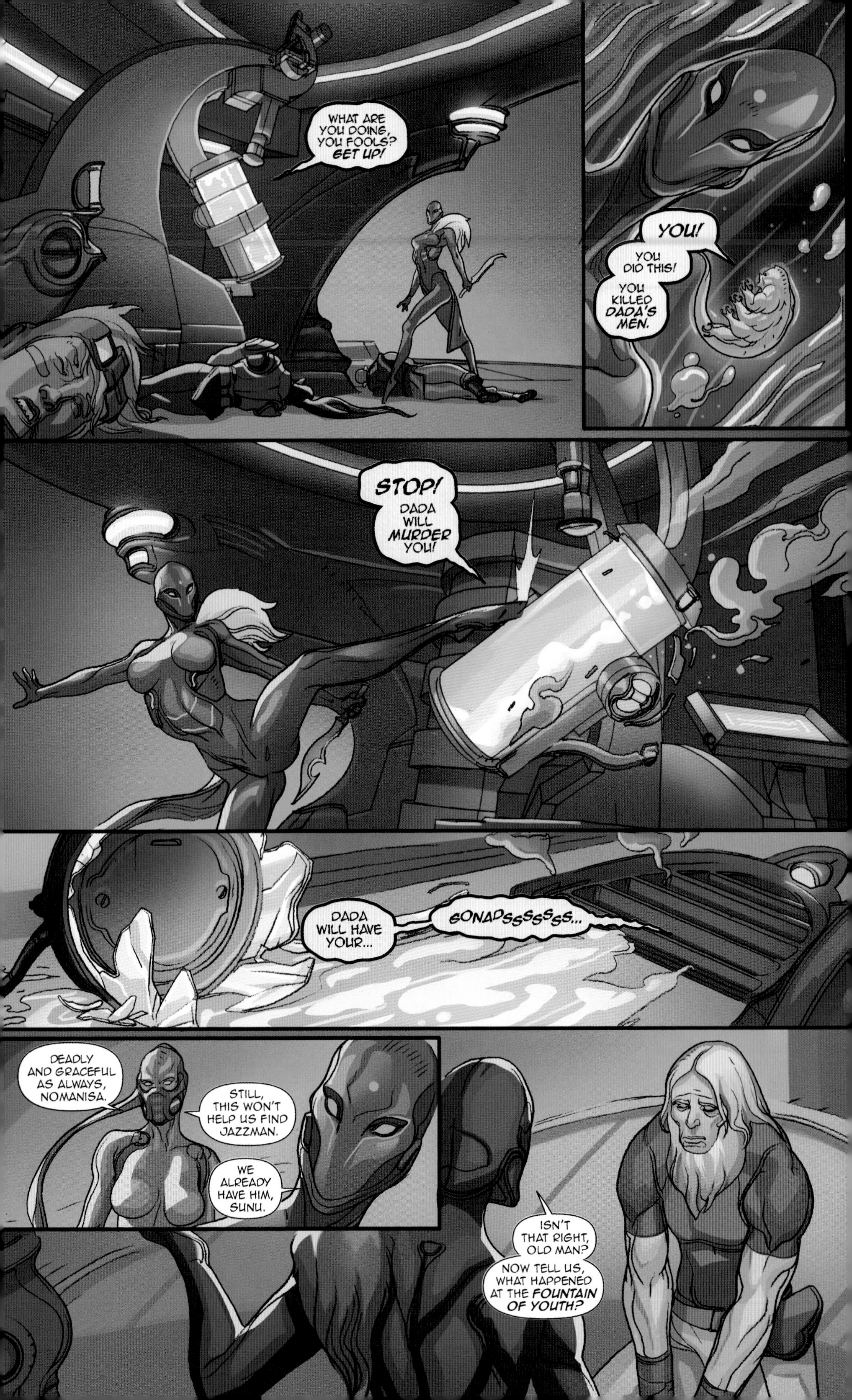
WHAT ARE YOU DOING, YOU FOOLS? GET UP!
YOU!
YOU DID THIS!
YOU KILLED DADA'S MEN.
STOP!
DADA WILL MURDER YOU!
DADA WILL HAVE YOUR...
GONADSSSSSSS...
DEADLY AND GRACEFUL AS ALWAYS, NOMANISA.
STILL, THIS WON'T HELP US FIND JAZZMAN.
WE ALREADY HAVE HIM, SUNU.
ISN'T THAT RIGHT, OLD MAN?
NOW TELL US, WHAT HAPPENED AT THE FOUNTAIN OF YOUTH?

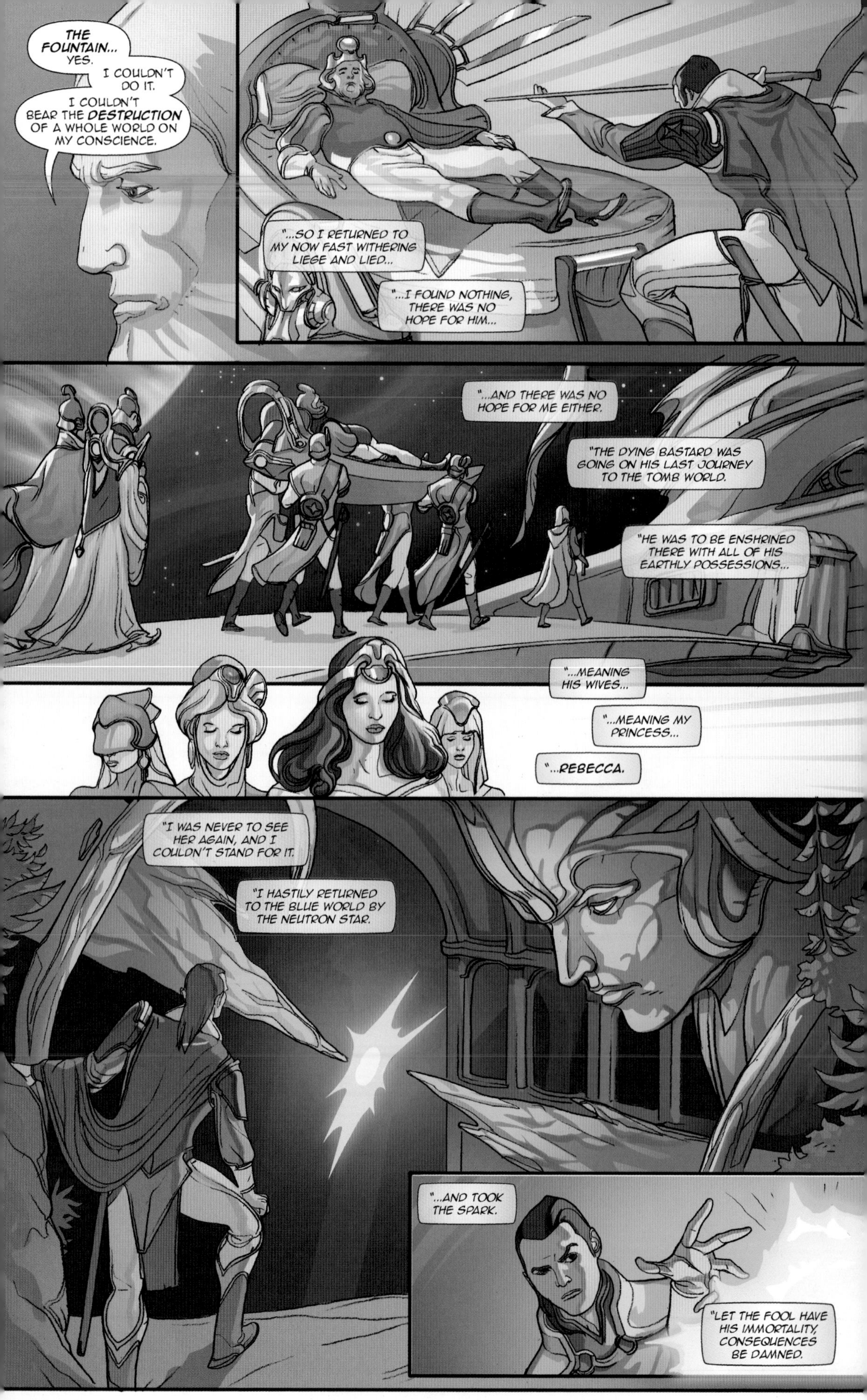
THE FOUNTAIN... YES.
I COULDN'T DO IT.
I COULDN'T BEAR THE DESTRUCTION OF A WHOLE WORLD ON MY CONSCIENCE.
"...SO I RETURNED TO MY NOW FAST WITHERING LIEGE AND LIED...
"...I FOUND NOTHING, THERE WAS NO HOPE FOR HIM...
"...AND THERE WAS NO HOPE FOR ME EITHER.
"THE DYING BASTARD WAS GOING ON HIS LAST JOURNEY TO THE TOMB WORLD.
"HE WAS TO BE ENSHRINED THERE WITH ALL OF HIS EARTHLY POSSESSIONS...
"...MEANING HIS WIVES...
"...MEANING MY PRINCESS...
"...REBECCA.
"I WAS NEVER TO SEE HER AGAIN, AND I COULDN'T STAND FOR IT.
"I HASTILY RETURNED TO THE BLUE WORLD BY THE NEUTRON STAR.
"...AND TOOK THE SPARK.
"LET THE FOOL HAVE HIS IMMORTALITY, CONSEQUENCES BE DAMNED.

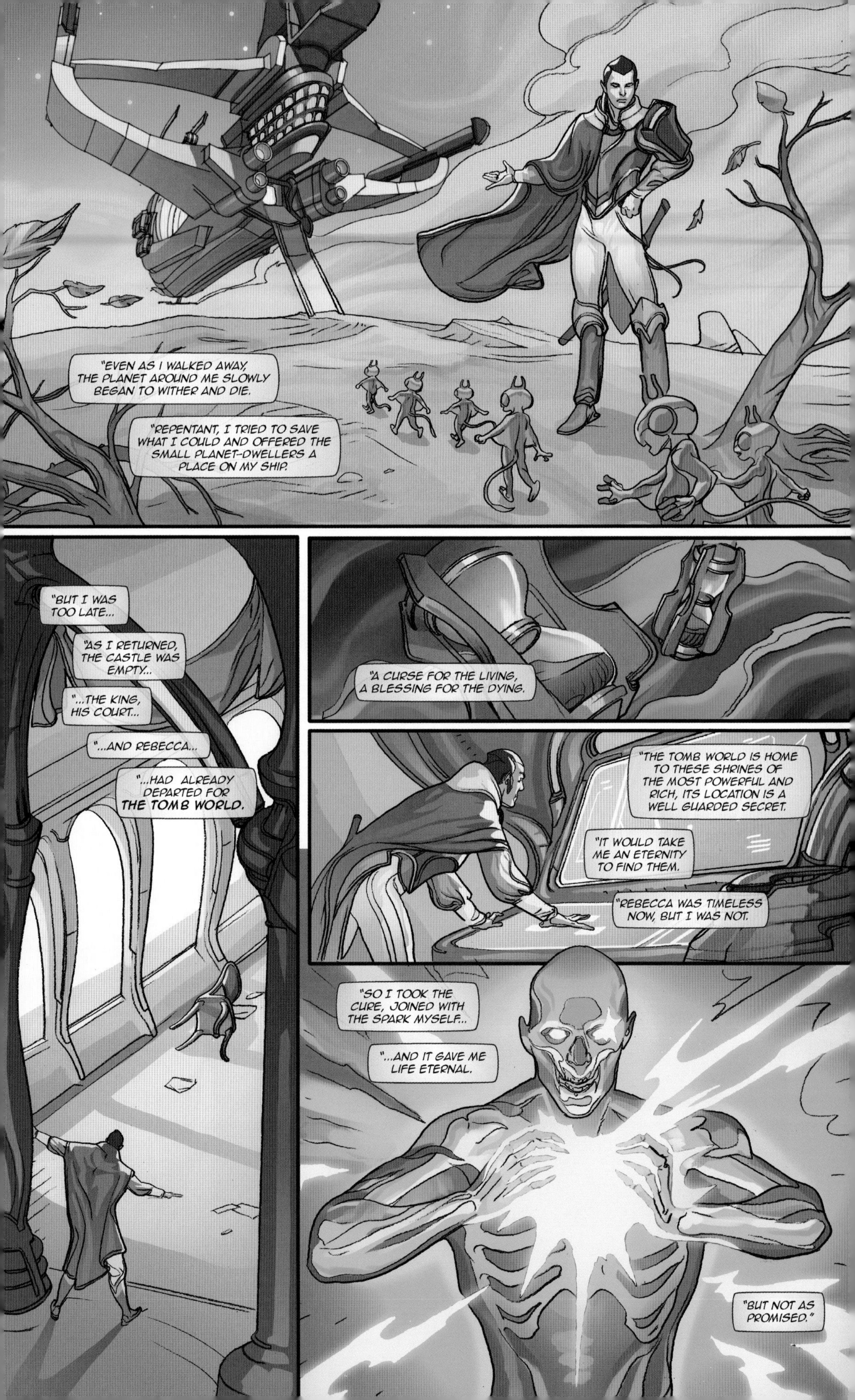
"EVEN AS I WALKED AWAY, THE PLANET AROUND ME SLOWLY BEGAN TO WITHER AND DIE.
"REPENTANT, I TRIED TO SAVE WHAT I COULD AND OFFERED THE SMALL PLANET-DWELLERS A PLACE ON MY SHIP.
"BUT I WAS TOO LATE...
"AS I RETURNED, THE CASTLE WAS EMPTY...
"...THE KING, HIS COURT...
"...AND REBECCA...
"...HAD ALREADY DEPARTED FOR **THE TOMB WORLD.**
"A CURSE FOR THE LIVING, A BLESSING FOR THE DYING.
"THE TOMB WORLD IS HOME TO THESE SHRINES OF THE MOST POWERFUL AND RICH, ITS LOCATION IS A WELL GUARDED SECRET.
"IT WOULD TAKE ME AN ETERNITY TO FIND THEM.
"REBECCA WAS TIMELESS NOW, BUT I WAS NOT.
"SO I TOOK THE CURE, JOINED WITH THE SPARK MYSELF...
"...AND IT GAVE ME LIFE ETERNAL.
"BUT NOT AS PROMISED."

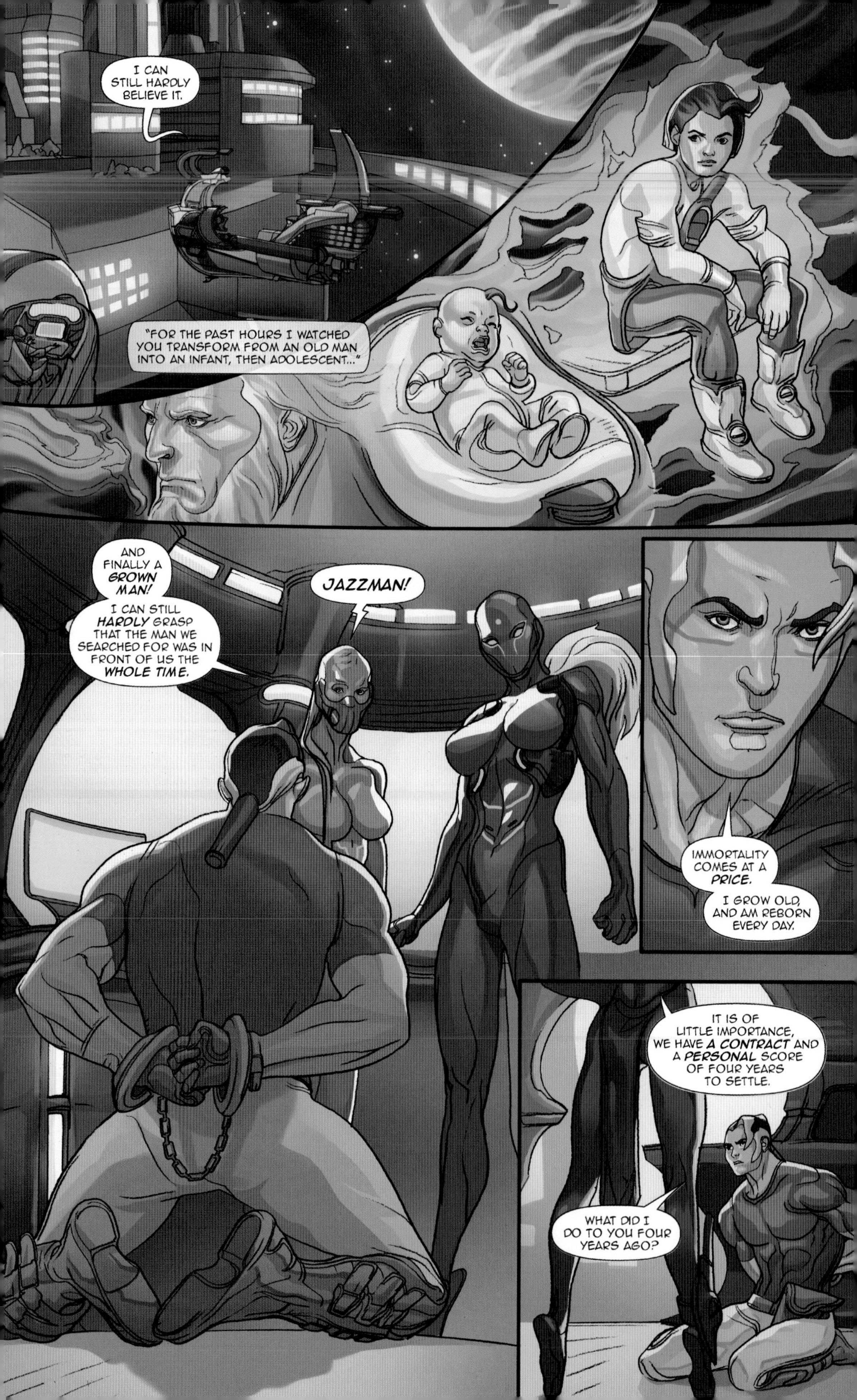
I CAN STILL HARDLY BELIEVE IT.
"FOR THE PAST HOURS I WATCHED YOU TRANSFORM FROM AN OLD MAN INTO AN INFANT, THEN ADOLESCENT..."
AND FINALLY A GROWN MAN!
I CAN STILL HARDLY GRASP THAT THE MAN WE SEARCHED FOR WAS IN FRONT OF US THE WHOLE TIME.
JAZZMAN!
IMMORTALITY COMES AT A PRICE.
I GROW OLD, AND AM REBORN EVERY DAY.
IT IS OF LITTLE IMPORTANCE, WE HAVE A CONTRACT AND A PERSONAL SCORE OF FOUR YEARS TO SETTLE.
WHAT DID I DO TO YOU FOUR YEARS AGO?

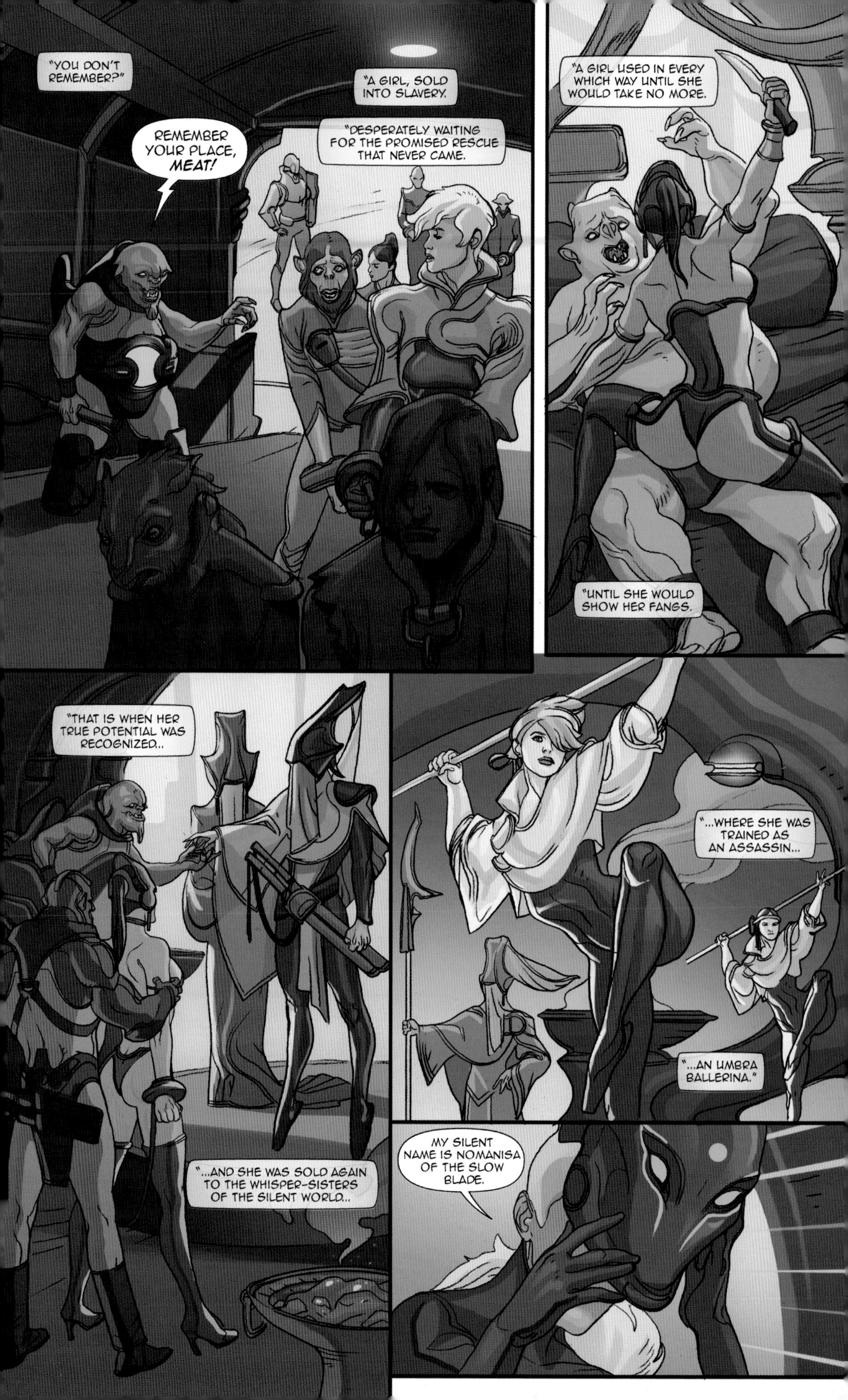
"YOU DON'T REMEMBER?"
REMEMBER YOUR PLACE, MEAT!
"A GIRL, SOLD INTO SLAVERY.
"DESPERATELY WAITING FOR THE PROMISED RESCUE THAT NEVER CAME.
"A GIRL USED IN EVERY WHICH WAY UNTIL SHE WOULD TAKE NO MORE.
"UNTIL SHE WOULD SHOW HER FANGS.
"THAT IS WHEN HER TRUE POTENTIAL WAS RECOGNIZED...
"...AND SHE WAS SOLD AGAIN TO THE WHISPER-SISTERS OF THE SILENT WORLD...
"...WHERE SHE WAS TRAINED AS AN ASSASSIN...
"...AN UMBRA BALLERINA."
MY SILENT NAME IS NOMANISA OF THE SLOW BLADE.

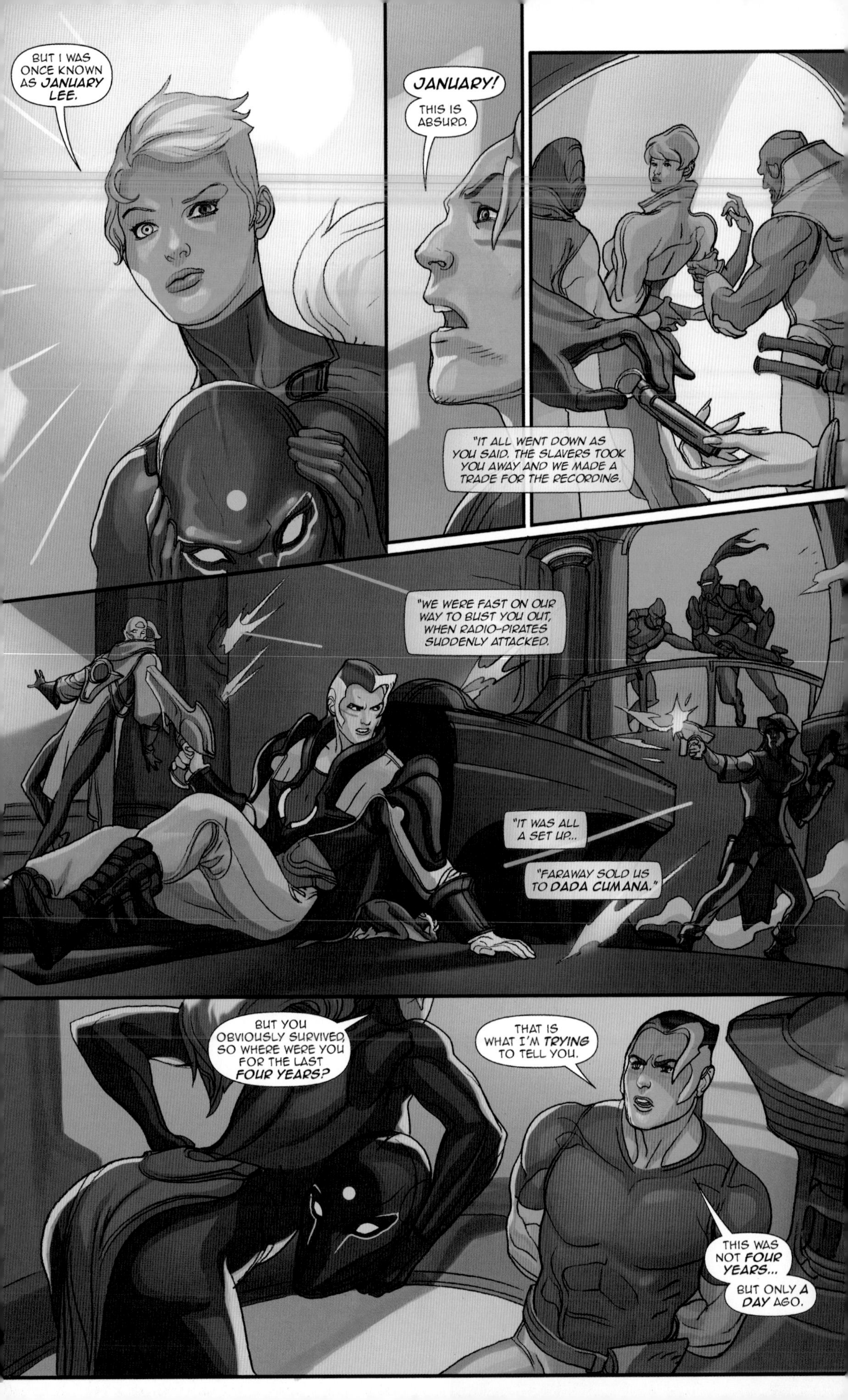
BUT I WAS ONCE KNOWN AS JANUARY LEE.
JANUARY!
THIS IS ABSURD.
"IT ALL WENT DOWN AS YOU SAID. THE SLAVERS TOOK YOU AWAY AND WE MADE A TRADE FOR THE RECORDING.
"WE WERE FAST ON OUR WAY TO BUST YOU OUT, WHEN RADIO-PIRATES SUDDENLY ATTACKED.
"IT WAS ALL A SET UP...
"FARAWAY SOLD US TO DADA CUMANA."
BUT YOU OBVIOUSLY SURVIVED, SO WHERE WERE YOU FOR THE LAST FOUR YEARS?
THAT IS WHAT I'M TRYING TO TELL YOU.
THIS WAS NOT FOUR YEARS...
BUT ONLY A DAY AGO.

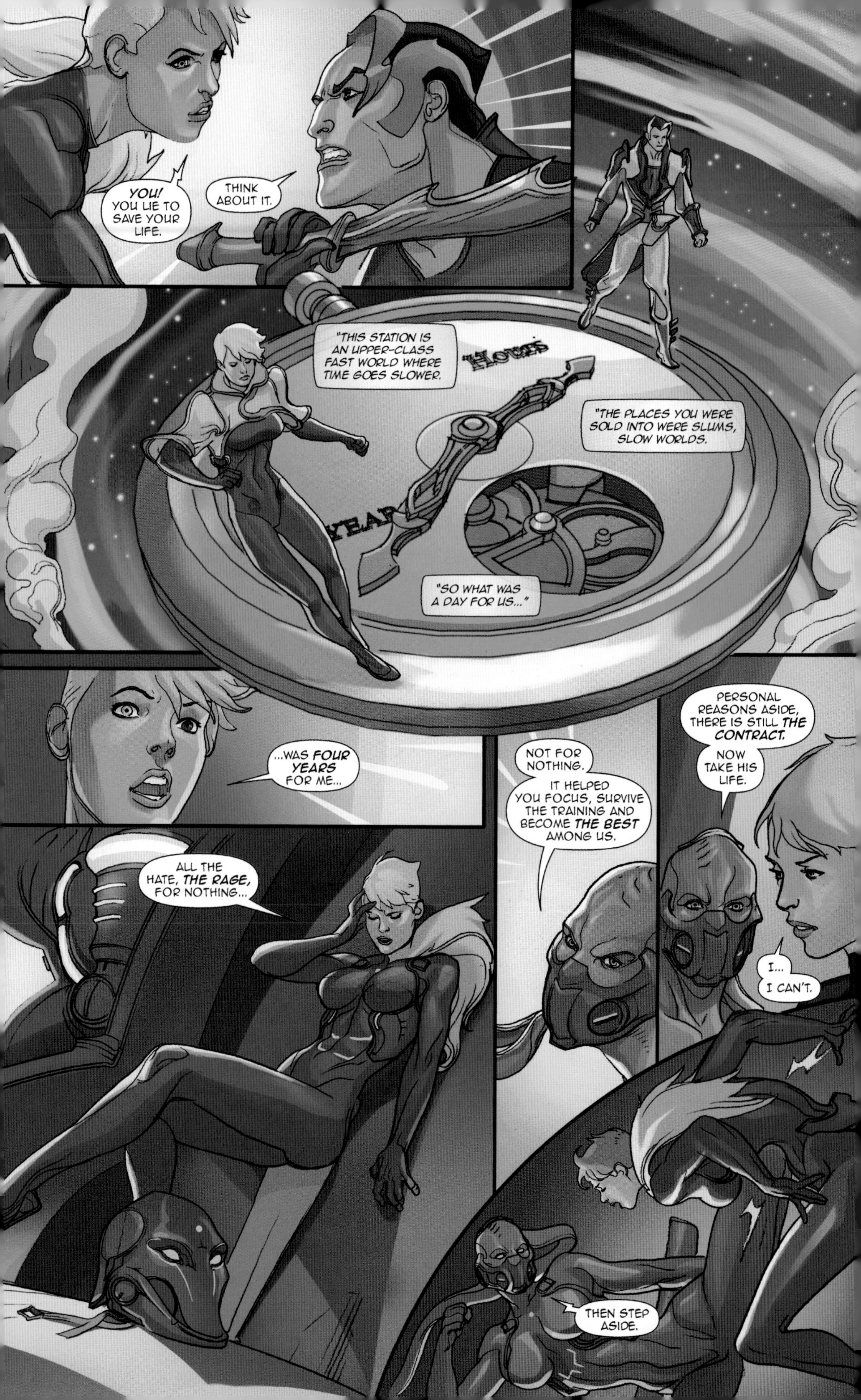
YOU! YOU LIE TO SAVE YOUR LIFE.
THINK ABOUT IT.
"THIS STATION IS AN UPPER-CLASS FAST WORLD WHERE TIME GOES SLOWER.
YEAR
"THE PLACES YOU WERE SOLD INTO WERE SLUMS, SLOW WORLDS.
"SO WHAT WAS A DAY FOR US..."
...WAS FOUR YEARS FOR ME...
ALL THE HATE, THE RAGE, FOR NOTHING...
NOT FOR NOTHING.
IT HELPED YOU FOCUS, SURVIVE THE TRAINING AND BECOME THE BEST AMONG US.
PERSONAL REASONS ASIDE, THERE IS STILL THE CONTRACT.
NOW TAKE HIS LIFE.
I... I CAN'T.
THEN STEP ASIDE.

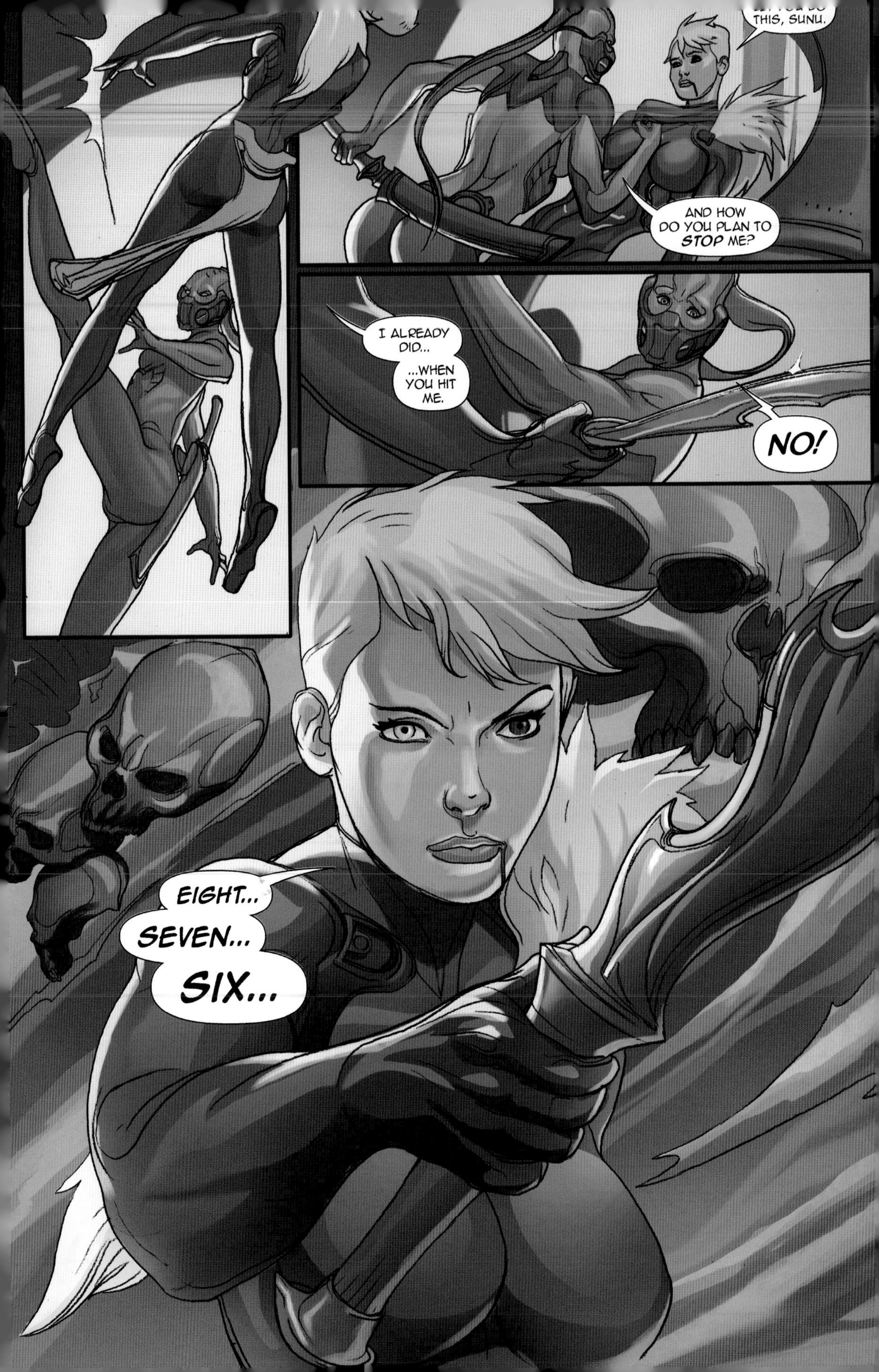
THIS, SUNU.
AND HOW DO YOU PLAN TO STOP ME?
I ALREADY DID...
...WHEN YOU HIT ME.
NO!
EIGHT...
SEVEN...
SIX...

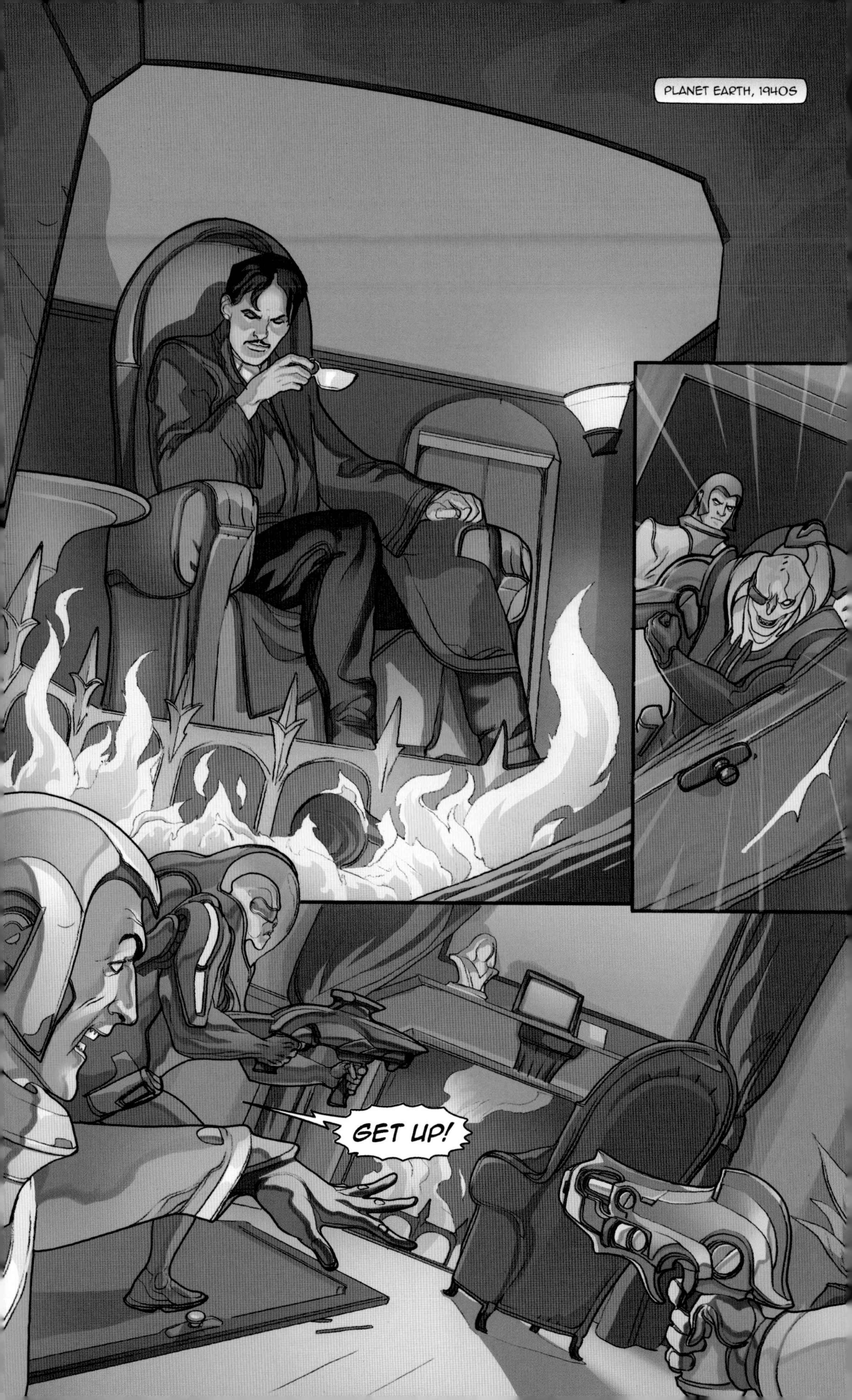
PLANET EARTH, 1940S
GET UP!

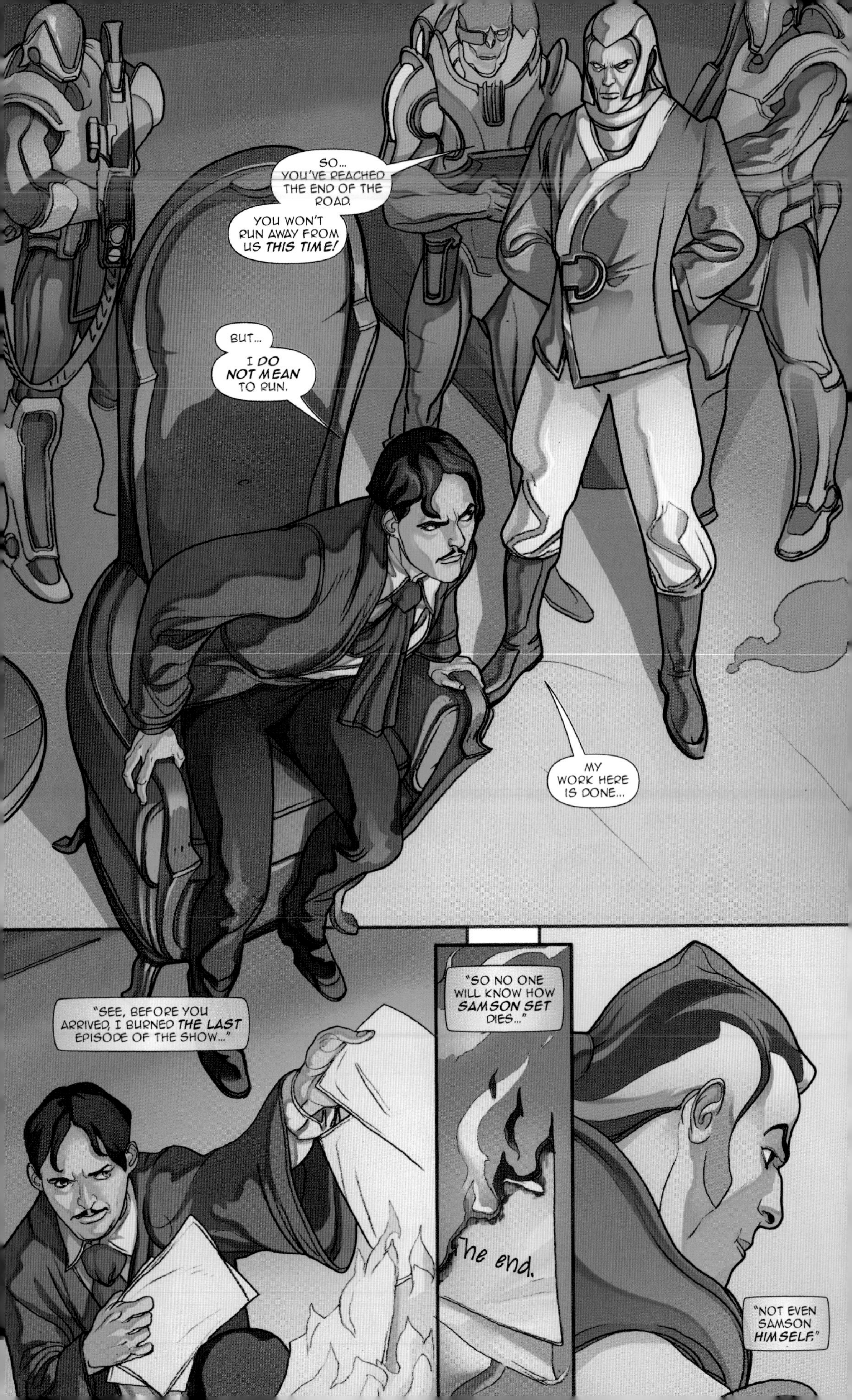
SO... YOU'VE REACHED THE END OF THE ROAD.
YOU WON'T RUN AWAY FROM US THIS TIME!
BUT...
I DO NOT MEAN TO RUN.
MY WORK HERE IS DONE...
"SEE, BEFORE YOU ARRIVED, I BURNED THE LAST EPISODE OF THE SHOW..."
"SO NO ONE WILL KNOW HOW SAMSON SET DIES..."
The end.
"NOT EVEN SAMSON HIMSELF."

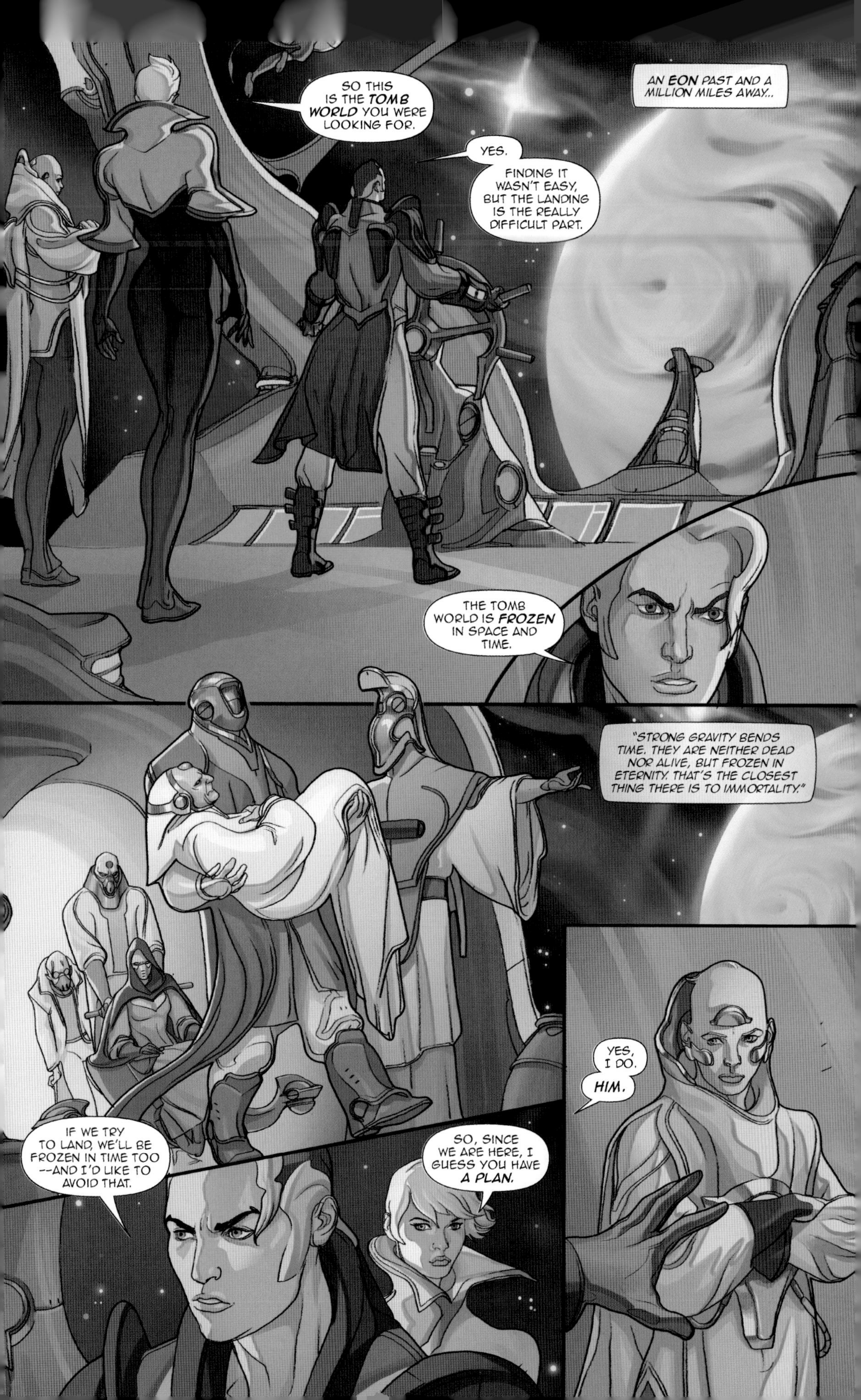
AN EON PAST AND A MILLION MILES AWAY...
SO THIS IS THE TOMB WORLD YOU WERE LOOKING FOR.
YES.
FINDING IT WASN'T EASY, BUT THE LANDING IS THE REALLY DIFFICULT PART.
THE TOMB WORLD IS FROZEN IN SPACE AND TIME.
"STRONG GRAVITY BENDS TIME. THEY ARE NEITHER DEAD NOR ALIVE, BUT FROZEN IN ETERNITY. THAT'S THE CLOSEST THING THERE IS TO IMMORTALITY."
IF WE TRY TO LAND, WE'LL BE FROZEN IN TIME TOO --AND I'D LIKE TO AVOID THAT.
SO, SINCE WE ARE HERE, I GUESS YOU HAVE A PLAN.
YES, I DO.
HIM.

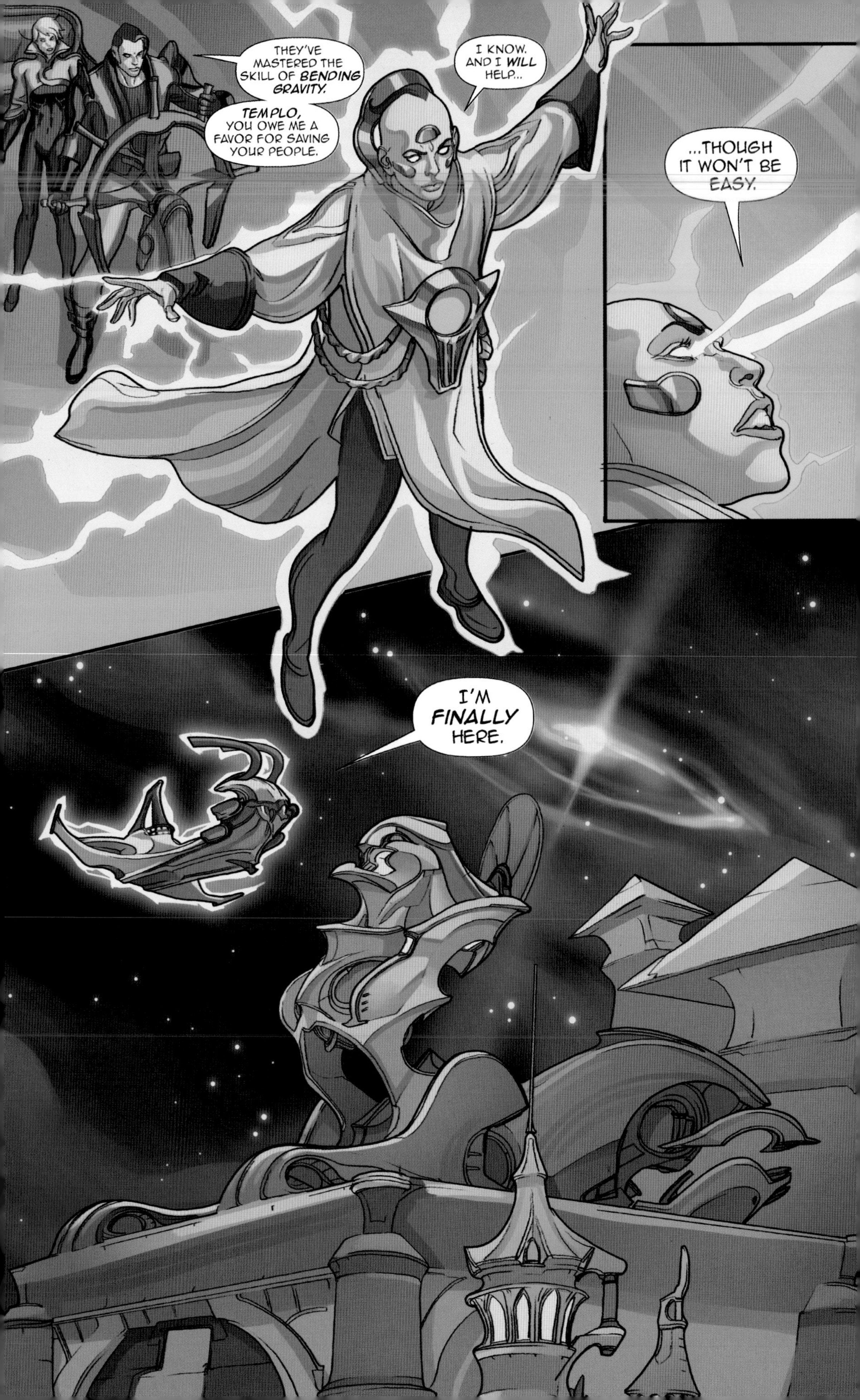
THEY'VE MASTERED THE SKILL OF BENDING GRAVITY.
TEMPLO, YOU OWE ME A FAVOR FOR SAVING YOUR PEOPLE.
I KNOW. AND I WILL HELP...
...THOUGH IT WON'T BE EASY.
I'M FINALLY HERE.

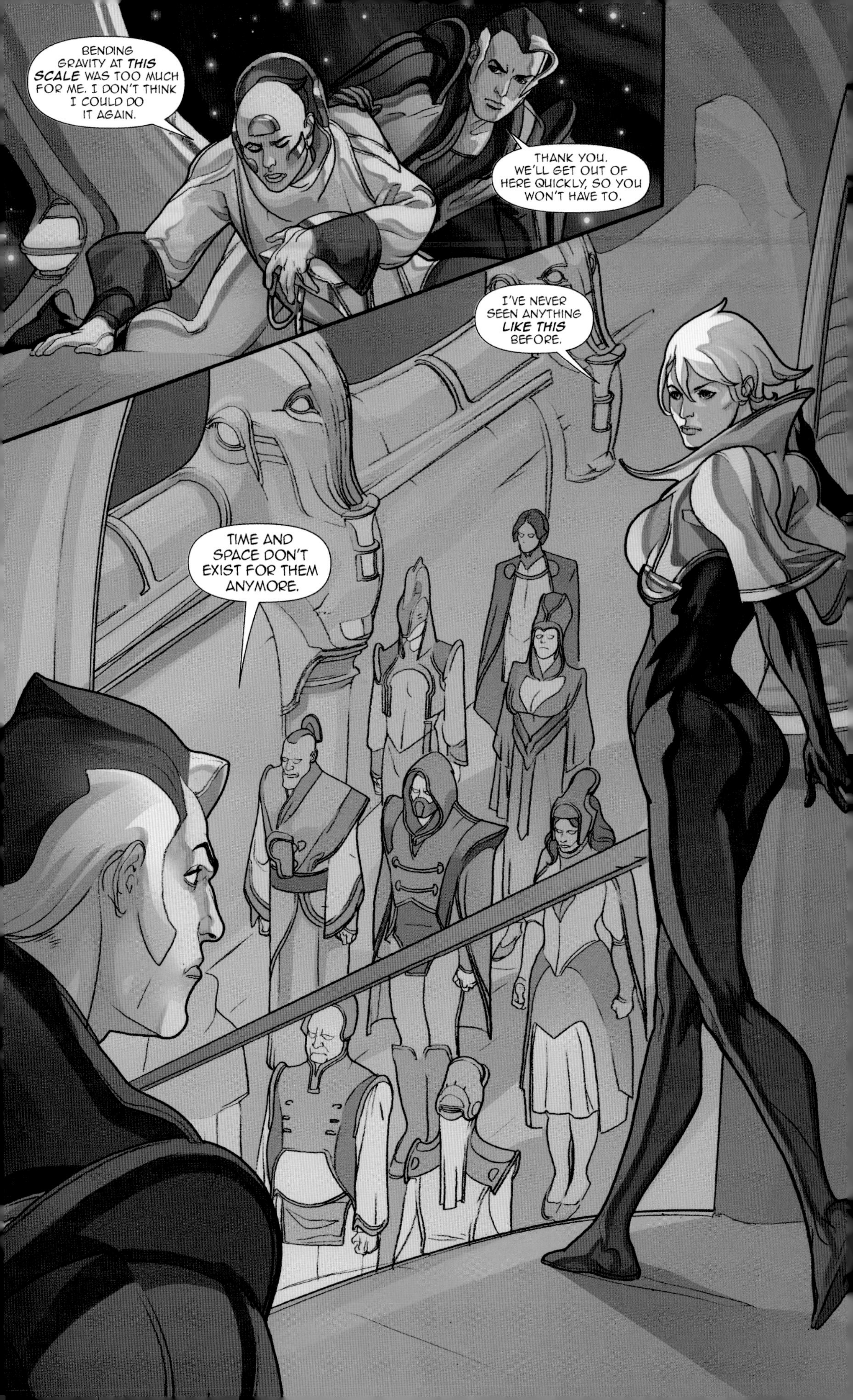
BENDING GRAVITY AT THIS SCALE WAS TOO MUCH FOR ME. I DON'T THINK I COULD DO IT AGAIN.
THANK YOU. WE'LL GET OUT OF HERE QUICKLY, SO YOU WON'T HAVE TO.
I'VE NEVER SEEN ANYTHING LIKE THIS BEFORE.
TIME AND SPACE DON'T EXIST FOR THEM ANYMORE.

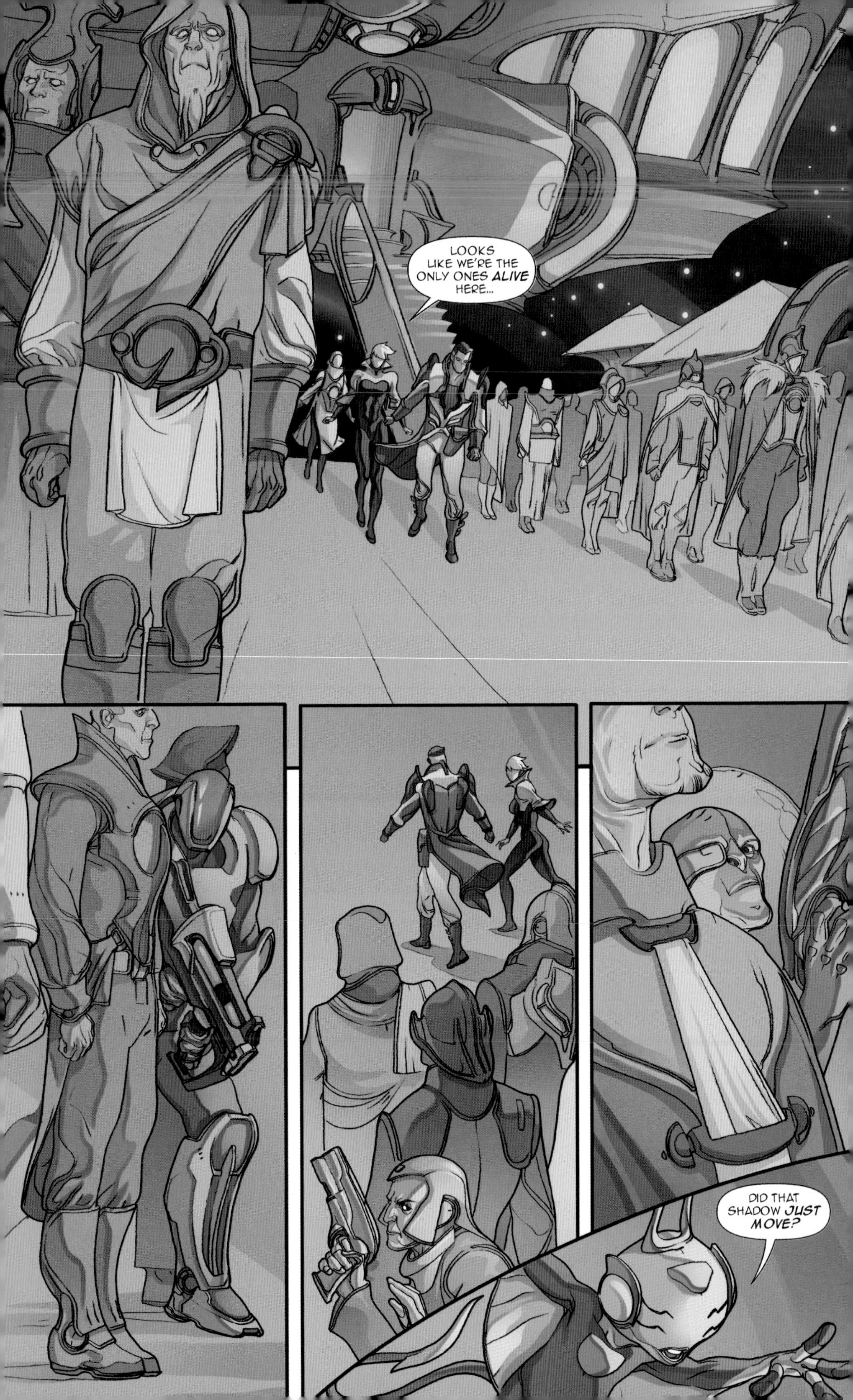
LOOKS LIKE WE'RE THE ONLY ONES ALIVE HERE...
DID THAT SHADOW JUST MOVE?

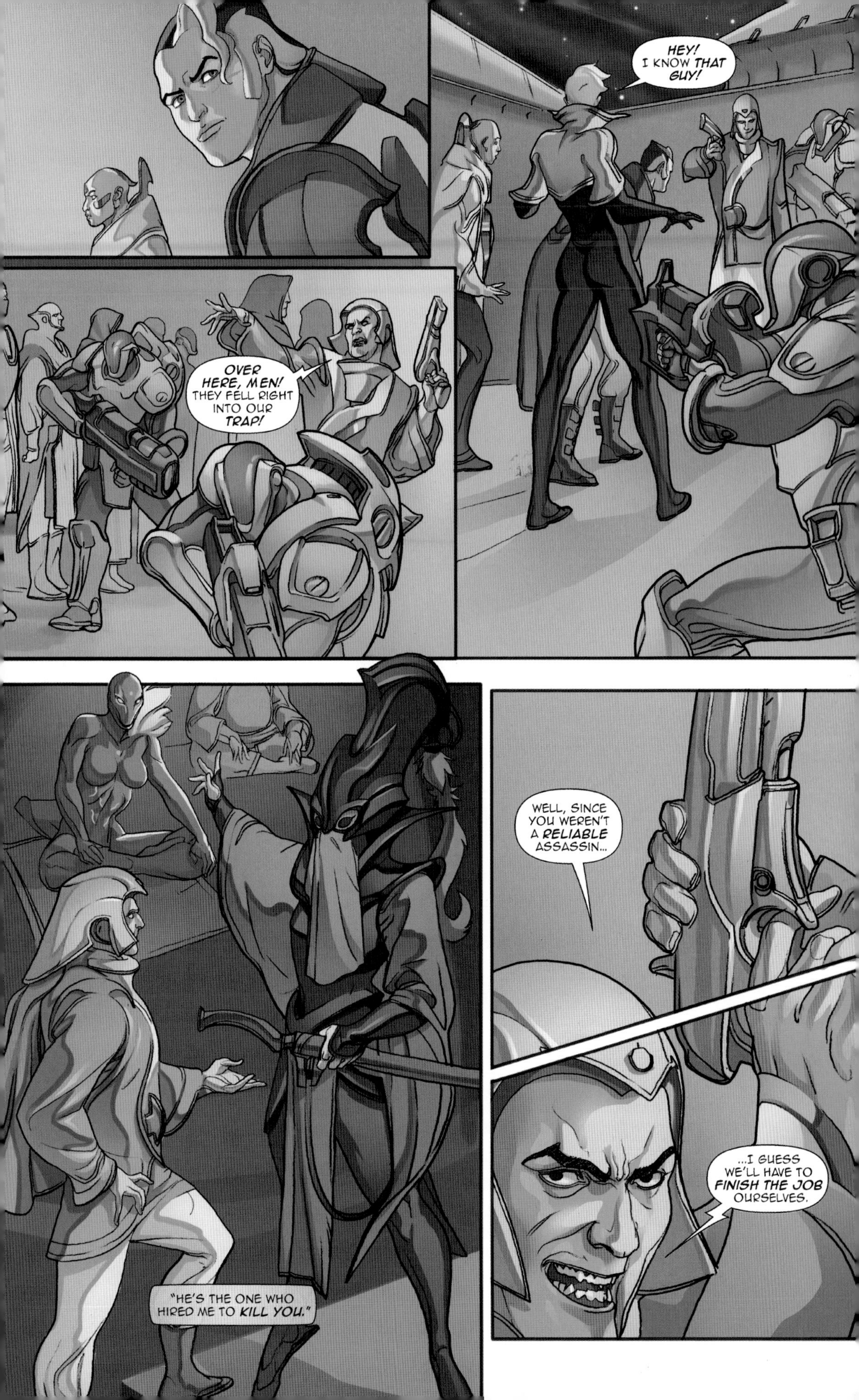
HEY! I KNOW THAT GUY!
OVER HERE, MEN! THEY FELL RIGHT INTO OUR TRAP!
"HE'S THE ONE WHO HIRED ME TO KILL YOU."
WELL, SINCE YOU WEREN'T A RELIABLE ASSASSIN...
...I GUESS WE'LL HAVE TO FINISH THE JOB OURSELVES.

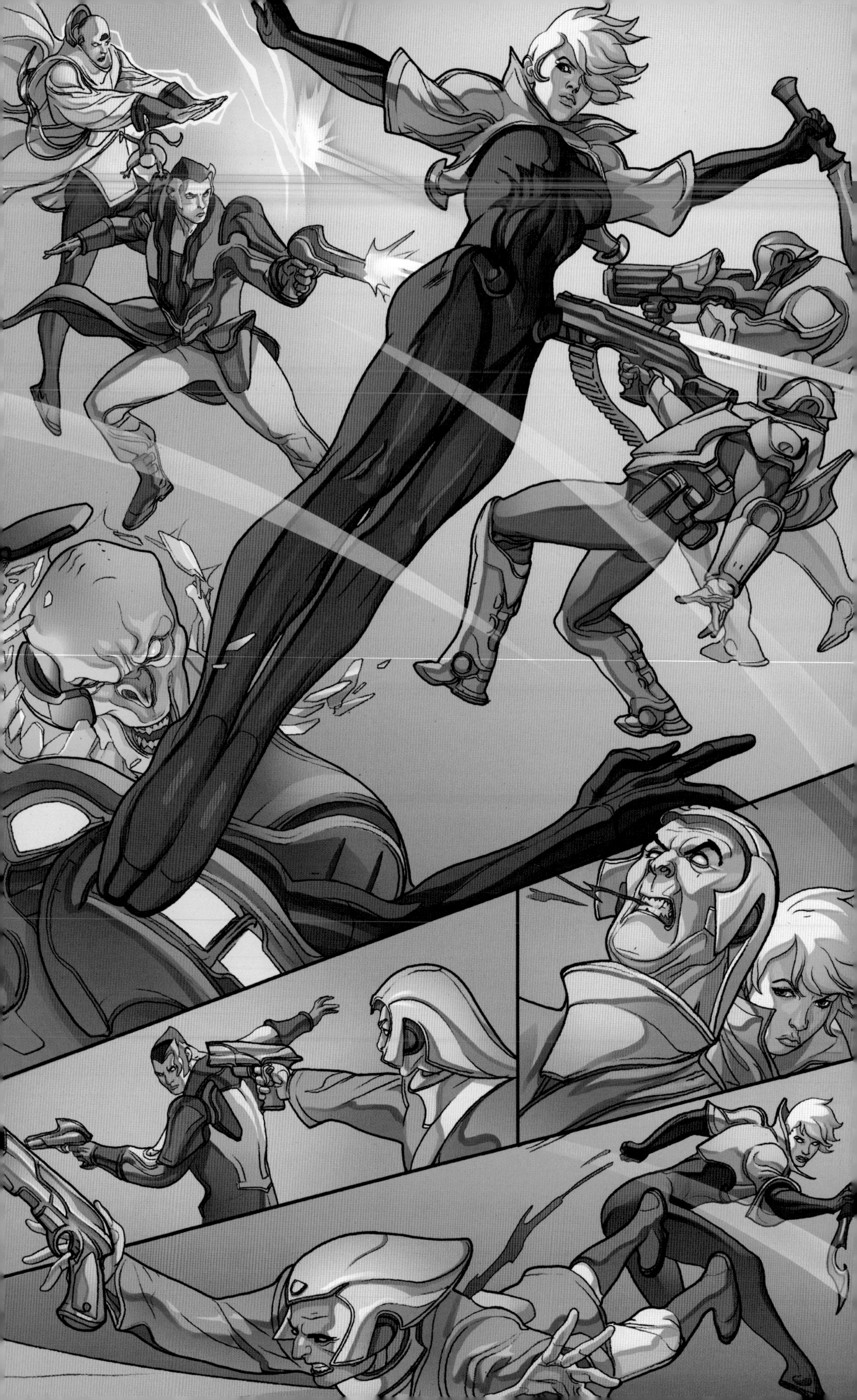

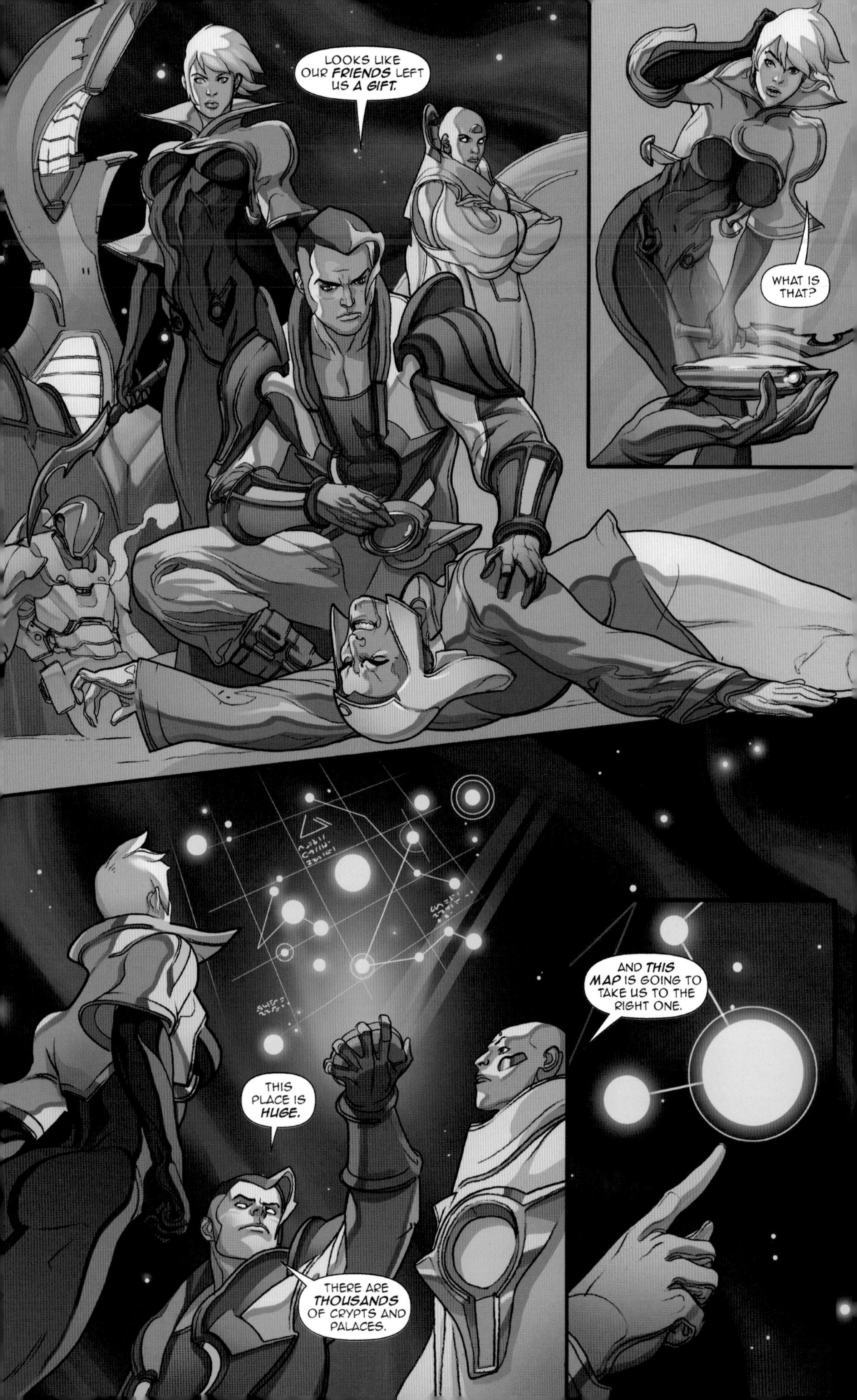
LOOKS LIKE OUR **FRIENDS** LEFT US **A GIFT.**
WHAT IS THAT?
THIS PLACE IS **HUGE.**
THERE ARE **THOUSANDS** OF CRYPTS AND PALACES.
AND **THIS MAP** IS GOING TO TAKE US TO THE RIGHT ONE.

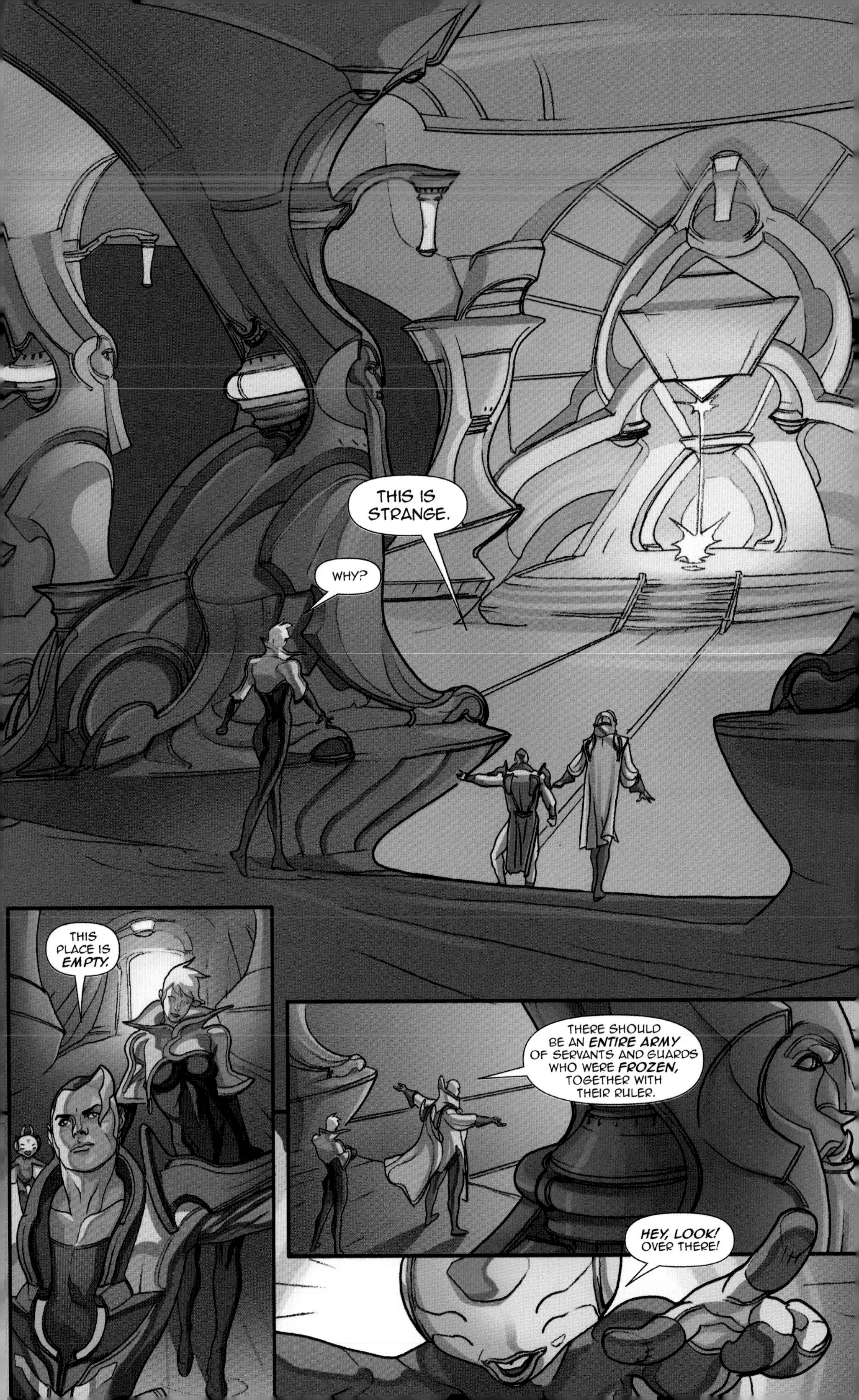
THIS IS STRANGE.
WHY?
THIS PLACE IS EMPTY.
THERE SHOULD BE AN ENTIRE ARMY OF SERVANTS AND GUARDS WHO WERE FROZEN, TOGETHER WITH THEIR RULER.
HEY, LOOK! OVER THERE!

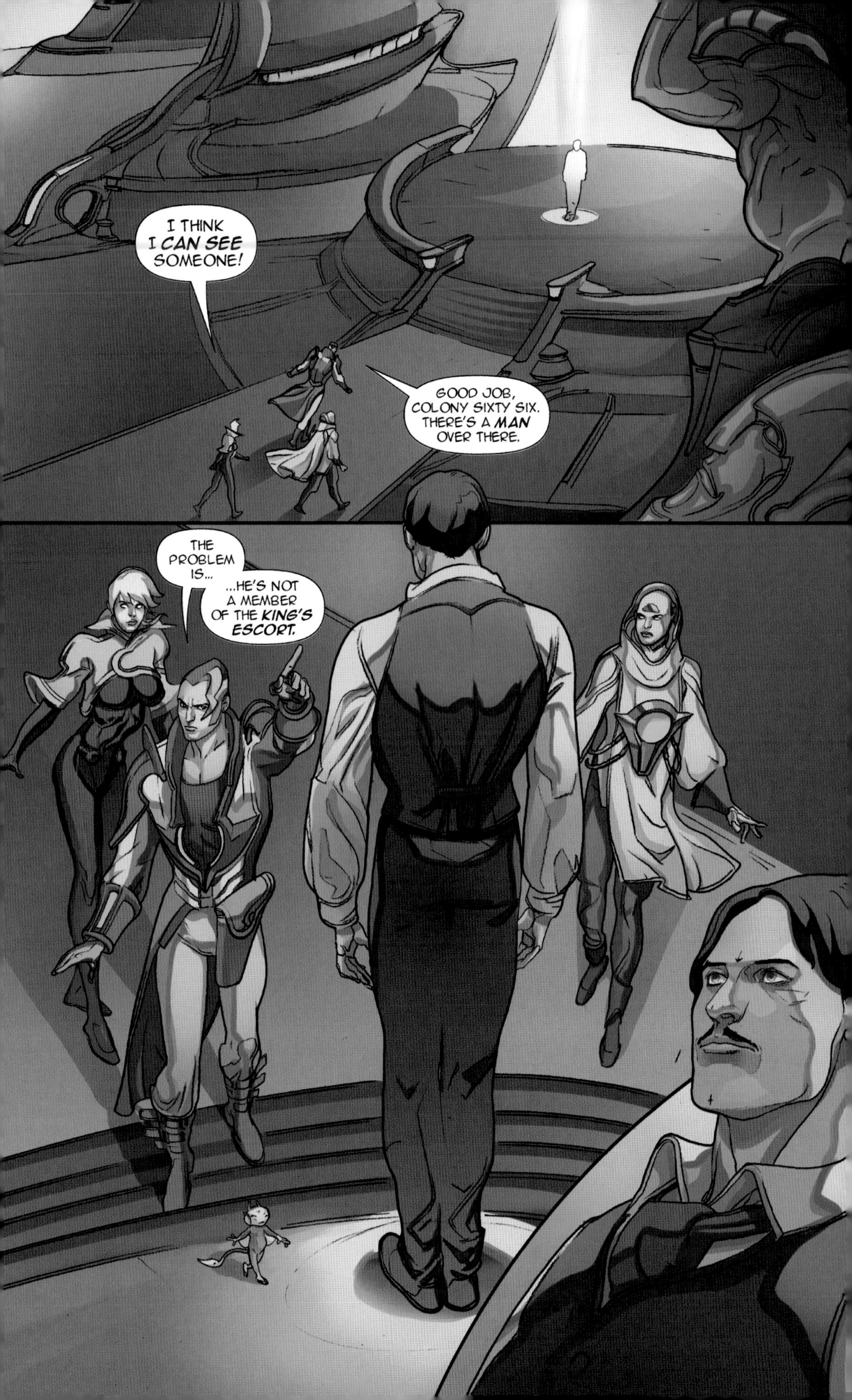

I THINK I CAN SEE SOMEONE!
GOOD JOB, COLONY SIXTY SIX. THERE'S A MAN OVER THERE.
THE PROBLEM IS...
...HE'S NOT A MEMBER OF THE KING'S ESCORT.

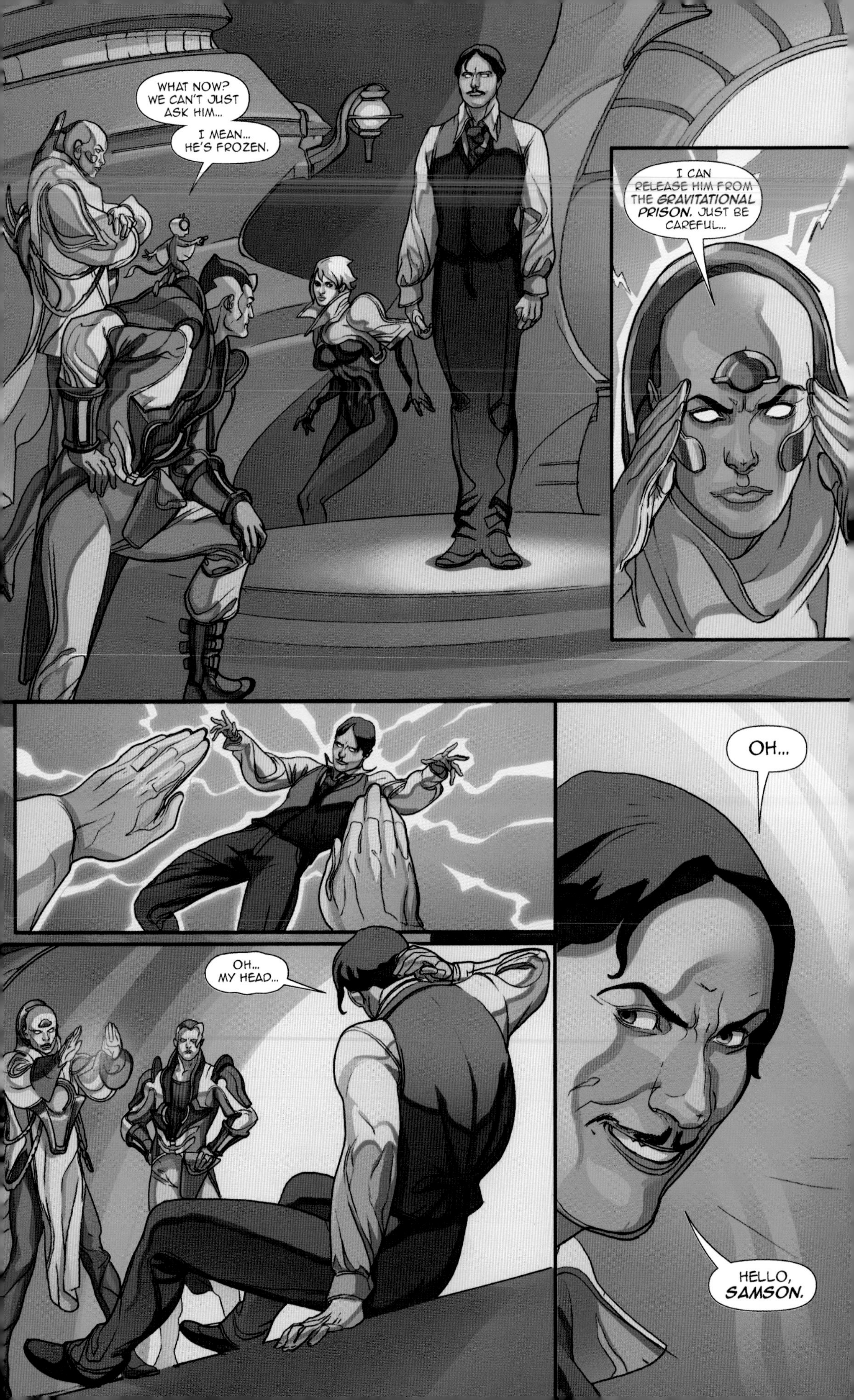
WHAT NOW? WE CAN'T JUST ASK HIM...
I MEAN... HE'S FROZEN.
I CAN RELEASE HIM FROM THE GRAVITATIONAL PRISON. JUST BE CAREFUL...
OH... MY HEAD...
OH...
HELLO, SAMSON.

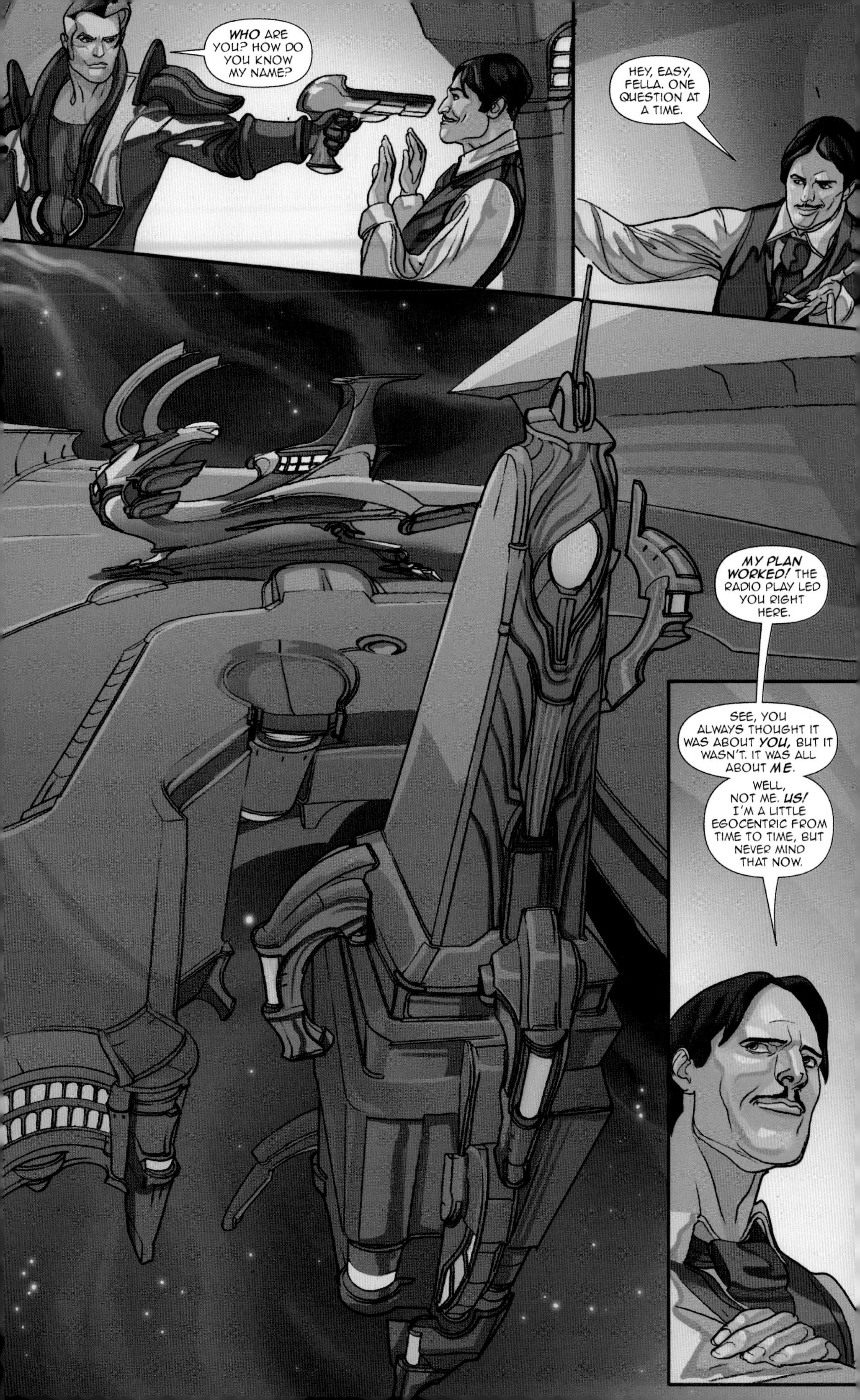
WHO ARE YOU? HOW DO YOU KNOW MY NAME?
HEY, EASY, FELLA. ONE QUESTION AT A TIME.
MY PLAN WORKED! THE RADIO PLAY LED YOU RIGHT HERE.
SEE, YOU ALWAYS THOUGHT IT WAS ABOUT YOU, BUT IT WASN'T. IT WAS ALL ABOUT ME.
WELL, NOT ME. US! I'M A LITTLE EGOCENTRIC FROM TIME TO TIME, BUT NEVER MIND THAT NOW.

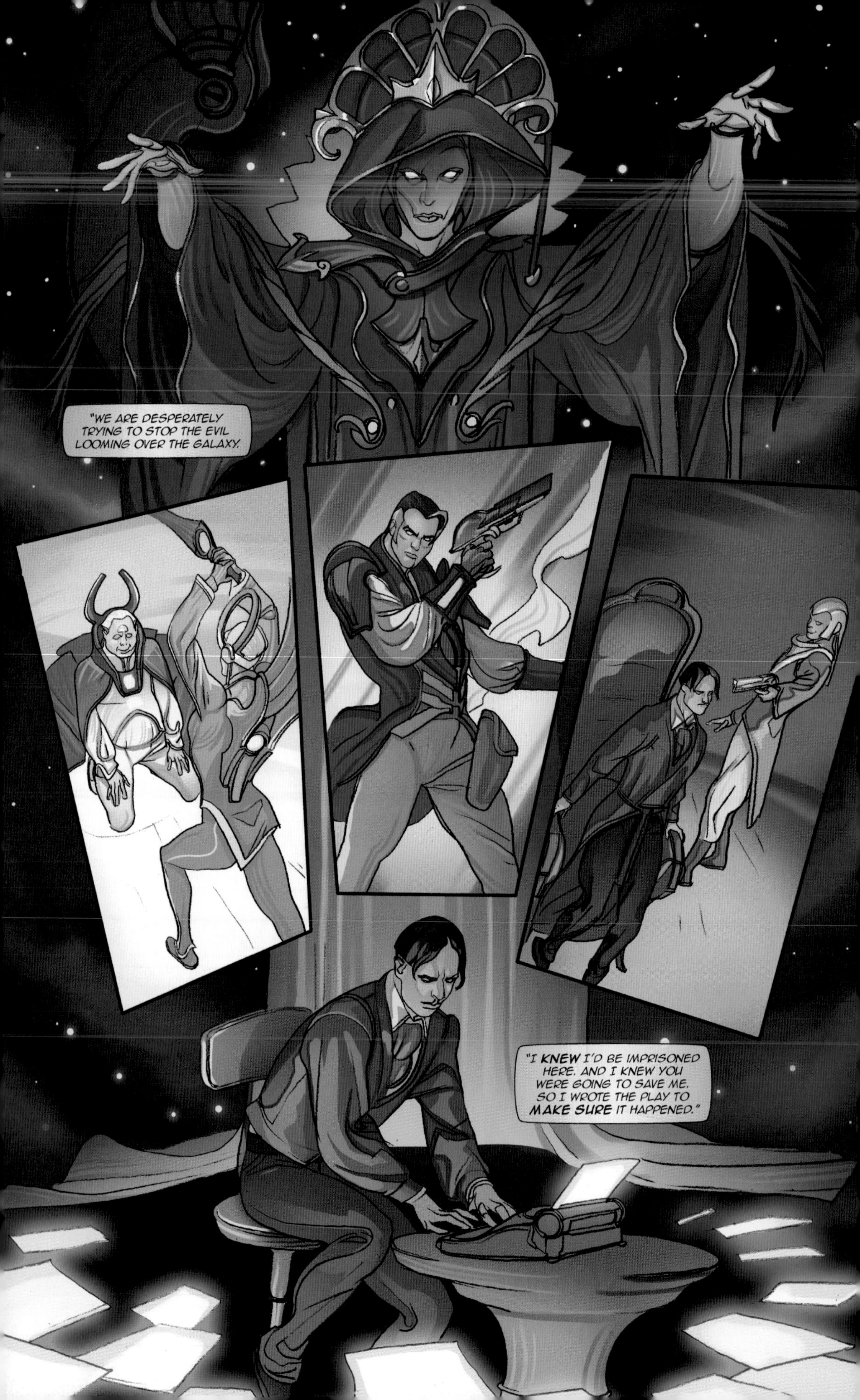
"WE ARE DESPERATELY TRYING TO STOP THE EVIL LOOMING OVER THE GALAXY.
"I **KNEW** I'D BE IMPRISONED HERE. AND I KNEW YOU WERE GOING TO SAVE ME. SO I WROTE THE PLAY TO **MAKE SURE** IT HAPPENED."

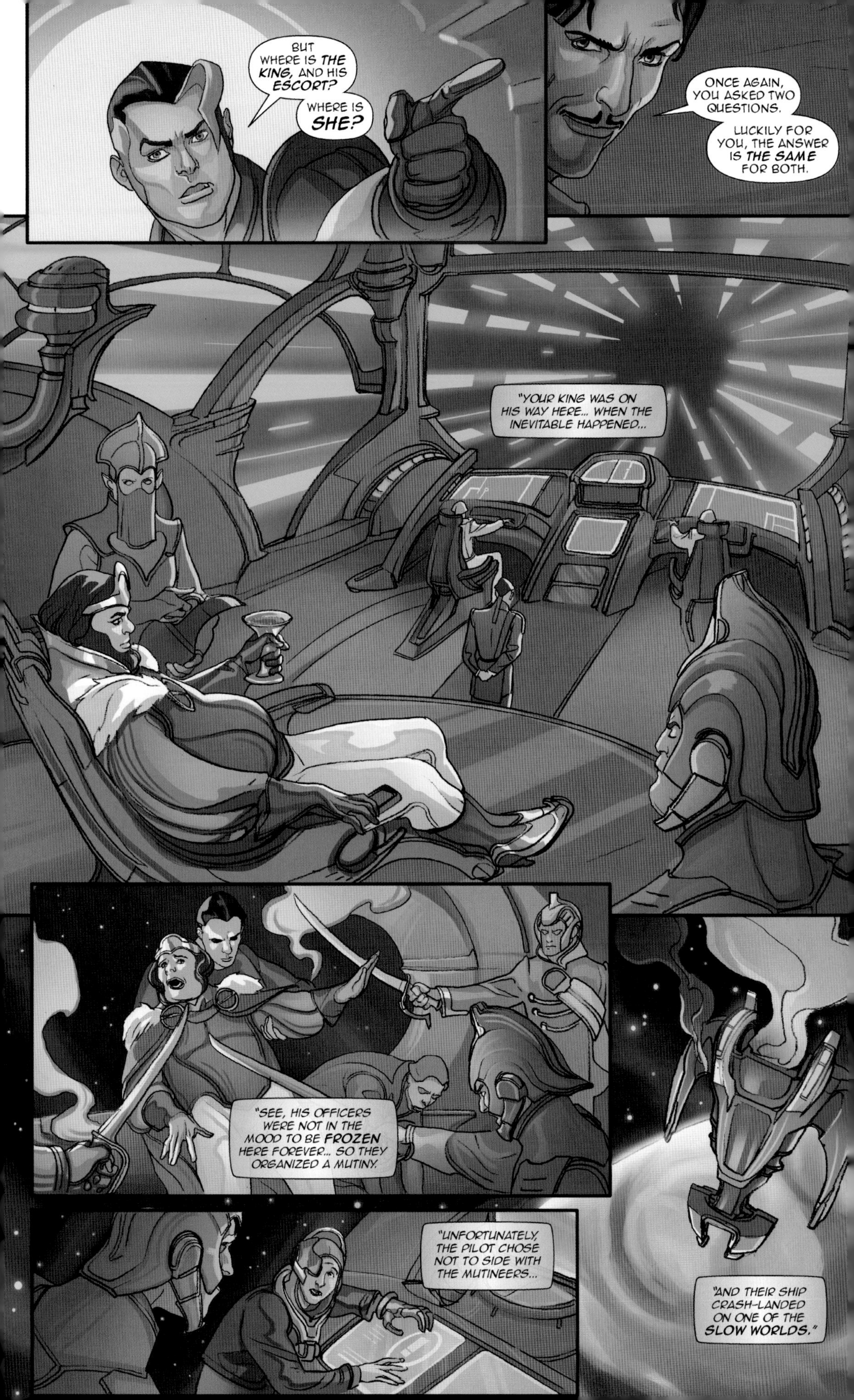

BUT WHERE IS THE KING, AND HIS ESCORT?
WHERE IS SHE?
ONCE AGAIN, YOU ASKED TWO QUESTIONS.
LUCKILY FOR YOU, THE ANSWER IS THE SAME FOR BOTH.
"YOUR KING WAS ON HIS WAY HERE... WHEN THE INEVITABLE HAPPENED...
"SEE, HIS OFFICERS WERE NOT IN THE MOOD TO BE FROZEN HERE FOREVER... SO THEY ORGANIZED A MUTINY.
"UNFORTUNATELY, THE PILOT CHOSE NOT TO SIDE WITH THE MUTINEERS...
"AND THEIR SHIP CRASH-LANDED ON ONE OF THE SLOW WORLDS."

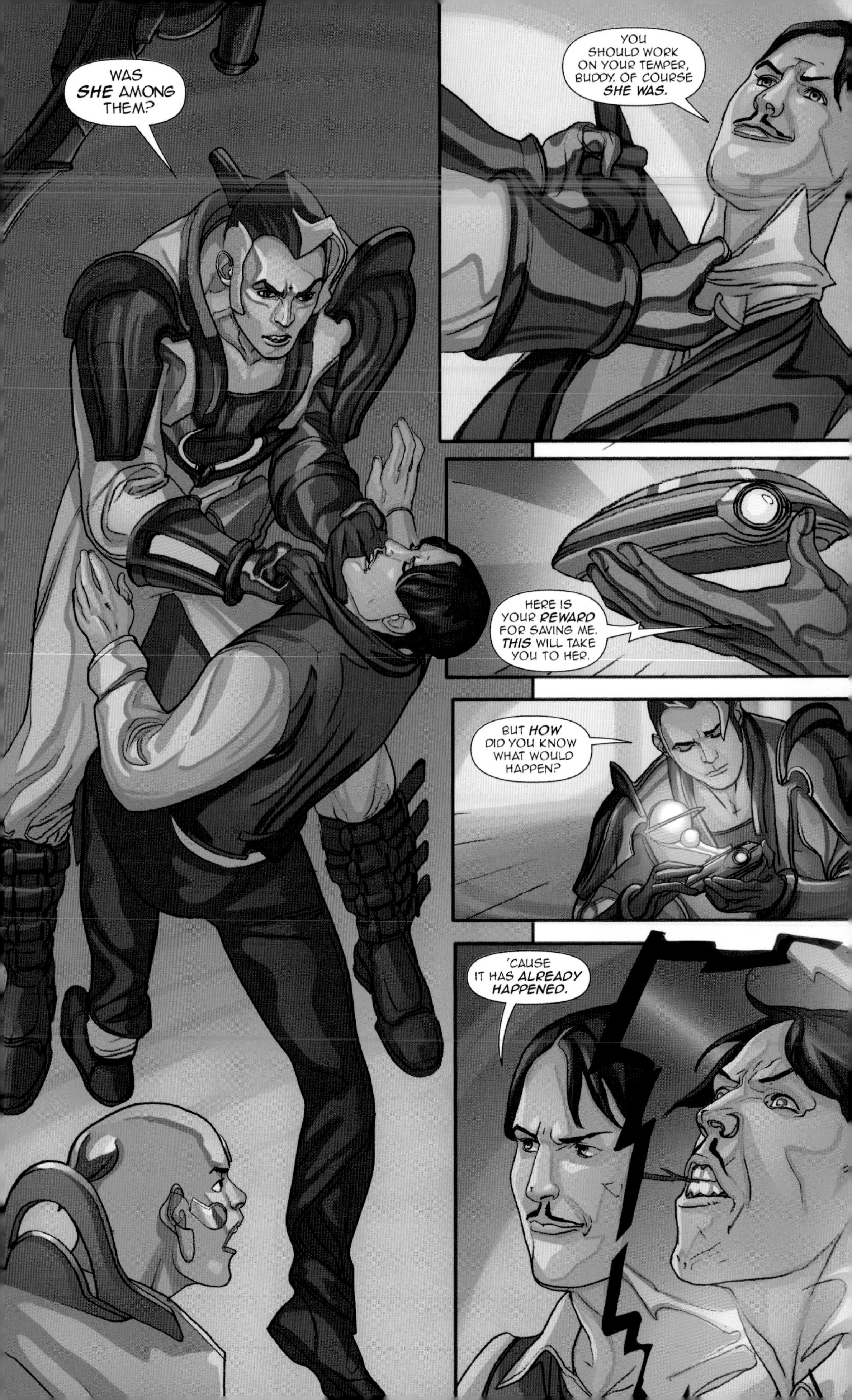
WAS SHE AMONG THEM?
YOU SHOULD WORK ON YOUR TEMPER, BUDDY. OF COURSE SHE WAS.
HERE IS YOUR REWARD FOR SAVING ME. THIS WILL TAKE YOU TO HER.
BUT HOW DID YOU KNOW WHAT WOULD HAPPEN?
'CAUSE IT HAS ALREADY HAPPENED.

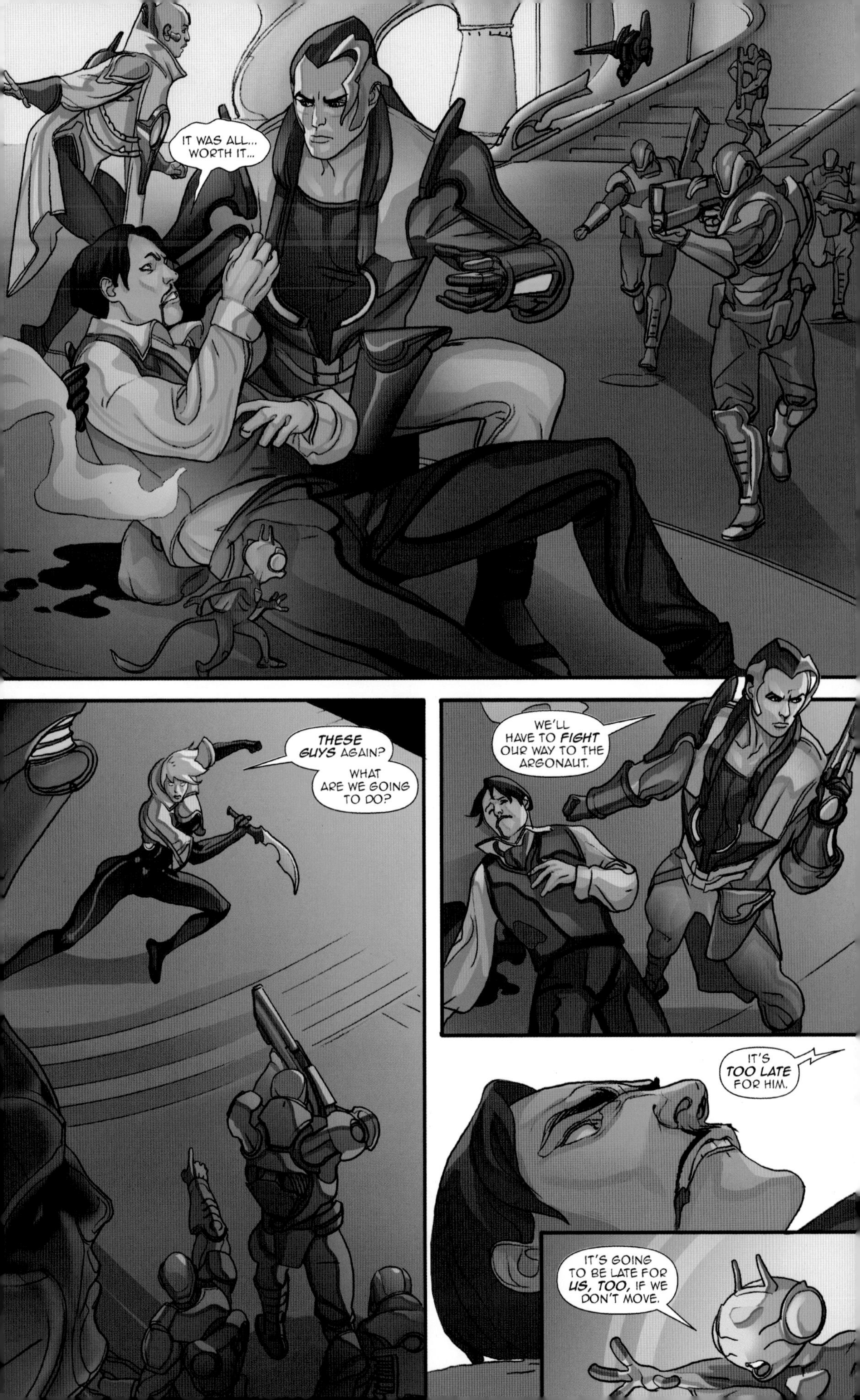
IT WAS ALL... WORTH IT...
THESE GUYS AGAIN?
WHAT ARE WE GOING TO DO?
WE'LL HAVE TO FIGHT OUR WAY TO THE ARGONAUT.
IT'S TOO LATE FOR HIM.
IT'S GOING TO BE LATE FOR US, TOO, IF WE DON'T MOVE.

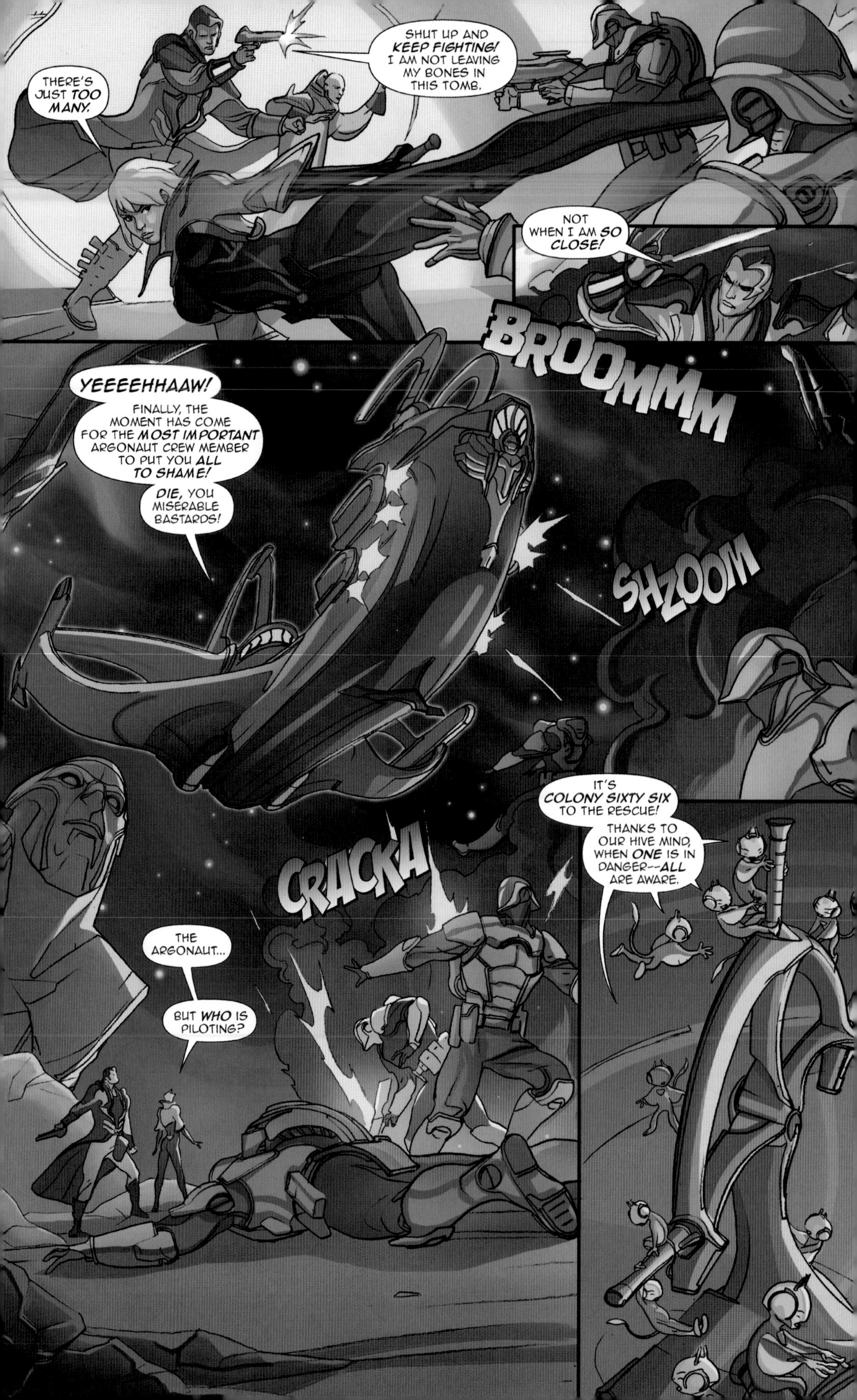
THERE'S JUST TOO MANY.
SHUT UP AND KEEP FIGHTING! I AM NOT LEAVING MY BONES IN THIS TOMB.
NOT WHEN I AM SO CLOSE!
BROOMMM
YEEEEHHAAW!
FINALLY, THE MOMENT HAS COME FOR THE MOST IMPORTANT ARGONAUT CREW MEMBER TO PUT YOU ALL TO SHAME!
DIE, YOU MISERABLE BASTARDS!
SHZOOM
CRACKA
THE ARGONAUT...
BUT WHO IS PILOTING?
IT'S COLONY SIXTY SIX TO THE RESCUE!
THANKS TO OUR HIVE MIND, WHEN ONE IS IN DANGER--ALL ARE AWARE.

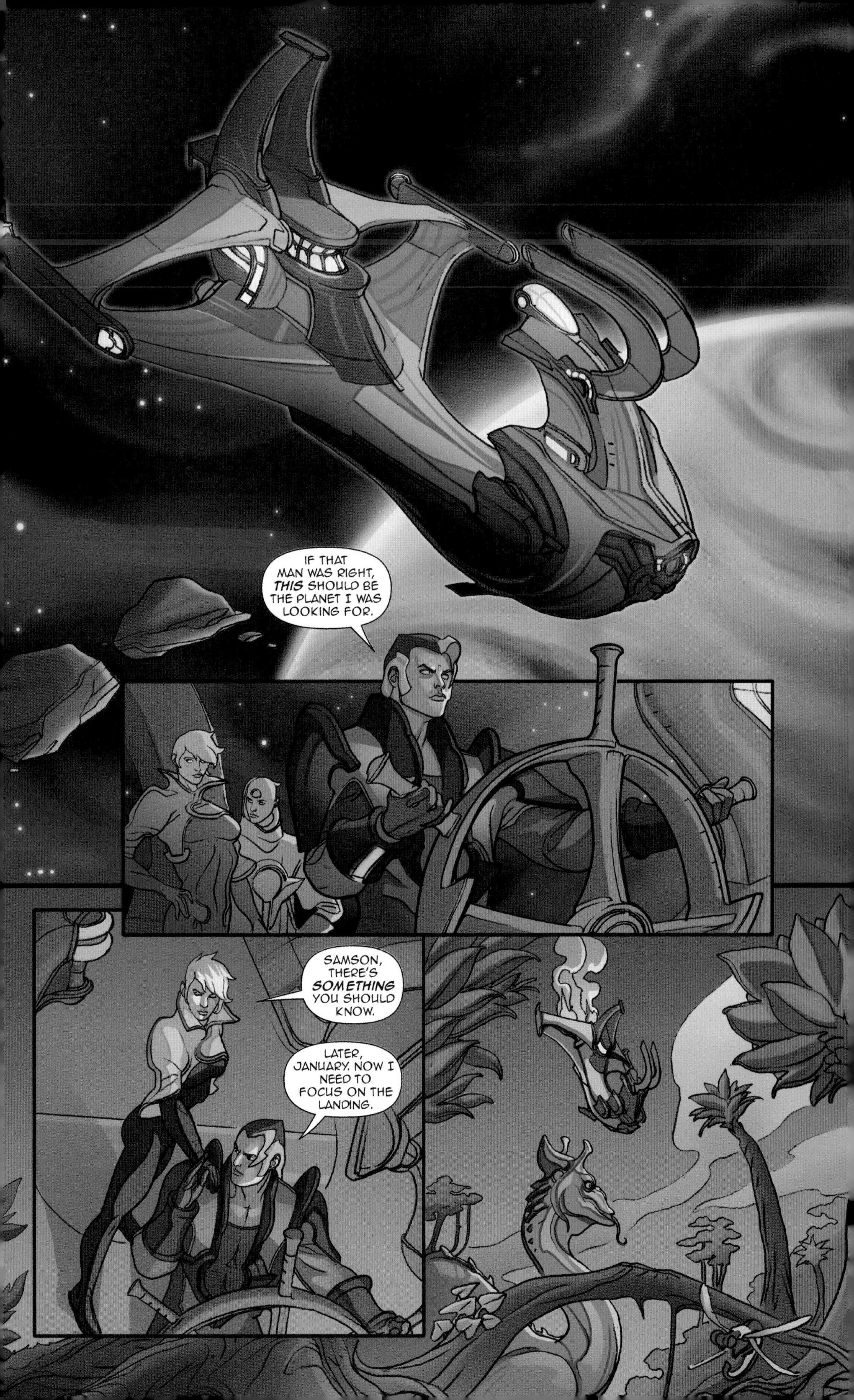
IF THAT MAN WAS RIGHT, THIS SHOULD BE THE PLANET I WAS LOOKING FOR.
SAMSON, THERE'S SOMETHING YOU SHOULD KNOW.
LATER, JANUARY. NOW I NEED TO FOCUS ON THE LANDING.

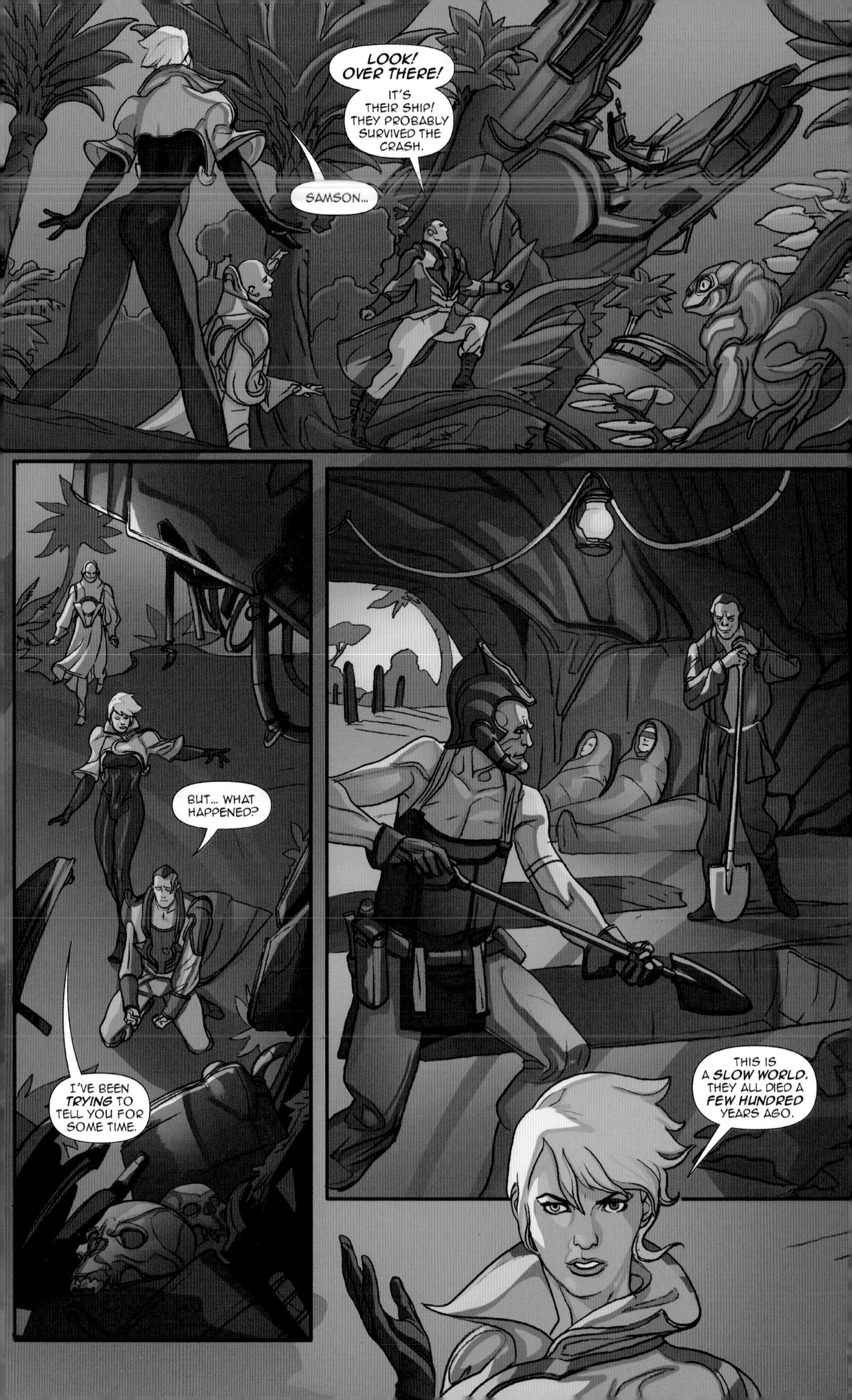
LOOK! OVER THERE!
IT'S THEIR SHIP! THEY PROBABLY SURVIVED THE CRASH.
SAMSON...
BUT... WHAT HAPPENED?
I'VE BEEN TRYING TO TELL YOU FOR SOME TIME.
THIS IS A SLOW WORLD. THEY ALL DIED A FEW HUNDRED YEARS AGO.

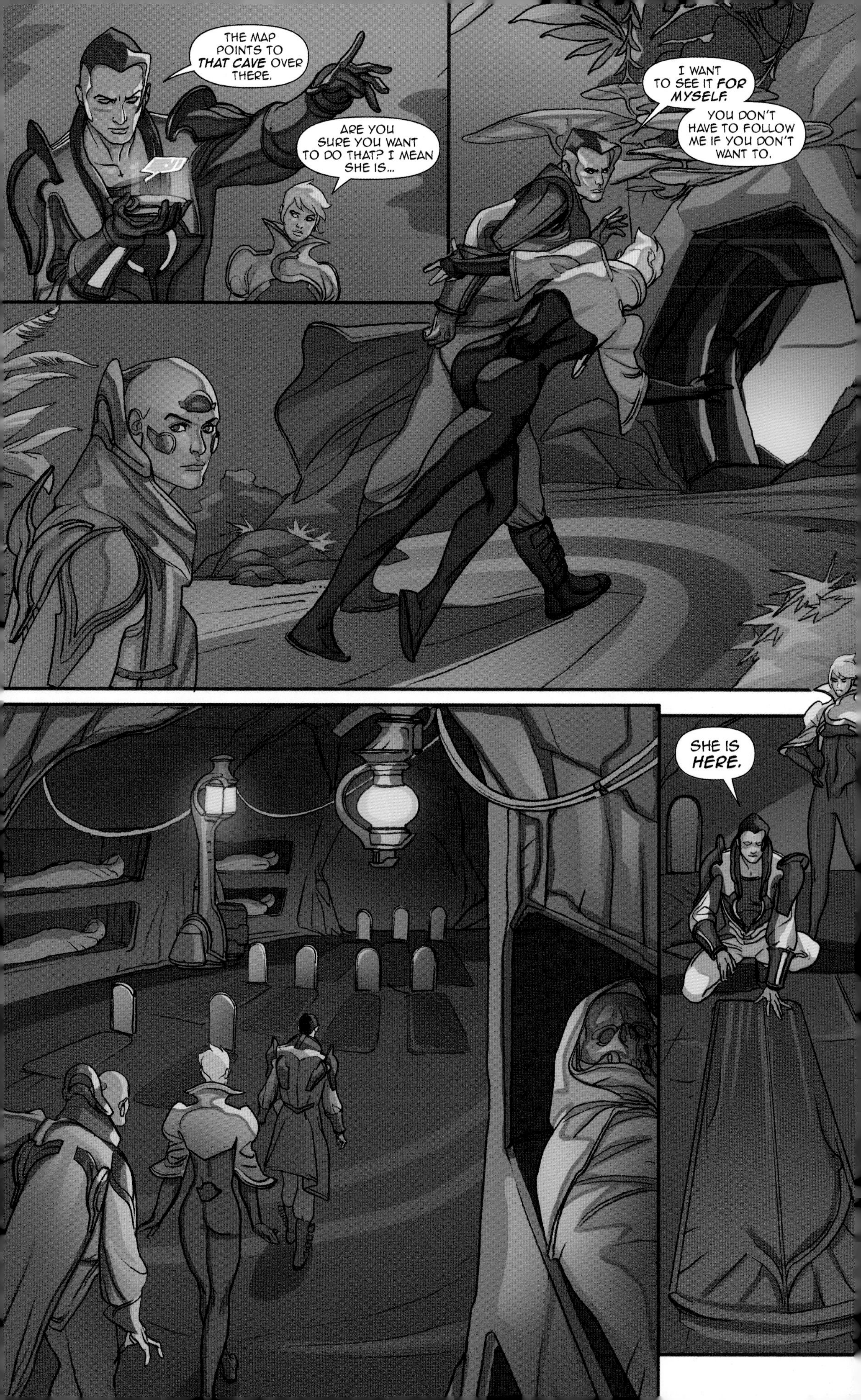
THE MAP POINTS TO THAT CAVE OVER THERE.
ARE YOU SURE YOU WANT TO DO THAT? I MEAN SHE IS...
I WANT TO SEE IT FOR MYSELF.
YOU DON'T HAVE TO FOLLOW ME IF YOU DON'T WANT TO.
SHE IS HERE.

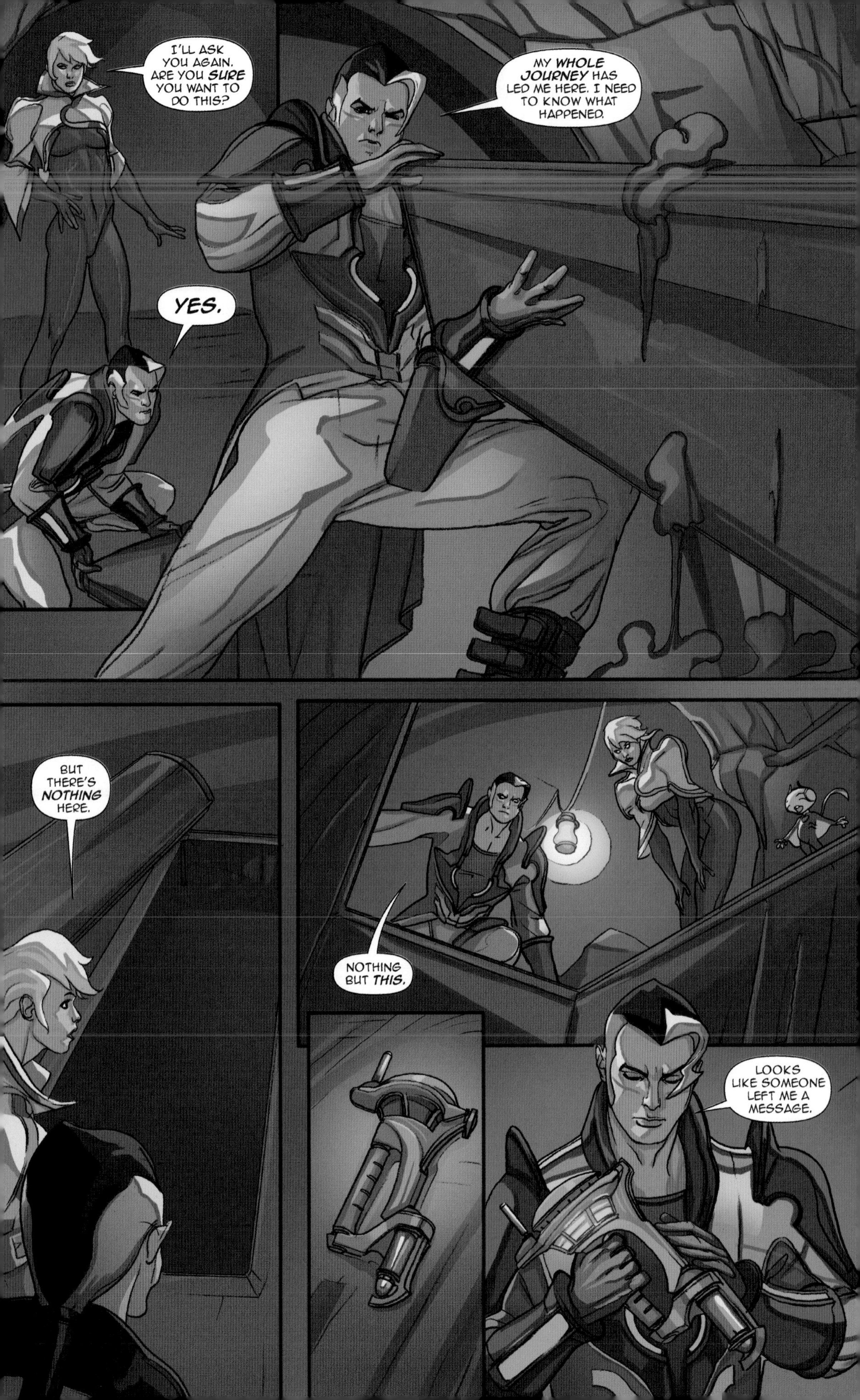
I'LL ASK YOU AGAIN. ARE YOU SURE YOU WANT TO DO THIS?
MY WHOLE JOURNEY HAS LED ME HERE. I NEED TO KNOW WHAT HAPPENED.
YES.
BUT THERE'S NOTHING HERE.
NOTHING BUT THIS.
LOOKS LIKE SOMEONE LEFT ME A MESSAGE.

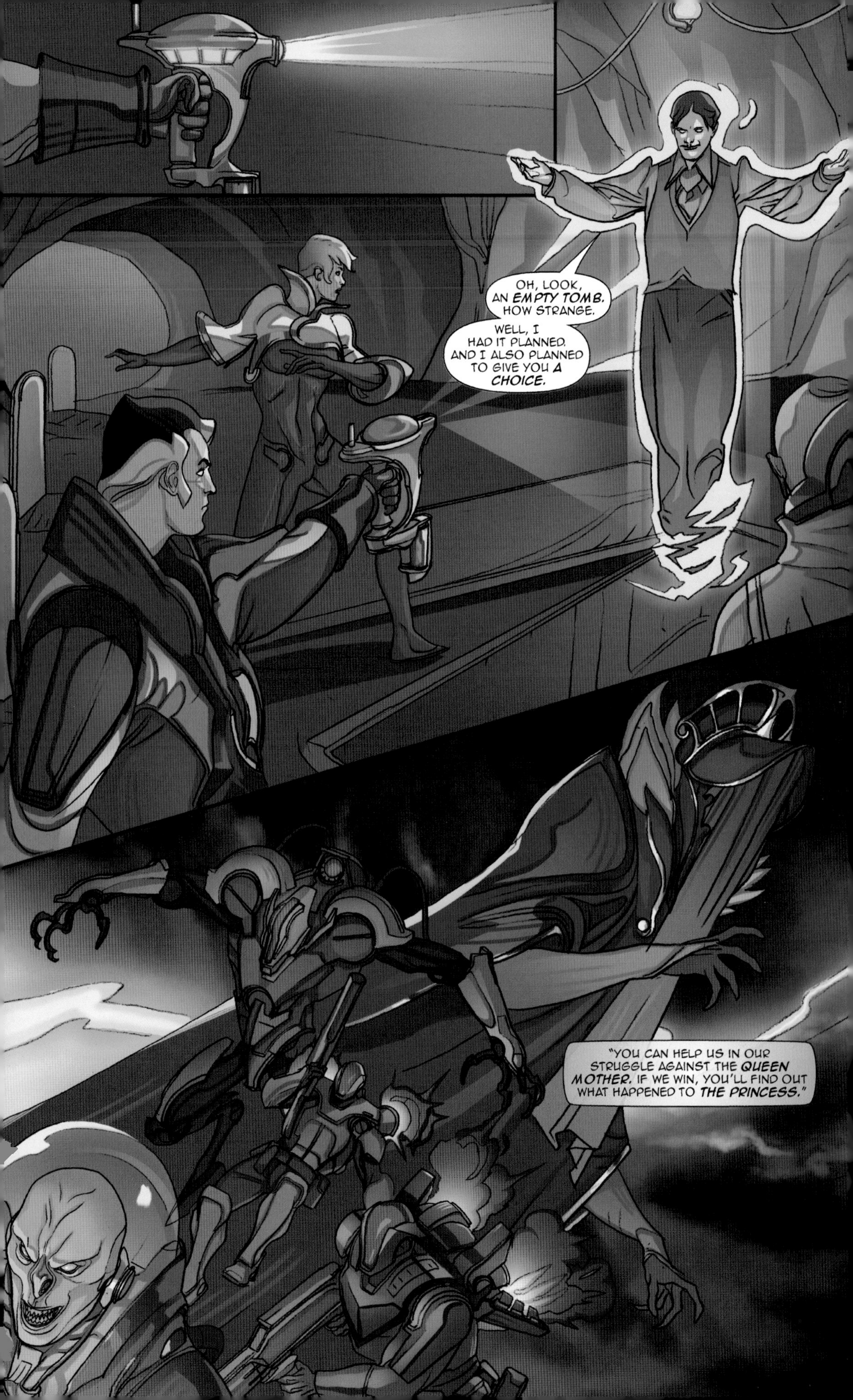

OH, LOOK, AN *EMPTY TOMB.* HOW STRANGE.
WELL, I HAD IT PLANNED. AND I ALSO PLANNED TO GIVE YOU *A CHOICE.*
"YOU CAN HELP US IN OUR STRUGGLE AGAINST THE *QUEEN MOTHER.* IF WE WIN, YOU'LL FIND OUT WHAT HAPPENED TO *THE PRINCESS.*"

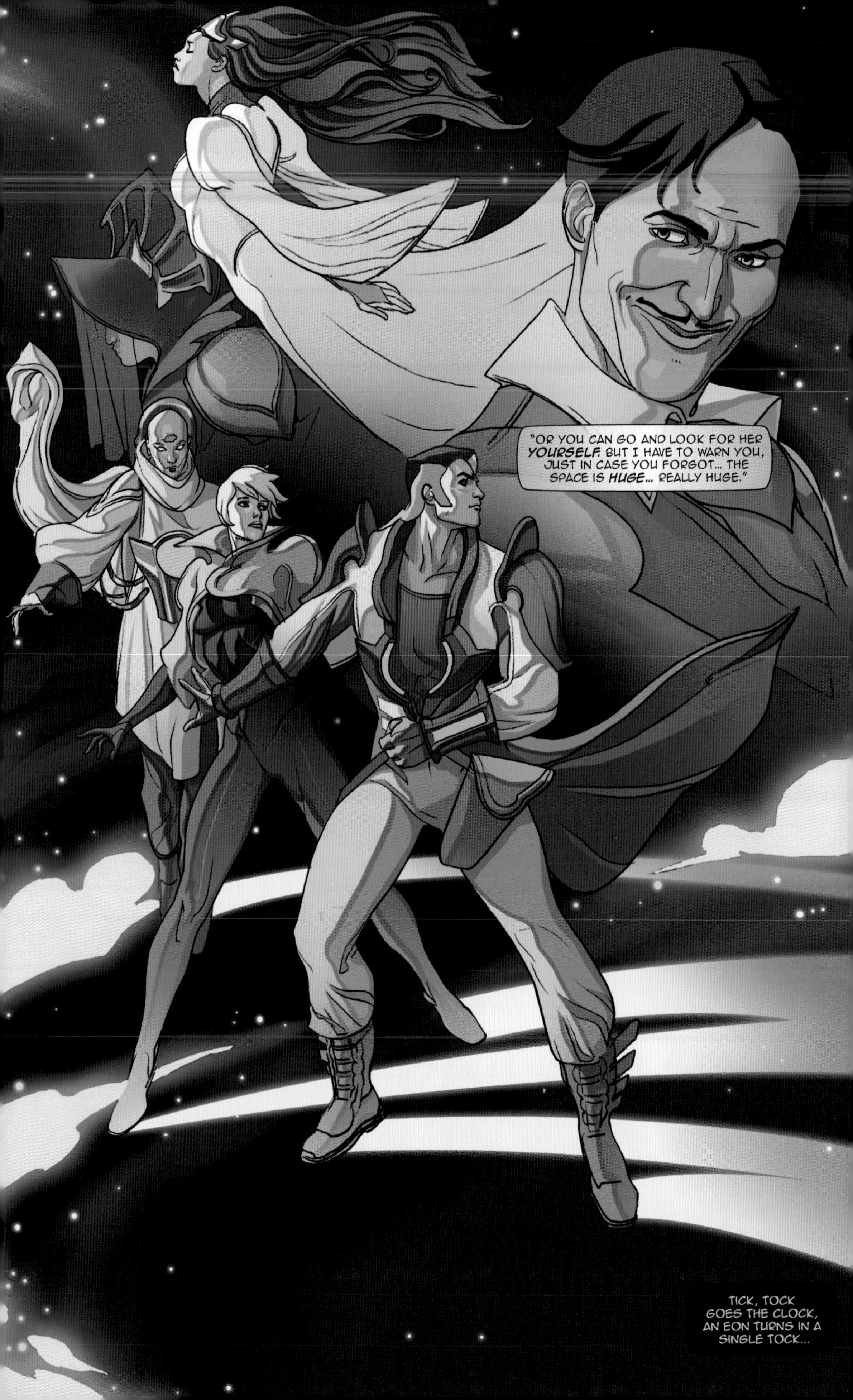
"OR YOU CAN GO AND LOOK FOR HER **YOURSELF.** BUT I HAVE TO WARN YOU, JUST IN CASE YOU FORGOT... THE SPACE IS **HUGE...** REALLY HUGE."
TICK, TOCK GOES THE CLOCK, AN EON TURNS IN A SINGLE TOCK...

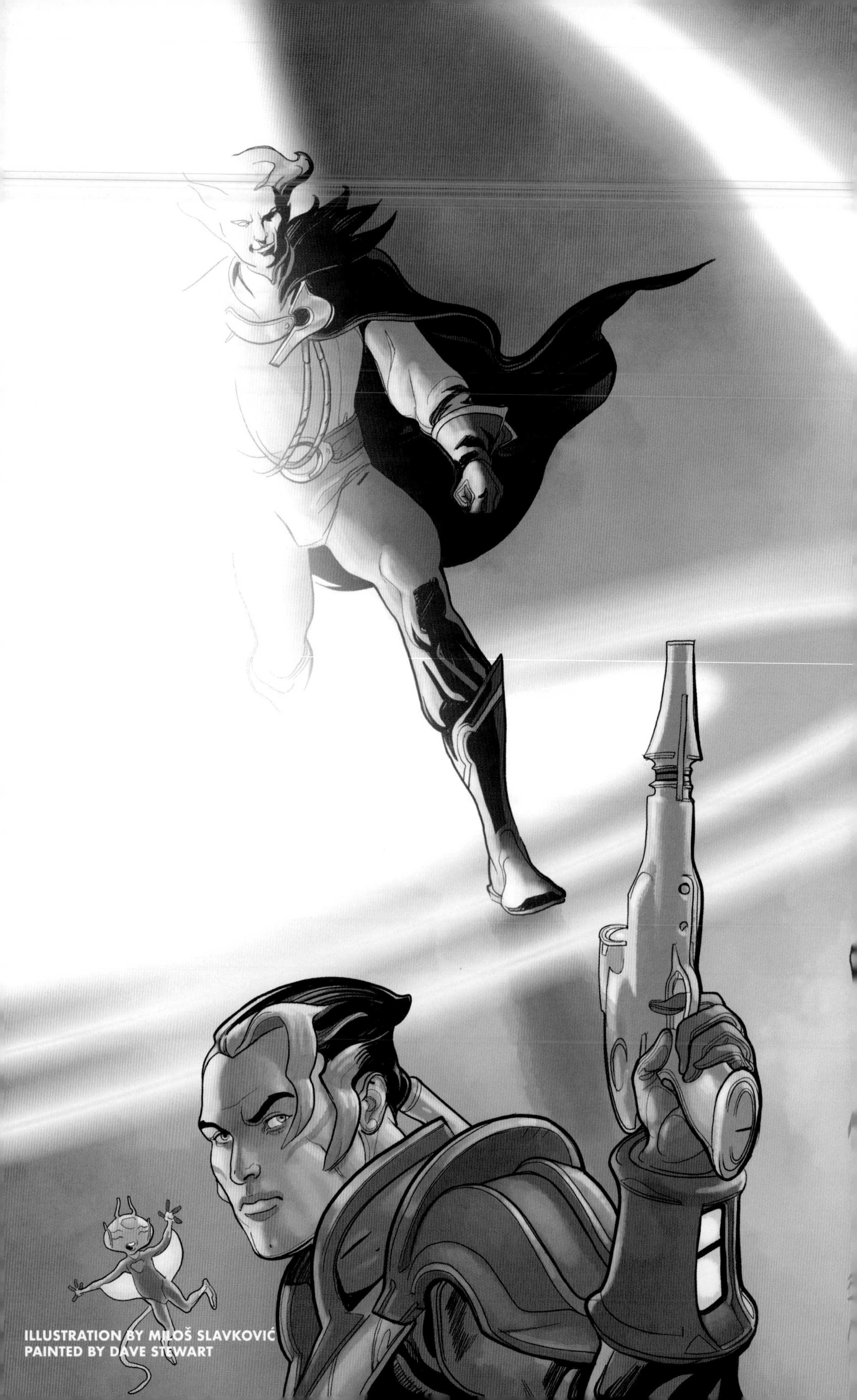
ILLUSTRATION BY MILOŠ SLAVKOVIĆ
PAINTED BY DAVE STEWART

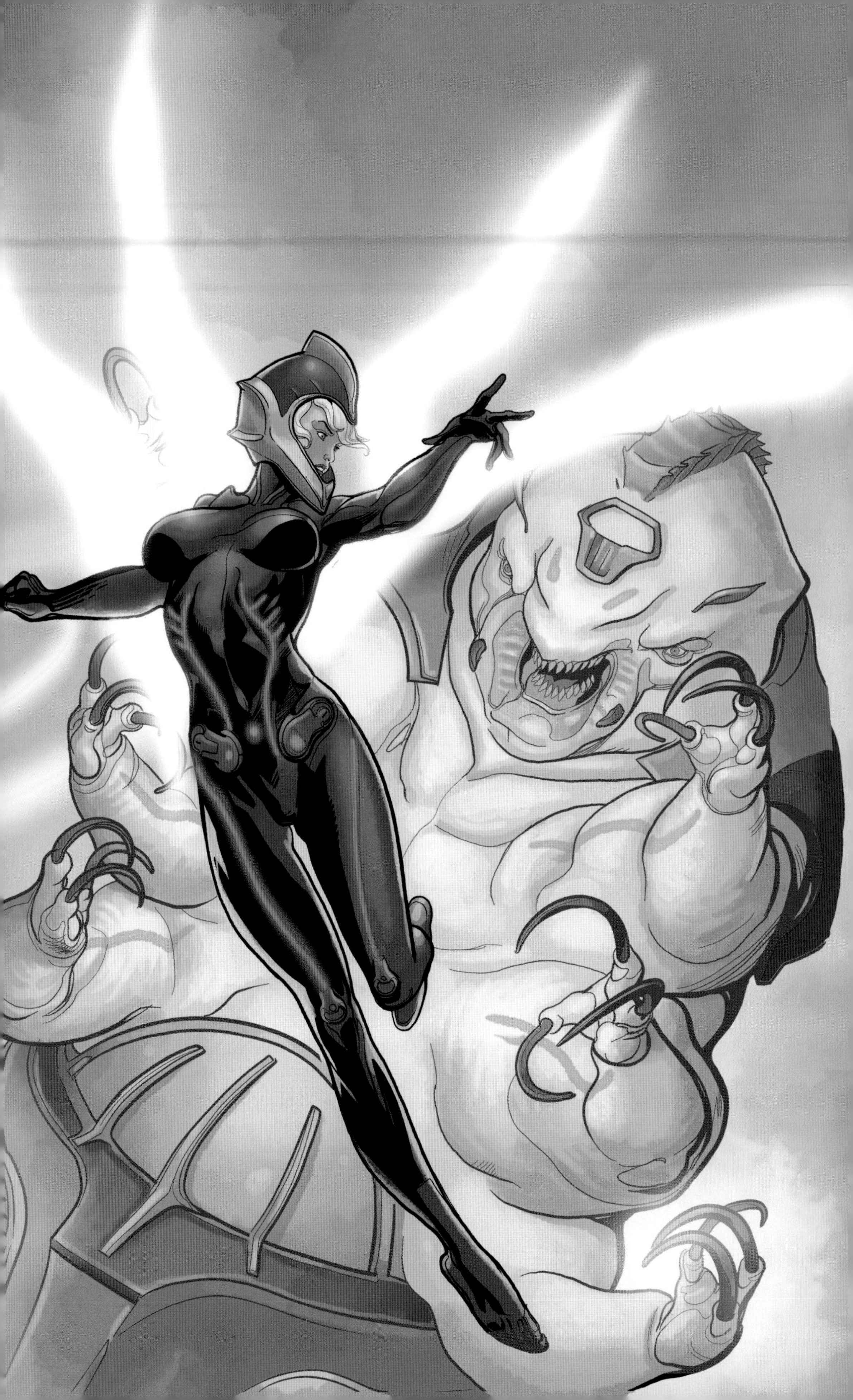

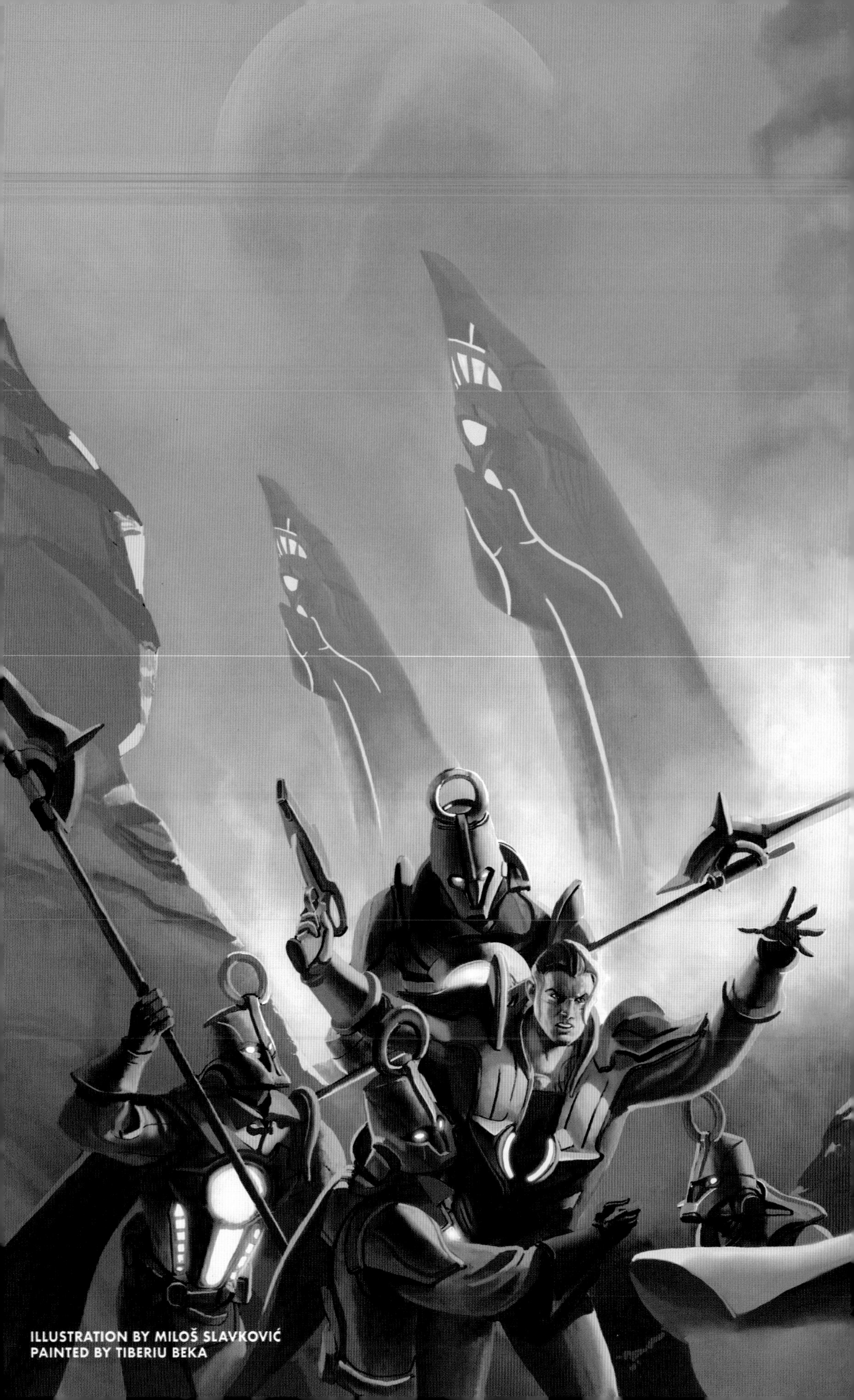

ILLUSTRATION BY MILOŠ SLAVKOVIĆ
PAINTED BY TIBERIU BEKA

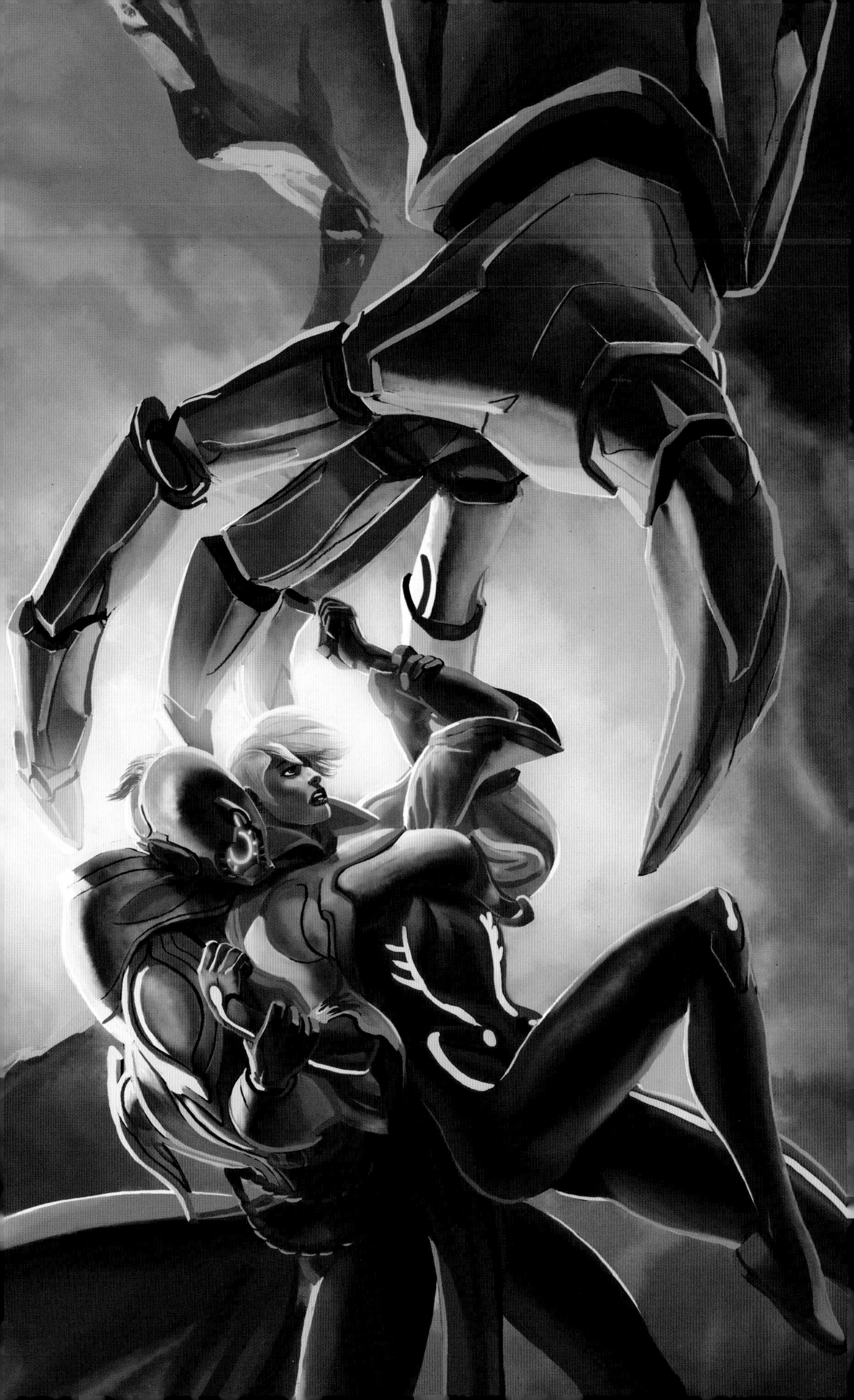

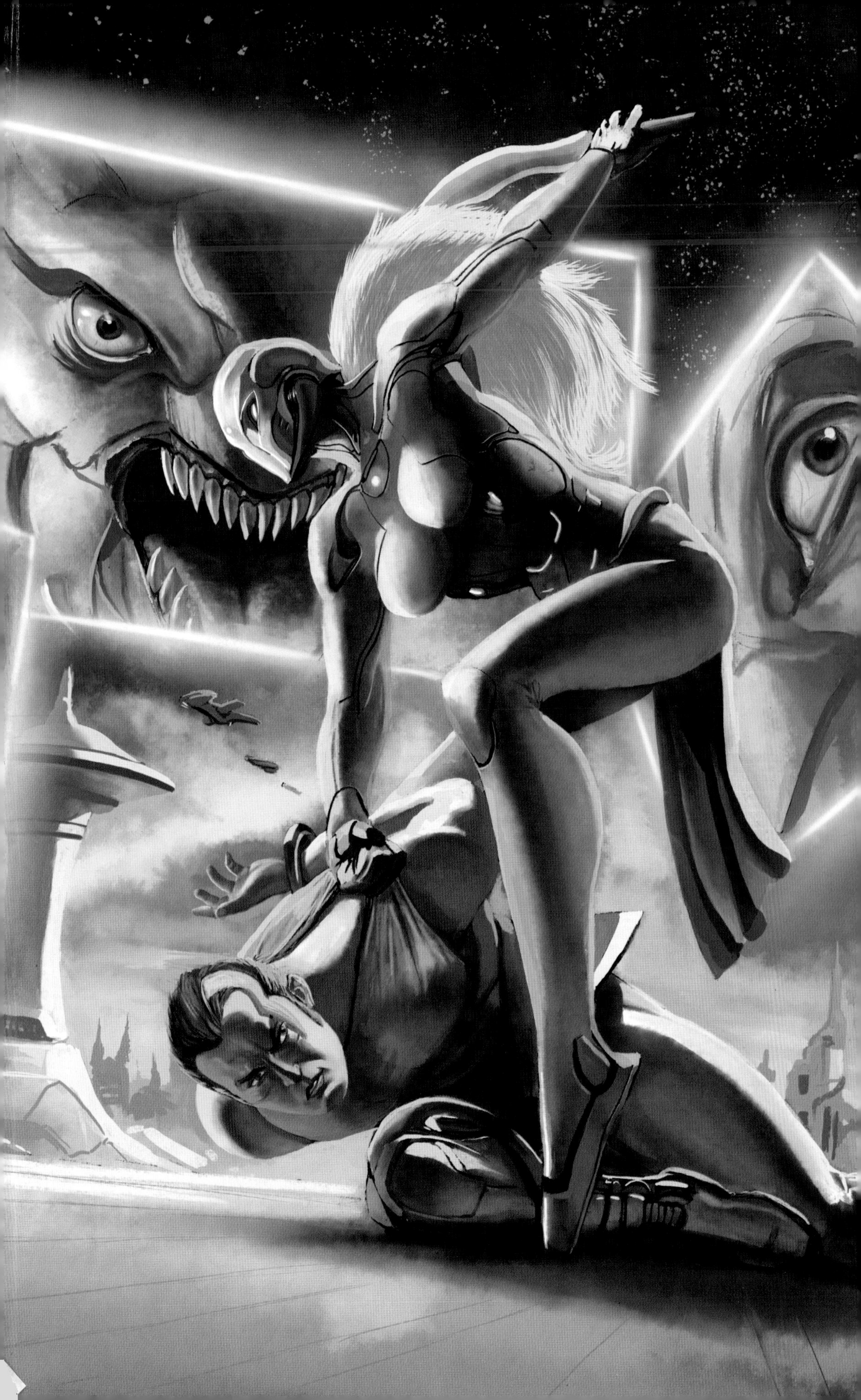

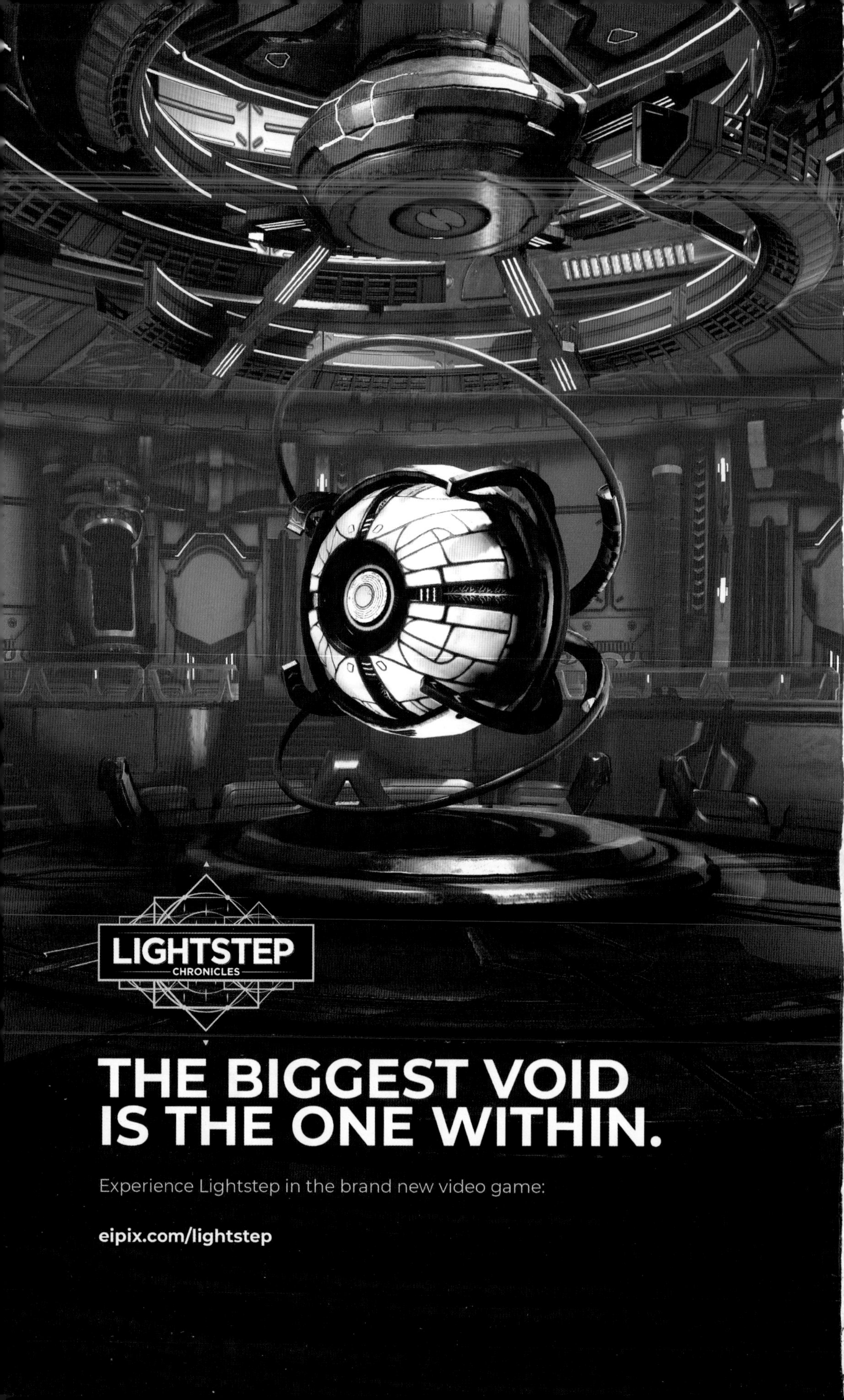
LIGHTSTEP
CHRONICLES
THE BIGGEST VOID
IS THE ONE WITHIN.
Experience Lightstep in the brand new video game:
eipix.com/lightstep